EXPLORING PRINTMAKING

A Practical Guide to Printmaking Techniques

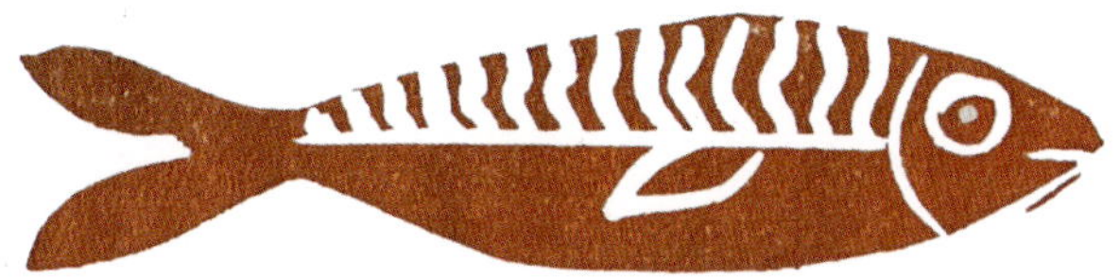

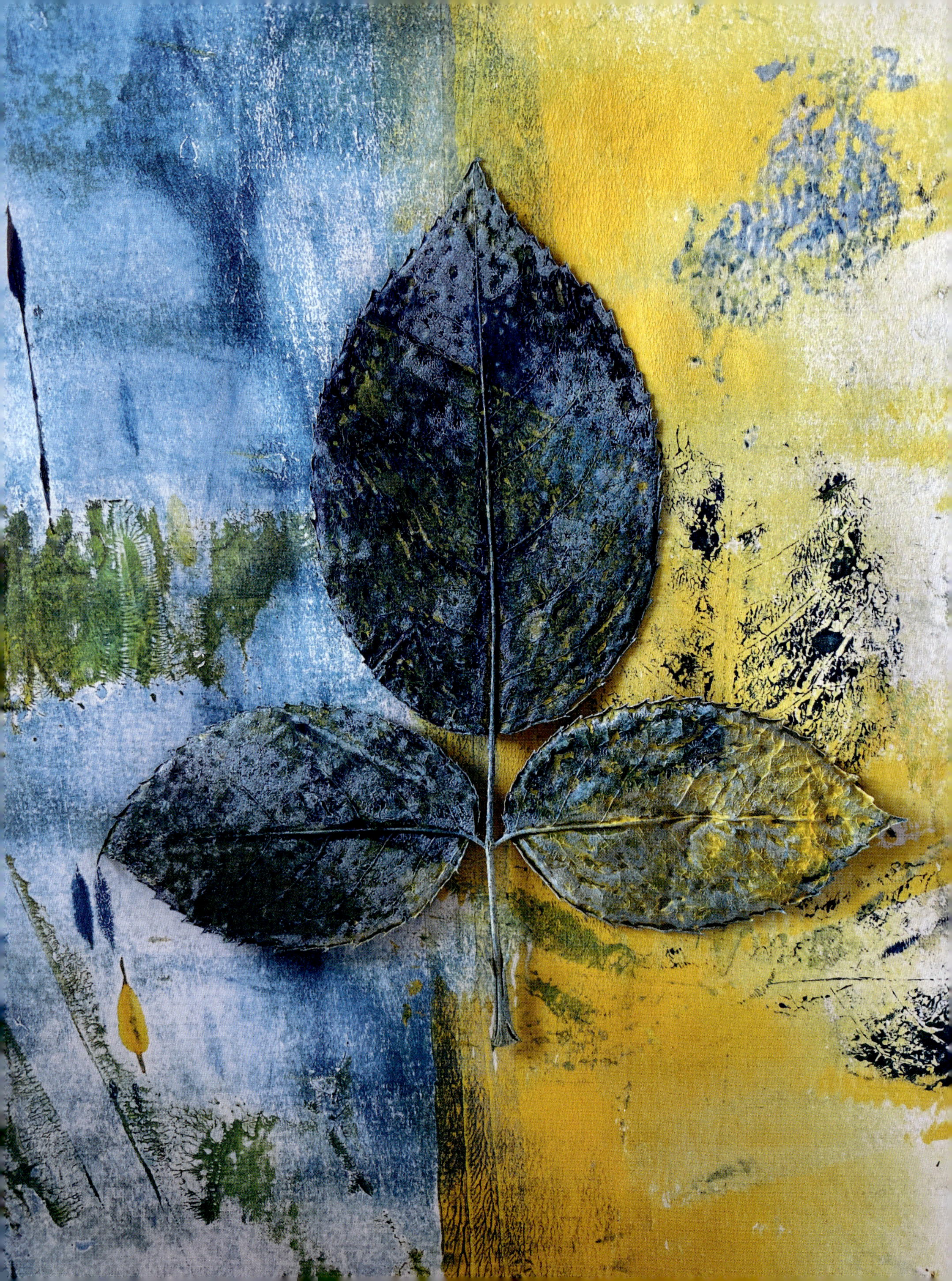

EXPLORING PRINTMAKING

A Practical Guide to Printmaking Techniques

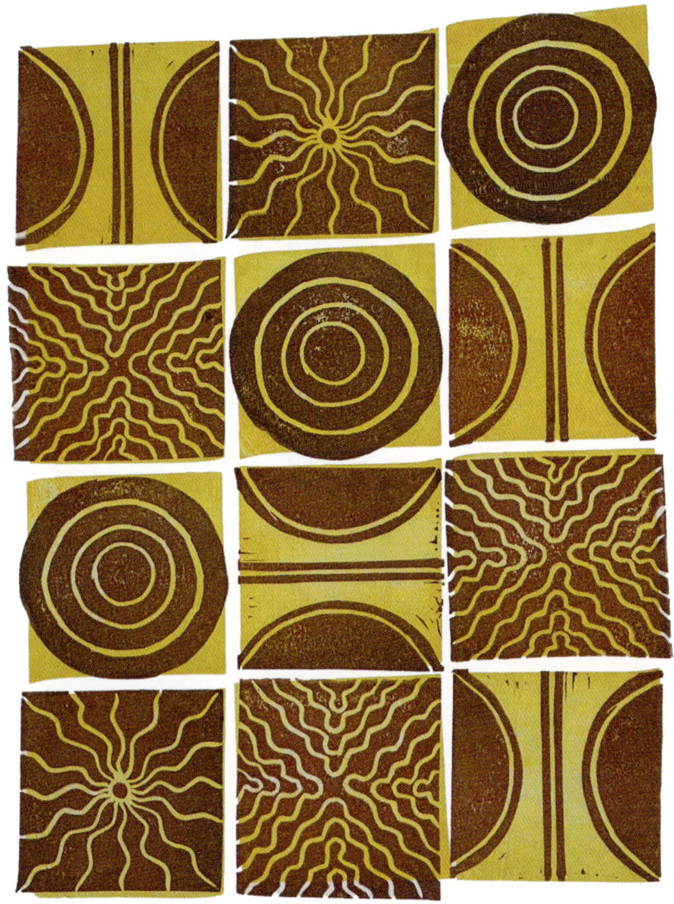

GILL THOMPSON

HERBERT PRESS

LONDON · OXFORD · NEW YORK · NEW DELHI · SYDNEY

HERBERT PRESS
Bloomsbury Publishing Plc
50 Bedford Square, London, WC1B 3DP, UK
29 Earlsfort Terrace, Dublin 2, Ireland

BLOOMSBURY, HERBERT PRESS and the Herbert Press logo are trademarks of
Bloomsbury Publishing Plc

First published in Great Britain in 2025

A catalogue record for this book is available from the British Library

Library of Congress Cataloguing-in-Publication data has been applied for

ISBN: PB: 978-1-7899-4302-3; eBook: 978-1-7899-4301-6

2 4 6 8 10 9 7 5 3 1

Design and layouts by Lorraine Inglis Design
Printed and bound in China by RR Donnelley Asia Printing Solutions Limited

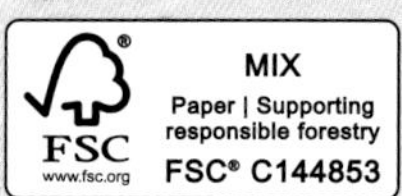

To find out more about our authors and books visit www.bloomsbury.com and sign up for
our newsletters

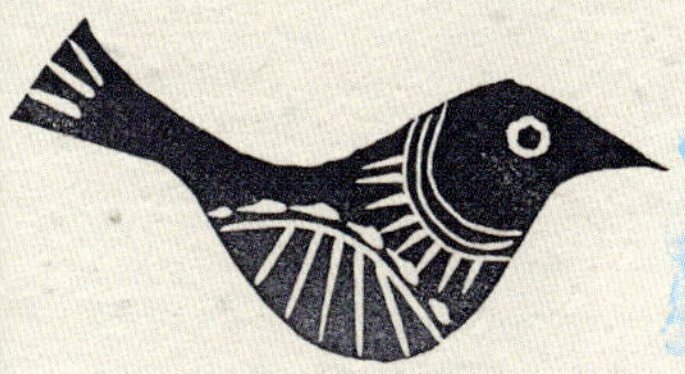

CONTENTS

INTRODUCTION

I am an artist and printmaker based on the Isle of Lewis in Scotland. My artwork is inspired by the beautiful coastal environment and reflects the shapes, colours and textures of the island. Before moving to Scotland, I lived and worked in Herefordshire. I brought up three children and worked full-time as a teacher but always managed to make space for creative projects.

I began linoprinting as a way of producing multiple sets of handmade cards for family and friends at Christmas. The dining room table would be covered by dozens of prints laid out to dry and the kitchen table was my workspace. Linoprinting was just the beginning — I explored other printmaking methods, using monoprinting to add interesting textures and marks to my paintings and collaging printed papers to create the backgrounds for mixed-media work. A chance meeting with another artist who used collagraph printing as her main technique motivated me to enrol on a printmaking course at the local art college and I have not looked back!

I have been printmaking now for more than 15 years, and I run workshops at the local art centre in Stornoway, in my studio and online. I still get inspired by new ideas and projects and enjoy experimenting and trying out ways of making an original print. There is always something new to learn, and different printmaking methods can be used to create prints with a range of features: linoprints are crisp and bold, whereas other print styles focus on texture or the drawn image, or become an atmospheric background.

This book is an introduction to the many ways of making a print without using a press. I will outline the different steps involved in making a print, from the initial idea, the drawing in your sketchbook, the planning stages, carving or constructing the plate, to inking up and finally printing on to paper or fabric.

This book is suitable for beginners who wish to try out various printmaking techniques, but it is also for more experienced artists and printmakers looking for ideas to develop their own practice. The techniques and projects have been used in the workshops that I teach, so they are tried and tested, and the step-by-step approach makes it easy for you to follow each printmaking project.

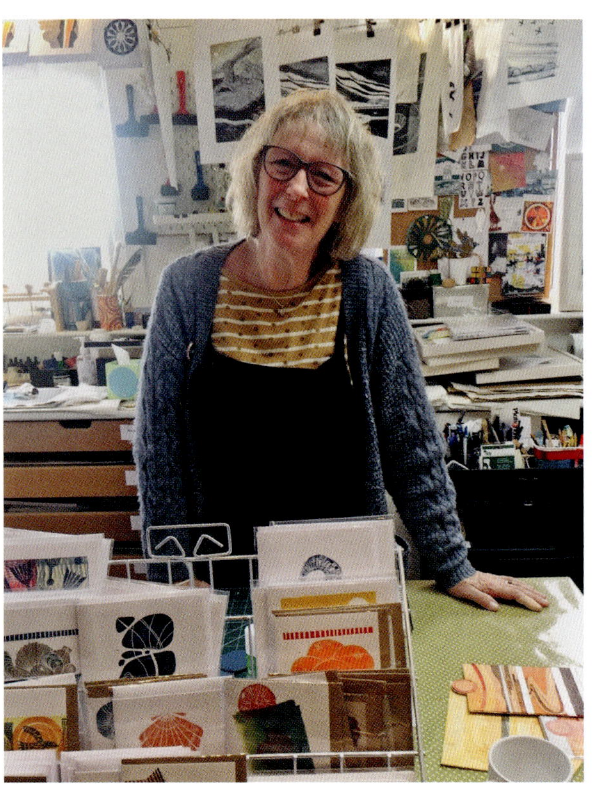

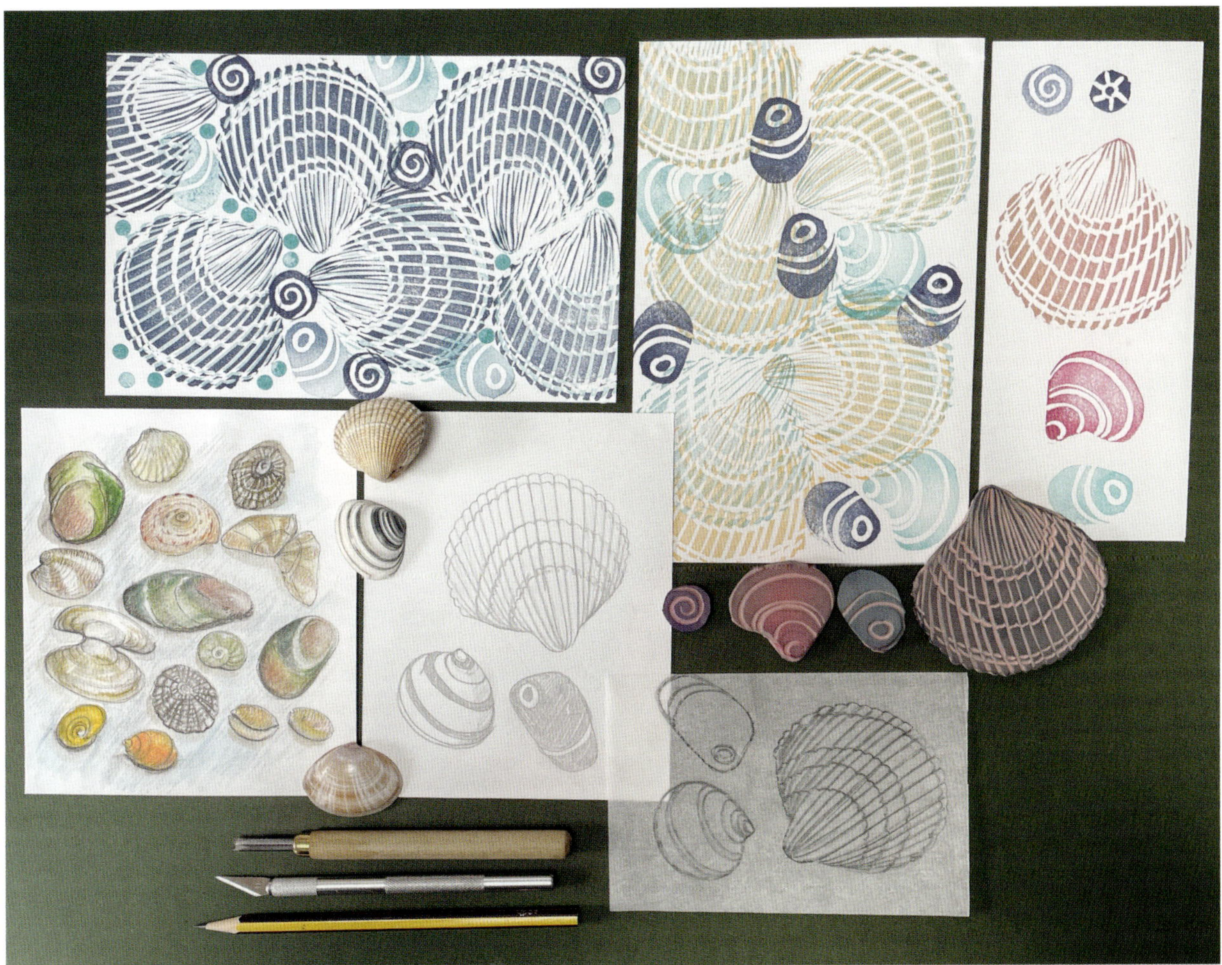

Once you have tried and practised different methods and have understood the skills involved, you can take them further, combining two or more techniques, making more complex printing plates or using the simpler designs in a range of creative ways. Part of the process is learning how to make the next print even better. If you think you would like to continue printmaking, there are many books that can guide you and give you more detail. You will also find plenty of tutorials online.

If you try out some or all of the printmaking activities in this book, you will accumulate a stack of printed papers. I have included projects and practical ways to use these. I never throw my prints away – they are the starting point for a creative project, giving me ideas when I am stuck, and are a great resource for making cards, book covers and collages.

I hope you find the print methods and activities fun and inspiring to do, and that you will choose at least one of the techniques to take further, developing a unique way of expressing yourself through print.

Gill Thompson

1
WHAT IS PRINTMAKING?

Printmaking is essentially a way of transferring an image or pattern from one surface to another using ink or paint. It is one of the earliest and most basic of artforms – a handprint on the wall of a cave, or prints made using cut potatoes or other fruit and vegetables.

Printmaking can be very simple, using a single colour and a basic shape or design. It can also be used to create a complex, multi-layered artwork requiring great skill and dexterity.

Some printmaking processes require a printing press, but the methods outlined in this book can all be achieved without a press and can be carried out in your home using tools and materials you have around the house and a few inexpensive pieces of equipment.

Whether you are starting out on your printmaking journey or developing and discovering new techniques, you will be rewarded as you reveal your print. There is always an element of surprise as you lift the paper and see what you have produced for the first time, and every print teaches you something new about the process.

People are often confused between original hand-printed work and commercial prints, which are copies of a piece of artwork. Many artists have giclée prints made of their artwork so they can sell limited-edition copies of their paintings; these prints are essentially good-quality photocopies (and only tend to be used by printmakers for book illustrations, cards or posters). By contrast, an original print (monoprint, relief print, collagraph, etching) is manually created

Opposite: Mixed media collage using monoprinted papers, acrylic paints and pastels.

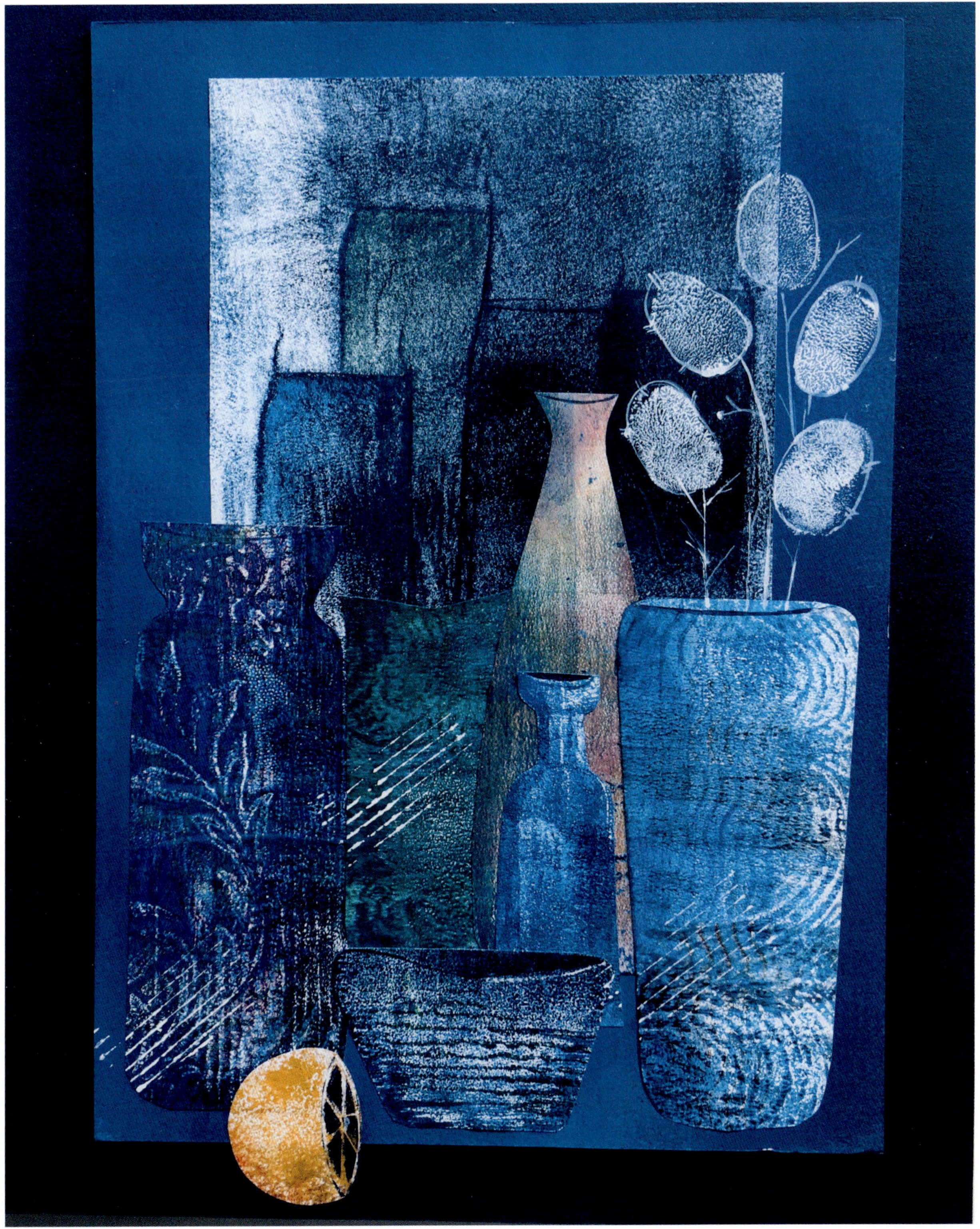

– drawn, carved, then, after a printing plate has been constructed, inked and printed by hand by the artist. A limited number of original prints using an identical design forms an edition. Although a print might be similar to others in an edition, there will always be slight variations, which makes each original print special and unique.

Printmaking techniques

- **Monoprinting** is the process of transferring an image or design from one surface to another to create a one-off print. This can be achieved in a variety of ways, but you can never reproduce the print exactly.

- **Relief printing** (used for linoprints, stamping and block prints) involves removing some of the surface of the printing block, leaving the remaining areas to be inked and printed.

- **Intaglio printing** (used for collagraph prints and etchings) works in the opposite way. The image or design is incised or carved into the surface of the printing block and the ink is applied, working it into the cut areas and marks.

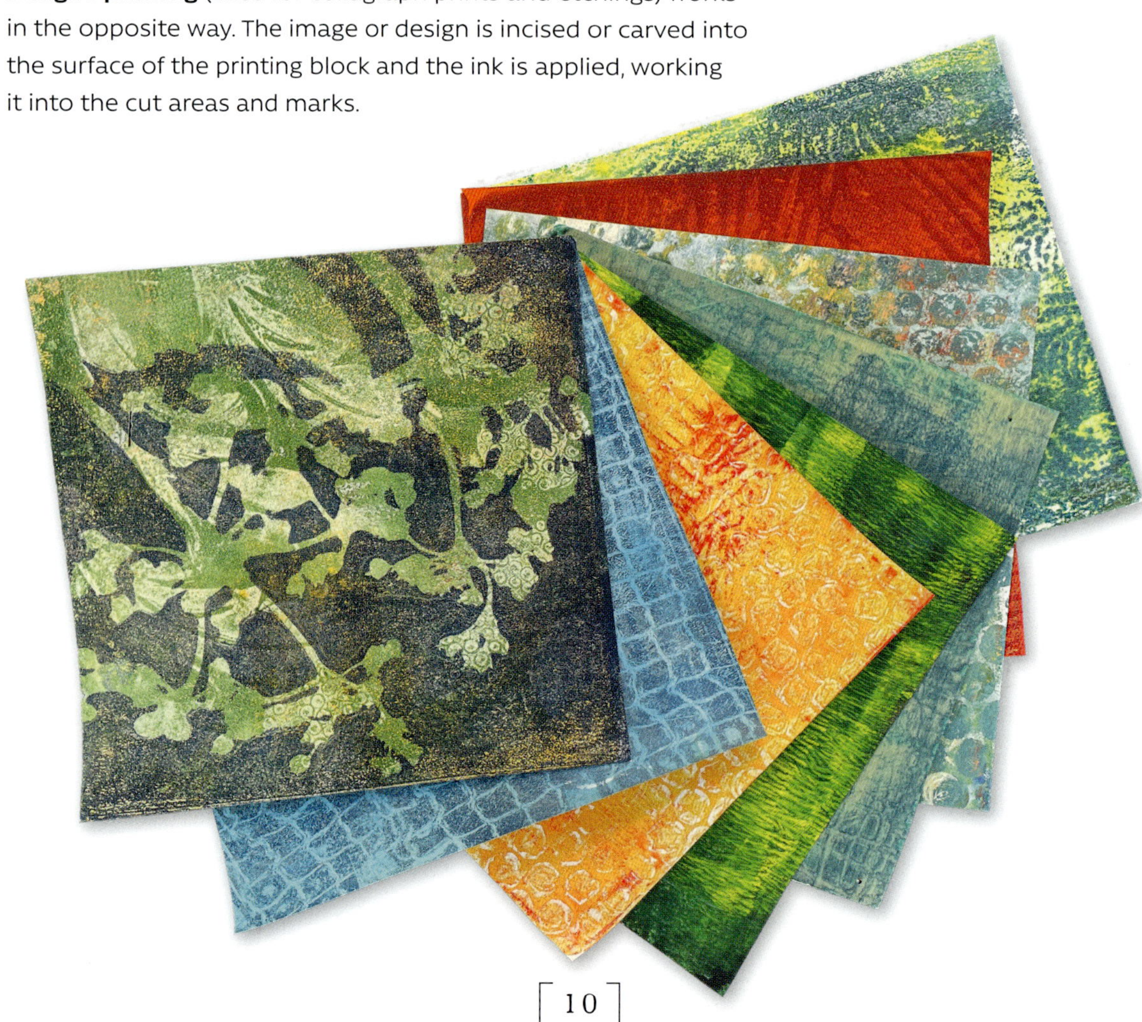

Below: **A small selection of hand-printed papers.**

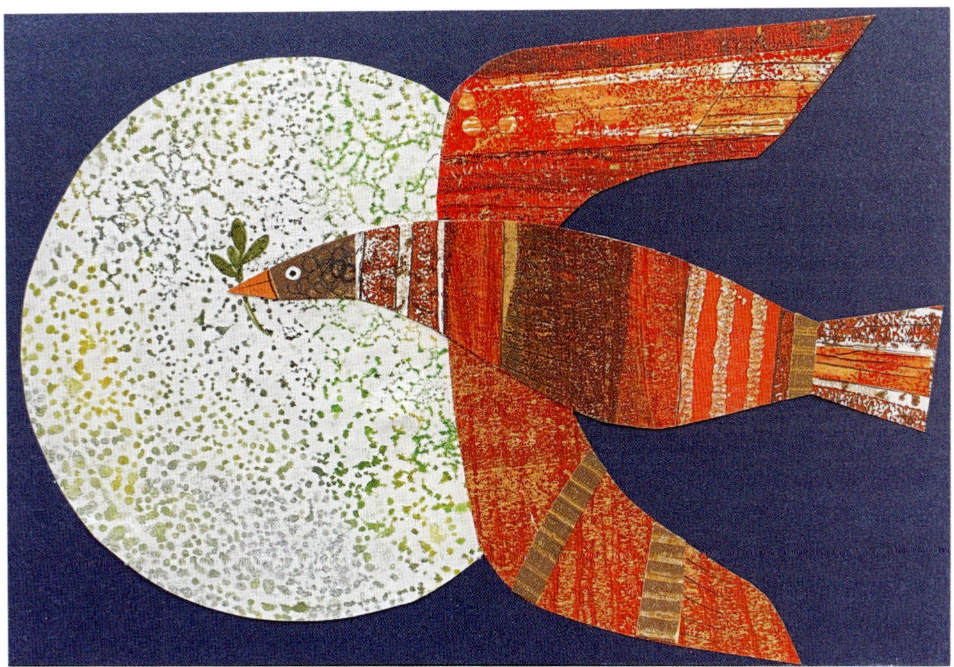

Above: Collaged design for a card using different hand-printed papers.

The block is then wiped, leaving the ink in the incisions and indentations, but removing most of the ink from the surface. In the case of collagraph printing, textures and shapes can be collaged on to the surface of the plate as well as having the incised areas.

- **Etching** is a printmaking technique which involves incising an image into the surface of the plate. Traditionally this is done using acid to create incisions in a metal plate.

- **Drypoint etching** is a simpler process using a sharp-pointed needle or tool to scratch the image into the surface of the plate, which could be an acetate sheet, Plexiglass®, a laminated card sheet or even Tetra Pak® packaging.

- **Eco printing** uses natural materials and dyes to transfer plant images, colours and shapes on to paper or fabric. Onion skins, 'iron water' made with rusty nails, or a collection of leaves can produce beautiful botanical prints which can be used in a variety of ways.

- **Anthotype printing and cyanotype printing** are processes that make simple images using the photosensitive properties of plants and vegetables (and chemicals, in the case of cyanotypes).

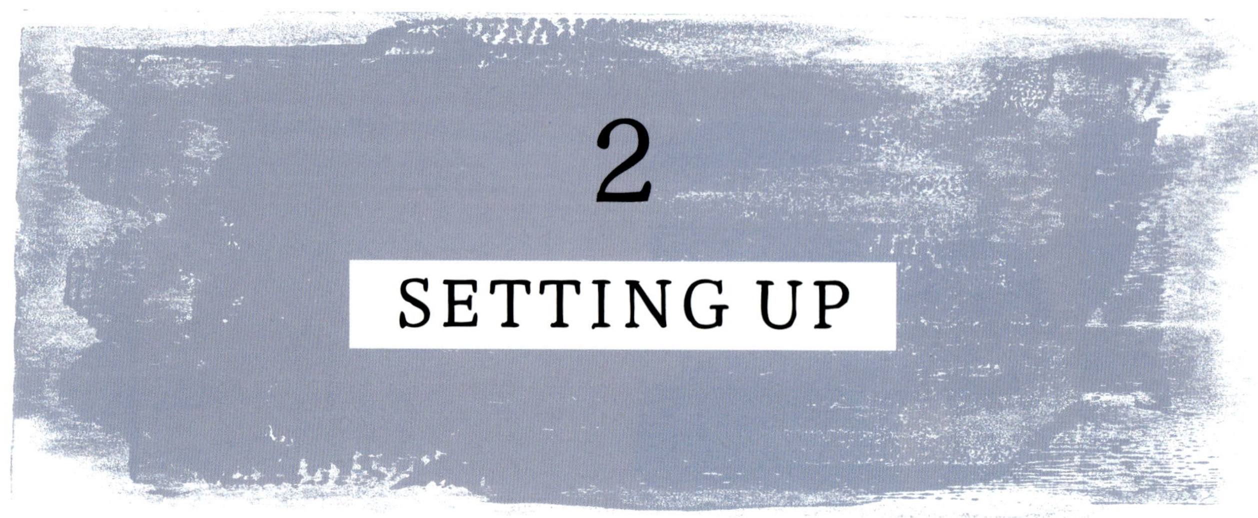

Preparing your workspace

Working at home can often mean using the kitchen table or a spare bedroom. If you are fortunate enough to have a designated area for being creative, that is ideal. Each of the printmaking methods has different requirements but you do not need a large area to carry out your work. However, for your safety and comfort, there are certain things which are necessary to consider for any project.

WORK SURFACE

- You need a firm, stable surface to work on, and it is best to cover it with newspaper and/or a wipeable tablecloth for protection.

- A cutting mat is the best way to protect your table from damage caused by sharp tools. Cutting mats also have a grid on the surface, which is helpful when drawing or cutting out materials.

- A chair that is at the right height for the table is important so that you can work in comfort. I work standing up for some printmaking activities, so I have a separate area of worktop which I use for inking up my lino plates and for monoprinting. This is my 'inky' area, and my table is for the cleaner activities.

LIGHTING

- You need good lighting to see what you are doing, particularly for finer work like carving relief printing plates.

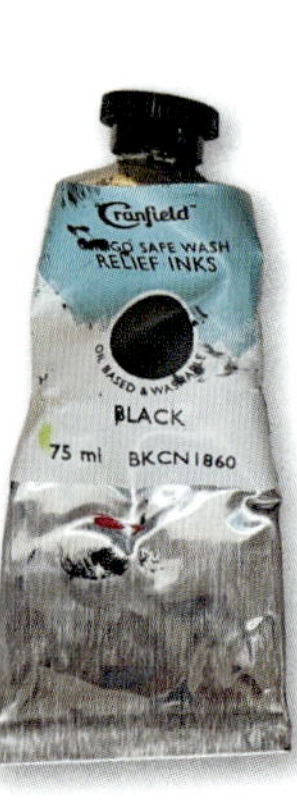

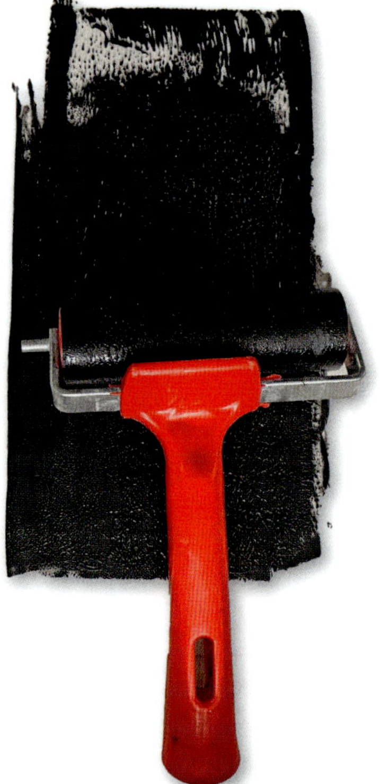

STORAGE

- A box or cupboard to keep your tools and materials in is essential so you can tidy everything away when you have finished, and store any sharp tools safely away from children or animals.

- Your paper needs to be stored flat, as do your finished prints, so bear that in mind when planning where to keep them. An empty drawer, a flat shallow box or an A3 art folder will keep paper and prints flat and dust-free.

- I have a concertina folder in which I store my printed papers. This allows me to sort them by colour and makes selecting paper for collages or card making much easier. You could make something similar with large envelopes or document folders.

- Gelatine plates (known as 'gel plates') need to be stored in their original containers, between the sheets of acetate that they came in – or with a sheet of plain paper on either printing surface – and enclosed in the plastic 'clam shell' package. If you use the acetate sheets, ensure that you squash out any air bubbles between the acetate and the surface of the gel plate as, over time, air bubbles can cause permanent indentations in the surface. I store the clam shell packs stacked on their sides in a box. If you lay them flat, don't put anything on top of them or you could damage the surface of the plates, which can affect your printing.

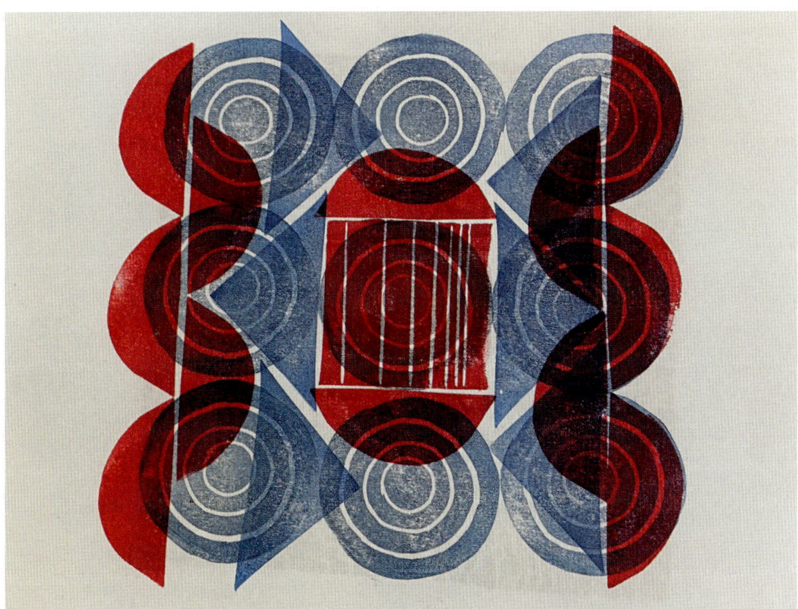

Right: **A combination of four different carved stamping blocks printed over each other.**

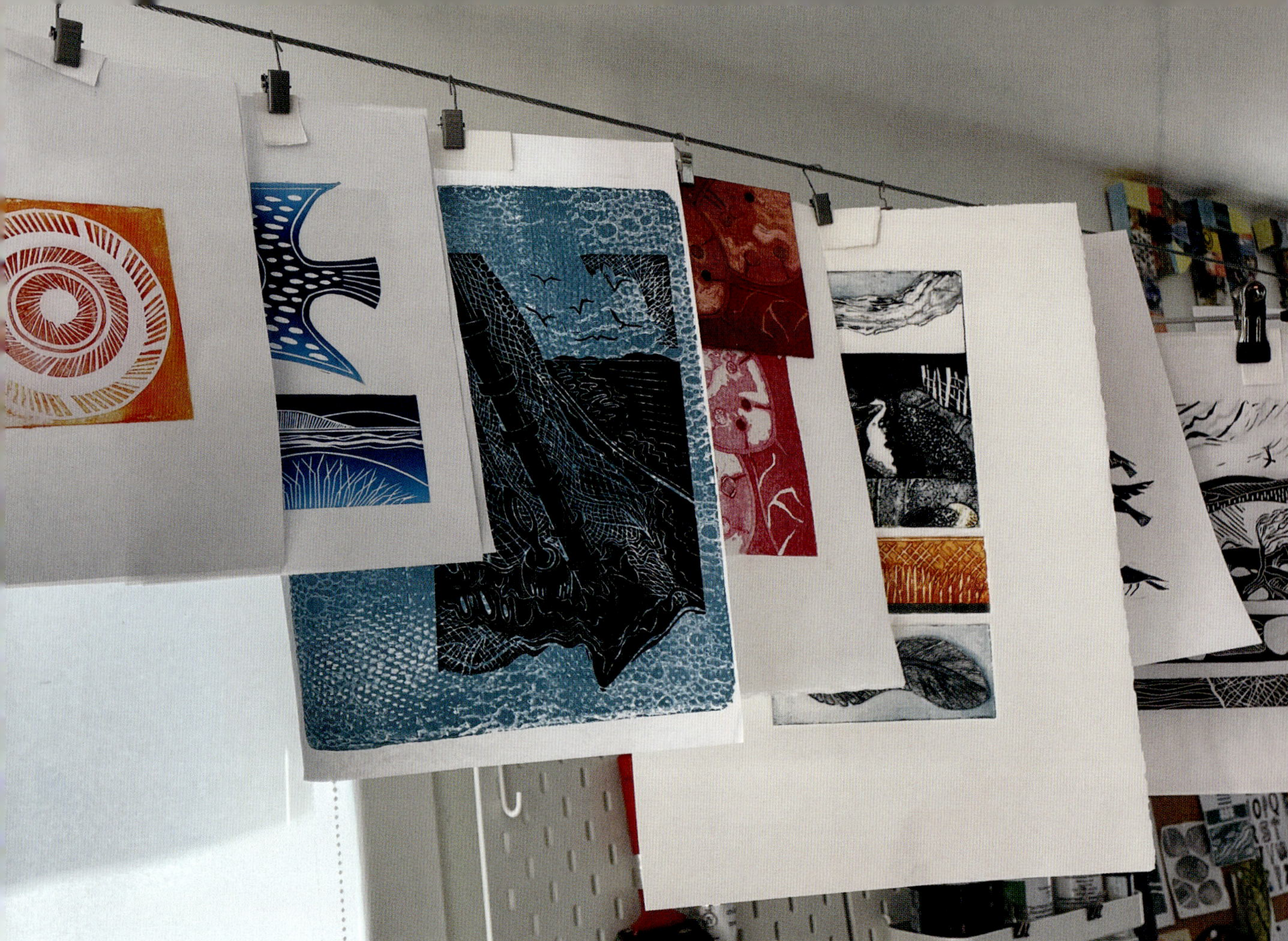

DRYING AREA

- You need an area to dry your prints as, with some of the print activities, you will be creating work that could take a while to dry and you do not want them to stick together or curl up. In colder temperatures, printing ink can take over a week to dry completely. A flat surface that is not likely to be disturbed is ideal. If you are able to set up a wire or cord stretched from one wall to another, work can be pegged up on this or on to a folding clothes dryer, out of the way and in a good current of air. There are various hanging systems available to buy but you can always improvise.

CLEANING UP

- Access to water is necessary for cleaning up after most printing activities. The printing inks I recommend (Caligo Safe Wash) are easily cleaned up using warm soapy water, once you have wiped the roller and inking slab with a rag and a little vegetable oil. Acrylic paints, providing they are not left to go hard on brushes or on a gel plate, can be cleaned in a bowl of soapy water. The gel plate needs to be washed gently, rinsed and blotted dry on an old, clean tea towel and then smeared with hand sanitiser gel before packing it away. This extends its life and ensures a good printing surface when you next use it. I suggest having a designated washing-up bowl for cleaning up your inky equipment, to save the kitchen sink.

■ Although not very eco-friendly, biodegradable baby wipes are useful for a quick clean-up of your fingers, worktop and the surface of the gel plate between paint layers or your inking tray or printing plate. Alternatively, keep some damp rags or cloths close to hand. I also keep a stack of cut-up cotton material (shirts, T-shirts, old pillowcases etc.) to use as rags.

Tools and materials

When you are getting started with printmaking, you only need a few basic tools. At this stage, it is advisable to go with inexpensive materials, and you can invest in better-quality versions if you decide to take your printmaking further. However, don't go for the cheapest tools as they can be frustrating to use and give disappointing results.

Putting together a basic set of materials and equipment that you are likely to use will save you time when you want to embark on one of the projects in this book. You may well already have some of these items, but others you may have to buy (see p.172). Within each of the projects there is also a list of all the tools and materials you will need to complete the activity.

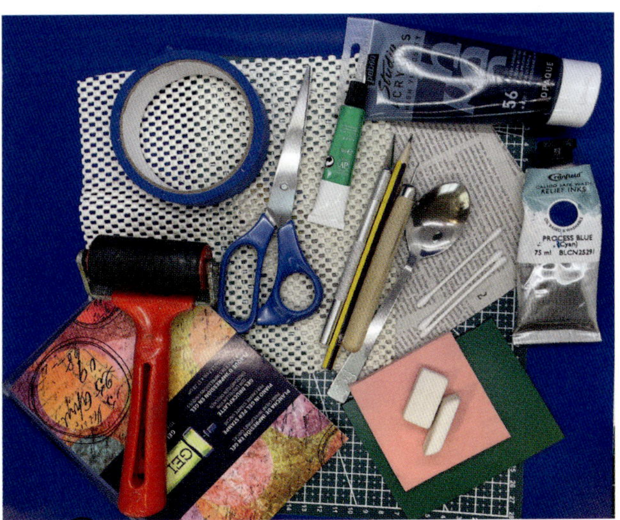

BASIC MATERIALS AND EQUIPMENT FOR PRINTMAKING

■ **non-slip mat** – (the kind you use on a tray to stop cups slipping) – when carving your lino or Speedy Carve™, this stabilises your carving block as you work.

■ **craft knife** – this has multiple uses for achieving crisp incisions and edges when cutting lino or for cutting and peeling in the relief collagraph activity. It is also used in several of the craft projects.

■ **scissors**

- **cutting tools** – (needed for lino, Speedy Carve™ and other materials such as erasers) – I suggest investing in a mid-range priced set to start with, as the cheaper versions can be very frustrating to use. Sets of Japanese carving tools with wooden handles or the Abig sets are ideal beginners' tools. You will mainly use tools with a V-shaped and U-shaped cutting blade. If you decide to continue with linoprinting, it is worth buying a couple of better-quality (and more expensive) tools, such as those made by Pfeil, which you can buy individually.

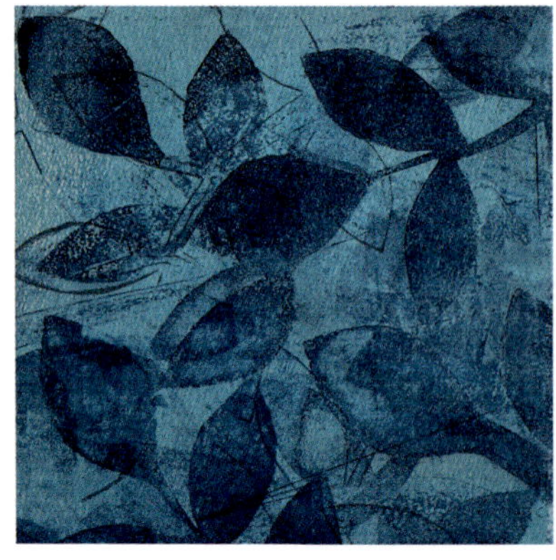

- **stationery** – pencils, fineliner pens, wax crayons, oil pastels, ruler, several large erasers, sharpener.

- **masking tape** – this can be used to fix your paper in place or to achieve a margin around your paper when printing.

- **double-sided sticky tape** – using this can be a quick and effective way of sticking pieces together for some of the projects.

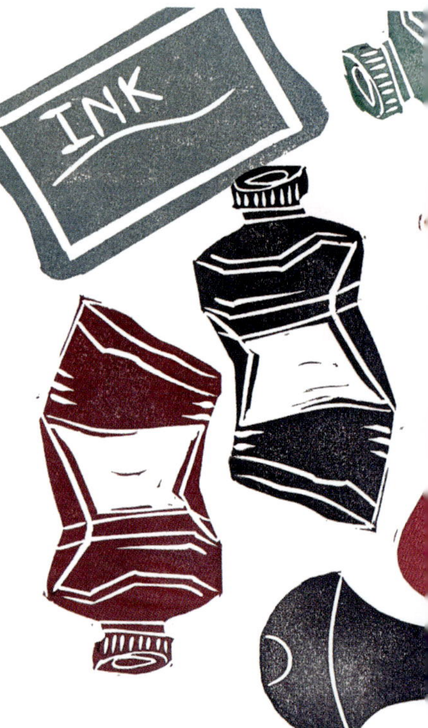

- **cling film and aluminium foil** – these can be used to create textured patterns.

- **cotton buds** – these can be used for drawing into paint or to remove unwanted paint or ink from a plate before printing.

- **PVA glue** – I use exterior-quality PVA as it dries with a waterproof finish.

- **scrap paper** – for placing under your work, for jotting down notes or trying out designs.

- **newspaper** – to protect your work surface.

- **tracing paper** – to trace an image from a photo, sketchbook or magazine and to transfer your image to the printing block.

- **white Tracedown® transfer paper** – use this to transfer your traced image to the lino block. It is placed between the tracing paper and the lino block, and you draw over the tracing, transferring a clear white image on to the surface of the lino.

- **sketchbook/notebook** – this is a useful resource for planning your prints, exploring mark-making, jotting down ideas and recording details of your prints (what you used, what worked, what you could change or improve on). I like an A4 book so I can print directly on the pages or stick printwork into it, but a smaller, more portable one is fine. (See also Susan Yeates' advice on p.22)

- **A4 white craft card** – use for bookmarks, cards, collages, etc.

- **printing paper** – a selection of papers is worth having to hand. If you are doing monoprinting, you can use ordinary copy paper, which is cheap and works well for collage. Cartridge paper is suitable for most of the print techniques in the book, as well as sketchbook paper. You can also get some great prints on tissue paper. For collagraph and drypoint etching, the paper needs to be dampened and a heavier paper (at least 200 gsm) is advisable – mixed media paper from a pad is ideal. Paper with a smooth surface works better than textured or handmade paper but you can always experiment with these if you have them.

- **cardboard** – mountboard is worth investing in as a plate for some of the print techniques. It is available in large sheets from most art and craft shops and suppliers. You might be able to get offcuts from a framing shop. Cereal packets, the card from the back of pads of paper and other forms of cardboard are very useful, easy to come by and worth saving from the recycling bin.

- **gelatine plate** – you can buy these in different sizes and shapes. I suggest going for 6 × 6 in. or 5 × 7 in. to begin with. You can also make your own gel plate with a mix of gelatine and glycerine (see p.170). Although this plate is more fragile than the commercial versions, it can be re-formed and reused if the surface gets damaged.

- **lino** – this is supplied in ready-cut pieces, A4 sheets or larger rolls. It can also be bought mounted on to wooden blocks. In colder temperatures, you will need to warm your lino by placing it on a radiator or a heat pad so that it is easier to carve.

- **Japanese Vinyl** – this is my favoured alternative to traditional lino and comes in sheets of various sizes. It is green on one side and blue on the other with a black core, enabling you to see where you have carved. It is slightly easier to carve into than traditional lino but gives a good, crisp image. If your workplace is cold, warming Japanese Vinyl will make it easier to cut pieces from a large sheet.

- **stamping block** – Speedy Carve™ is a pink carving block for stamp carving and printing, and comes in pieces of different sizes. There are other makes of printing blocks, but this is chunky and easy to carve into.

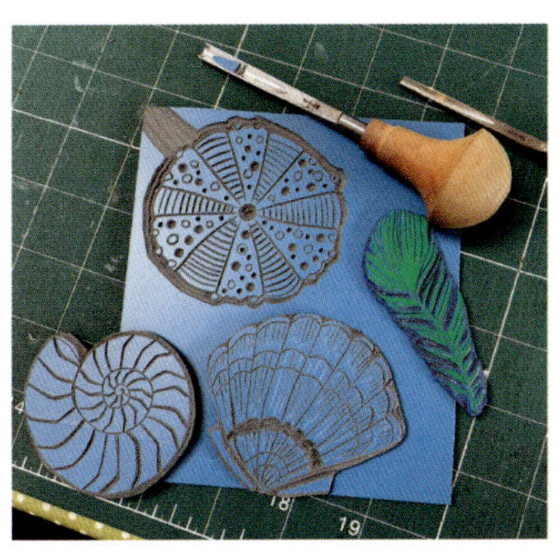

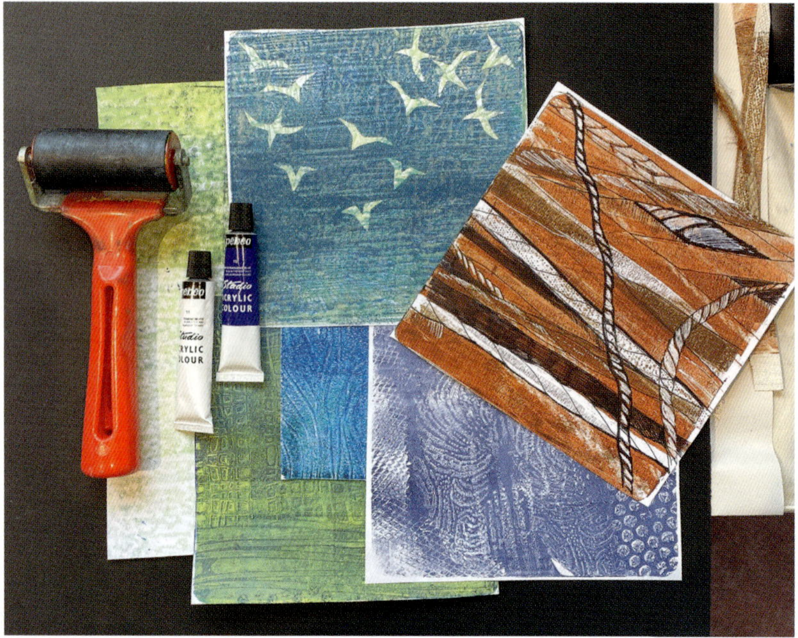

- **rollers (brayers)** – these are needed for applying ink or paint. You can buy very cheap rollers, but I advise choosing medium-priced versions which, with care, will last you a long time. Make sure you clean the roller thoroughly after each use as dried paint or ink is hard to remove and affects the surface of the roller.

- **spoon or baren** – burnish your linoprint (rubbing over the paper to pick up the ink from the lino block) using a wooden or metal spoon or any smooth flat object. I have a glass decanter stopper with a flat top which works really well. Printmaking suppliers sell a variety of different barens.

- **paints** – these are suitable for monoprinting and gel-plate printing and you can use any basic acrylic paints. Different brands of paint have different properties that affect how they work on the gel plate but you will work out how to use them as you try out the activities. Warm, dry weather will mean that they dry on the plate faster and colder temperatures mean you may need to wait longer for a layer to dry before you roll the next colour on to the plate.

- **inks** – for the purposes of the print activities in this book, I suggest using Caligo Safe Wash inks. These can be bought in individual tubes and, although oil-based, clean up easily with soap and water. They are more rewarding to use than the water-based inks that dry

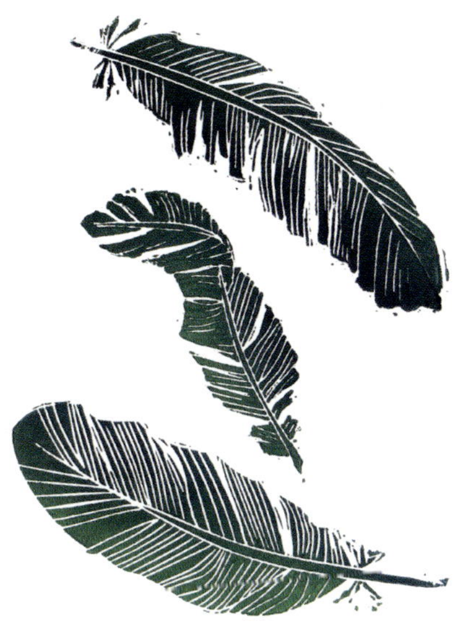

very fast and have a dull, matt finish. Start with a small selection of inks – black and white and two or three other colours such as process blue, process yellow and process red. These will enable you to mix a good range of other colours.

■ **knife or plastic spatula** – this is useful for mixing inks.

■ **inking tray** – you will need a flat, wipeable slab for mixing paints and inks – this can be a sheet of acrylic, a smooth glass worktop saver or a smooth flat tile. You can also buy plastic inking trays at craft stores.

■ **ink pads** – these can be bought inexpensively in sets or individually, and come in a wide range of colours and sizes.

MATERIALS FOR MARK-MAKING

As the print techniques described in the book are essentially experimental, it's worth assembling a stash of items for mark-making and adding texture. You may be surprised to discover how many everyday materials you can use:

■ juice and milk cartons (washed and flattened out)
■ lids from jars and bottles
■ small packaging boxes
■ meat and vegetable trays with a textured base
■ bubble wrap
■ plastic netting from fruit and vegetable bags
■ old credit cards (also great for spreading ink)
■ clothing labels
■ toilet roll tubes
■ old keys
■ clothes pegs
■ forks
■ kitchen utensils
■ corks
■ textured wallpaper samples
■ corrugated card
■ stencils (bought or handmade)
■ paper clips
■ string
■ cotton reels
■ fabric scraps
■ lace
■ ribbons
■ children's construction bricks
■ vegetable pieces (half an onion or a carrot, a wedge of cabbage or a piece of cauliflower)
■ leaves, ferns and grasses (fresh or pressed between layers of newspaper)
■ feathers

As you begin experimenting with print techniques, you may well find yourself collecting all sorts of items with interesting shapes and textures, in case they come in handy.

3

BEFORE YOU GET STARTED

There are a few important things that you need to know before you start printmaking.

Health and safety

Some of the activities involve tools that are sharp such as lino cutting tools, an etching needle or a craft knife. Here are some tips to avoid injuries:

- Use a non-slip mat (available on a roll from hardware and camping shops) when carving.

- Always carve away from the hand that is holding your carving block. Try to get into the habit of holding the block in place with your non-carving hand behind the cutting tool.

- Consider buying a bench hook. This is a simple device that fits to the edge of your work table and has a ledge you can push your block against when carving. They are available to buy or can be made if you are handy with woodworking tools.

- Take care when using craft knives; the blades are extremely sharp and can give a nasty cut – replace the plastic cap after using and move the knife to a container away from your immediate work area.

- When you are not using your tools, place them away from your work area so you don't inadvertently cut yourself.

- Keep plasters and hygienic wipes to hand, just in case you cut yourself.

- Have a comfortable chair and a worktable which is the right height for you. For inking up and monoprinting, consider working standing up at a worktop (as I do), so that you don't hunch over as you work, putting a strain on your shoulders, back and neck.

- Take regular breaks to relax and move around. Give your hands a good shake, roll your shoulders back and forth, and step away from your workplace.

- Work in a good light – if your overhead light is not bright enough, a table lamp that can be angled on your work area is very useful.

Using a sketchbook

If you are new to printmaking, it is a good idea to buy a sketchbook right away – sketching should be an integral part of your printmaking process and your drawings will be a valuable resource for projects to come. Whilst you can take a photo of landscapes, objects or plants, sketching connects you to your subject in a different way, translating what you see into a series of marks and shapes. It is a very personal method of recording your thoughts and ideas, and everyone will work differently. There are no rules and no right or wrong ways of filling your pages, as long as it makes sense to you and is useful for developing your skills and informing future work. A sketchbook is a tool rather than an album of finished work.

Sketchbooks can be used for jotting down ideas as they come to mind. I make simple drawings of things I want to develop into prints and I paste in images from magazines and photos that I feel could be inspiration for future work. I also print directly into the sketchbook and make notes about past projects, such as how I went about planning a print, what went well and what could be improved. These are invariably very useful to look back on.

A sketchbook can therefore have a range of different important functions and can be:

- where you record something you see that you would like to use

- where you make rough drawings representing the chief features of an object or scene

- where you translate what you see into a series of marks and shapes

- a reference to help you develop a piece of work

- where you experiment with printmaking materials to try different techniques

- a record of the stages of making a print for future reference

- a record of colour combinations that you see

- where you try out mark-making ideas

- where you develop your observational skills.

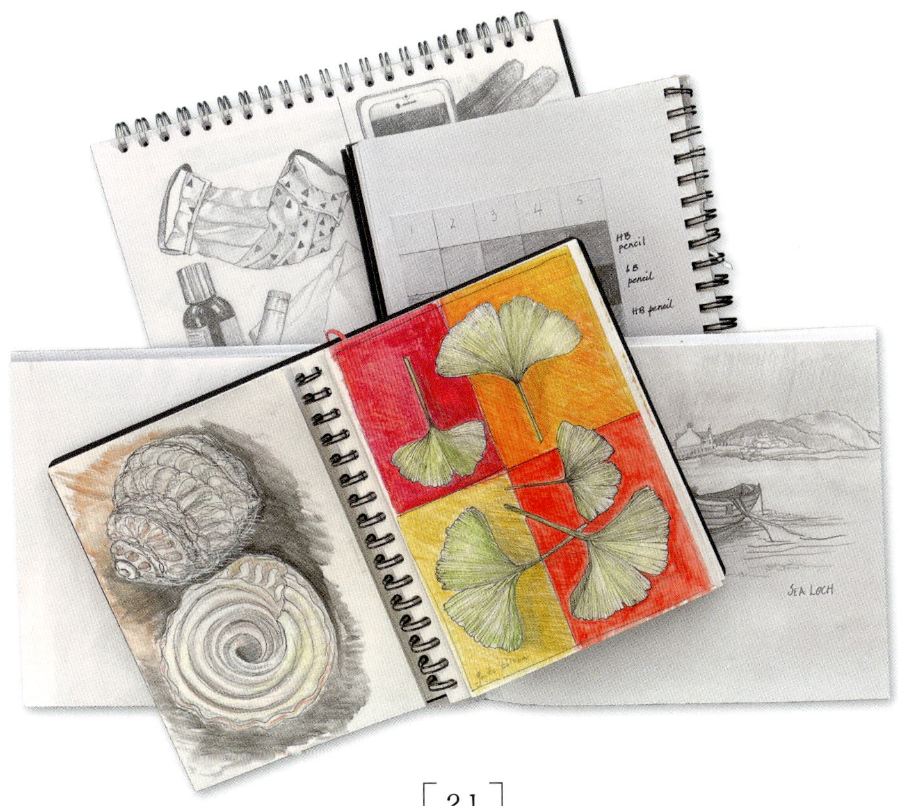

Susan Yeates — printmaker

'As an artist and printmaker, sketchbooks have always been an important part of my creative practice. In fact, I would say that they are the foundation to my creativity and are the one thing I cannot function without. Sketchbooks are the place for me to explore ideas, doodle things I see and make notes for future works. I have hundreds of them in my home studio, of all shapes and sizes. My sketchbooks are filled with messy marks, unplanned doodles, random sketches, disorganised drawings, intuitive paintings and hurried scribbles. These pages provide a plethora of ideas to draw from when I wish to start a new print.

'My biggest tip would be to start with a small sketchbook and a single pencil. Always keep this on you and sketch anything that interests you throughout your day. Make sure you can fit your sketches into those small pockets of time during your day to build up a regular habit – just two to five minutes is enough. Within a few weeks, you will have plenty of ideas to play with for simple prints.'

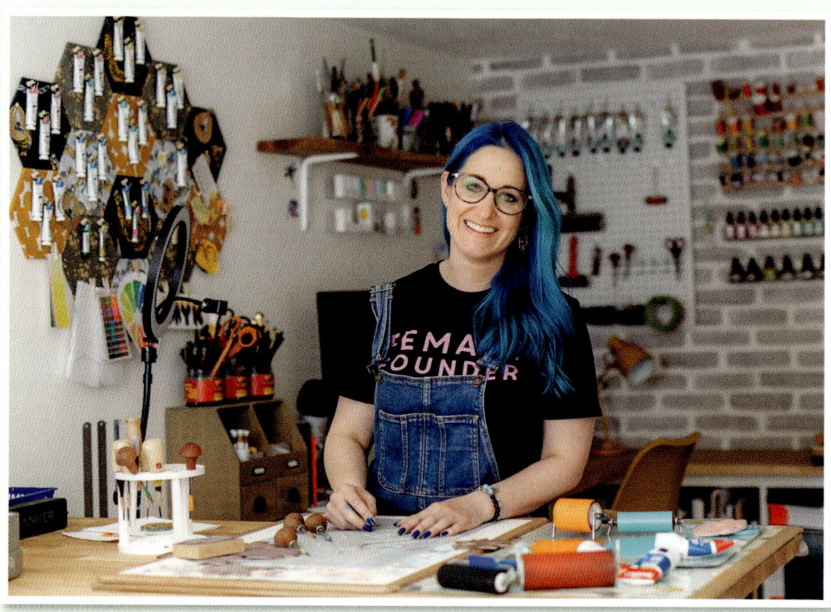

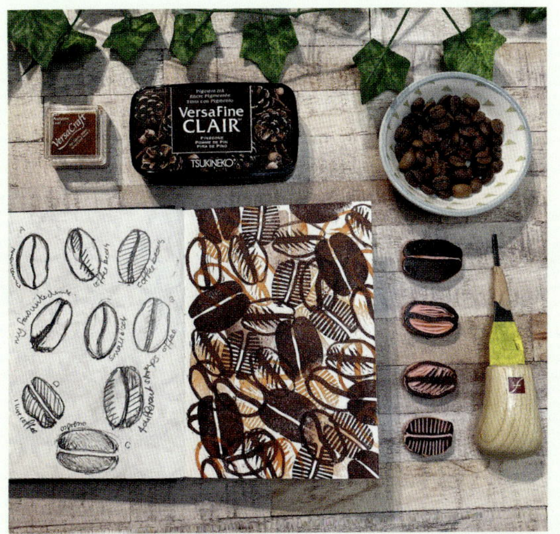

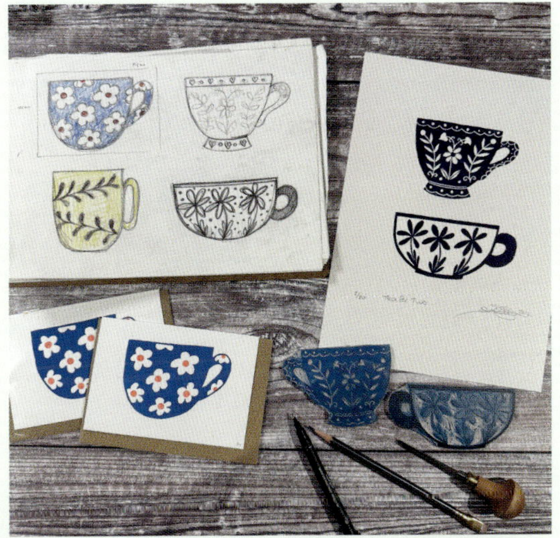

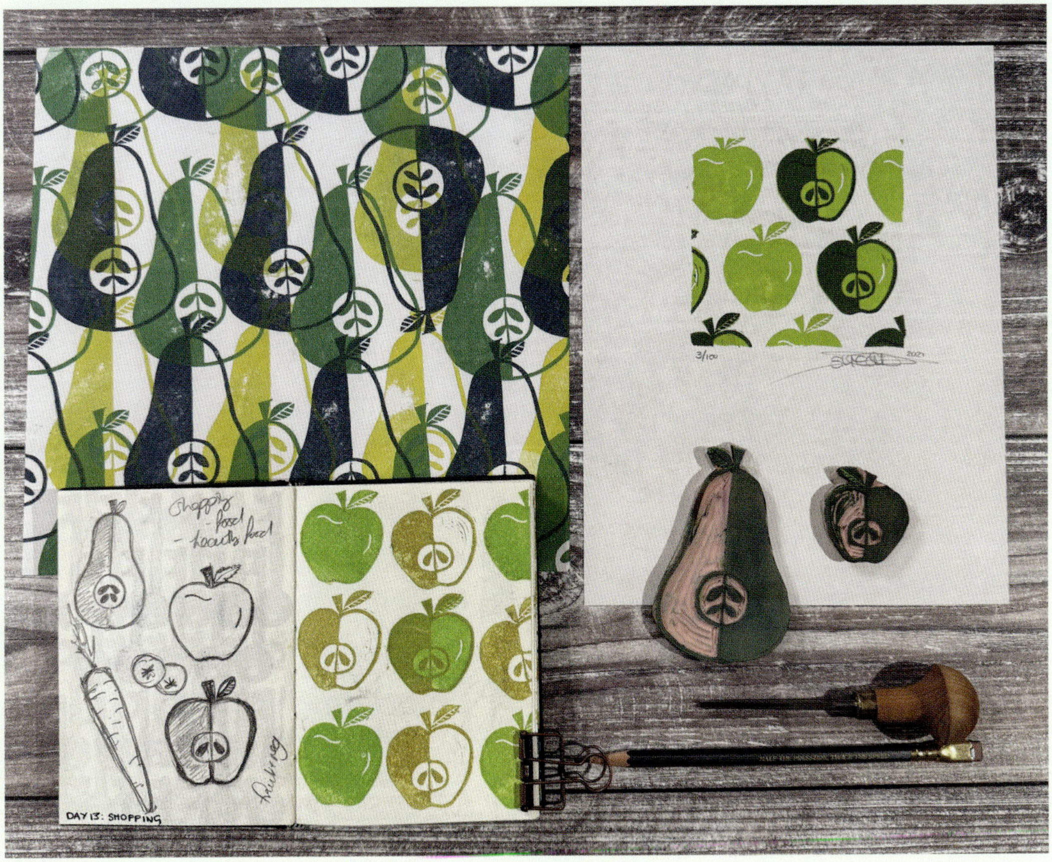

Knowing where to begin

Each chapter in this book is a starting point and describes the basic processes in a specific print method and the skills needed, which you can then try out by doing the activities provided. Once you have done some practising, you can then use your own ideas and find inspiration by looking at the work of other artists and printmakers. You may decide to focus on leaves and flowers from your garden or park, pebbles and seashells, local buildings or still-life compositions using objects from around your home. You might choose to employ your printmaking skills to make Christmas or birthday cards or posters for a community event. The projects in Chapter 12 (p.142) give ideas for using your prints creatively and you will surely think of many more once you get started.

Simple is best

When you begin making prints, it is important to experiment with simple images whilst you get your head around the processes. Once you have understood what marks your tools can make or how different materials will print, you can move on to more detailed and complex designs.

Your initial drawing needs to be pared down to the basic shapes, and you should think in terms of creating tonal qualities with different marks. This will be explained in the chapter on linocut (see Chapter 6, p.64).

When making a linoprint, working out which areas to carve out and which to leave comes with practice and although you will make mistakes, you will learn from them. Don't expect perfection right from the start but aim to improve with each new attempt.

Printing in reverse

Your linoprint or stamp print will print in reverse – this means that you will need to flip the image as you transfer it to the lino or another type of printing block. This is particularly important if you are printing words or numbers or an image of a recognisable building or place. Draw the image in your sketchbook or on paper, trace it with a pencil and tracing paper and then flip the tracing over so that you transfer it in reverse. This way, your print will be as you drew the original image, and any words or numbers will be the right way round.

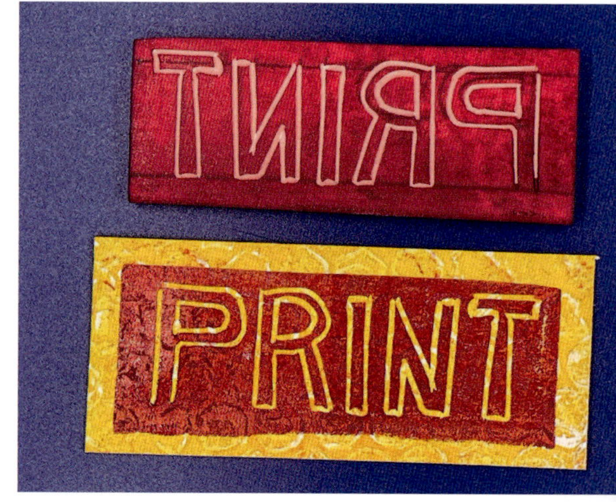

4

MONOPRINTING

A monotype or monoprint is essentially one of a kind: 'mono' comes from the Greek word *monos*, which means 'one', and 'type' comes from the Latin *typus*, meaning 'kind' or 'form'. Monoprinting is a way of creating a one-off image, and there are many techniques that you can use. No two prints are alike, although images can be similar, depending on the materials you use. The appeal lies in the unique quality of the marks made, the ability to create a layered effect and the production of work that is spontaneous and vibrant. There are many different ways in which you can create monoprints, and you can use a variety of media, such as acrylic paints, watercolour paints or printing inks.

Monoprints make excellent backgrounds to use for drawing into or for journalling. They can be cut and collaged to create cards and pictures. As unique prints, they also look great displayed in a frame. Here are some techniques for you try out and then develop using some of the creative projects in Chapter 12 (see p.142).

Mark-making with found objects

Mark-making is a simple form of printing, and you can experiment using a collection of objects from around the home and some ink pads or printing ink.

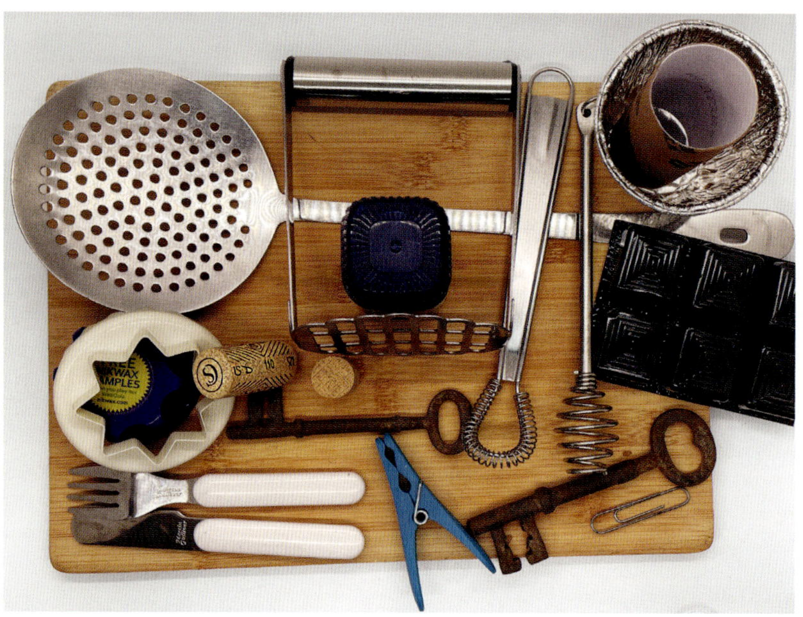

YOU WILL NEED

- selection of found objects with interesting shapes or textures (for example, bottle tops, toilet roll tubes, pieces of card, forks, kitchen utensils, children's construction bricks, corks, plastic meat and vegetable trays or vegetable pieces such as half an onion or carrot, a wedge of cabbage or a piece of cauliflower)
- printing paper (copy paper, sketchbook paper, cartridge paper or any smooth paper)
- small blocks of wood
- printing ink
- ink pads
- inking tray or slab
- roller (brayer)
- string or rubber bands
- double-sided tape
- sponge (optional)
- disposable gloves (optional)
- damp cloth or baby wipes (optional)
- warm soapy water

1. Set out your equipment and materials so they are easy to access. This can be a messy activity so have a damp cloth or baby wipes to hand or wear disposable gloves.

2. Squeeze some printing ink on to your inking tray and roll it out thinly with the roller. (a)

3. Dip the objects into the ink and then use them to make marks on the paper. (b)

4. Try different ways of making patterns using your objects. You can squash a toilet roll tube to vary the shape it makes. (c)

5. The tines of a fork, corks and bottle tops make interesting shapes. (d)

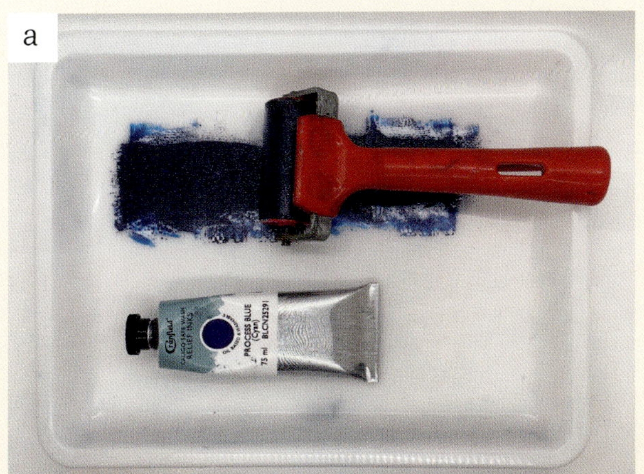

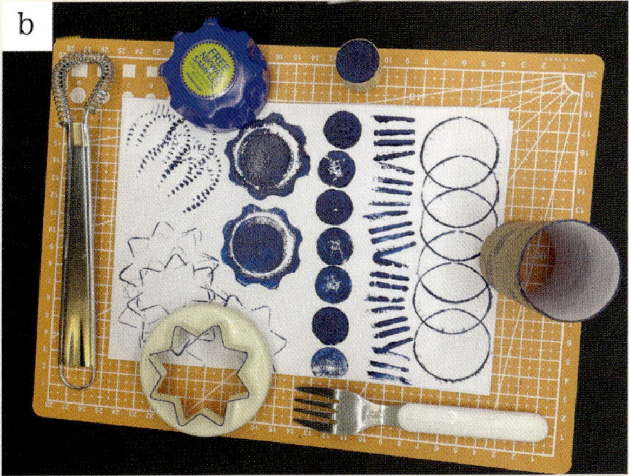

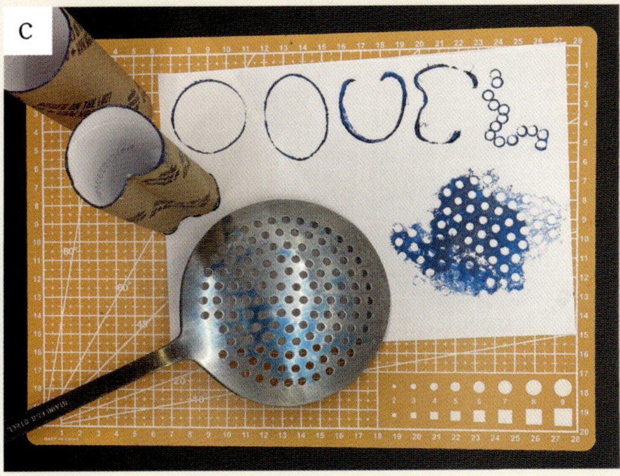

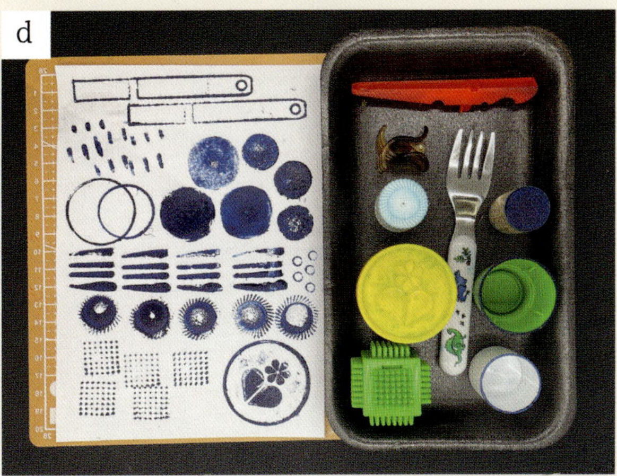

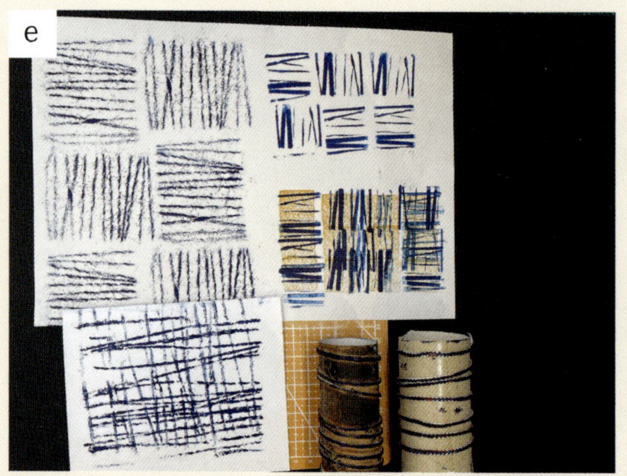

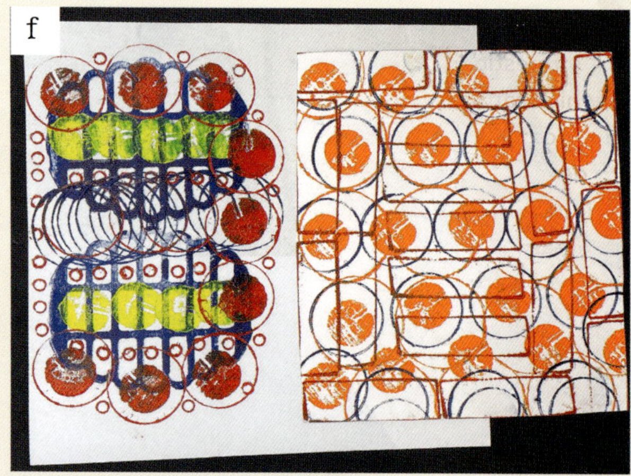

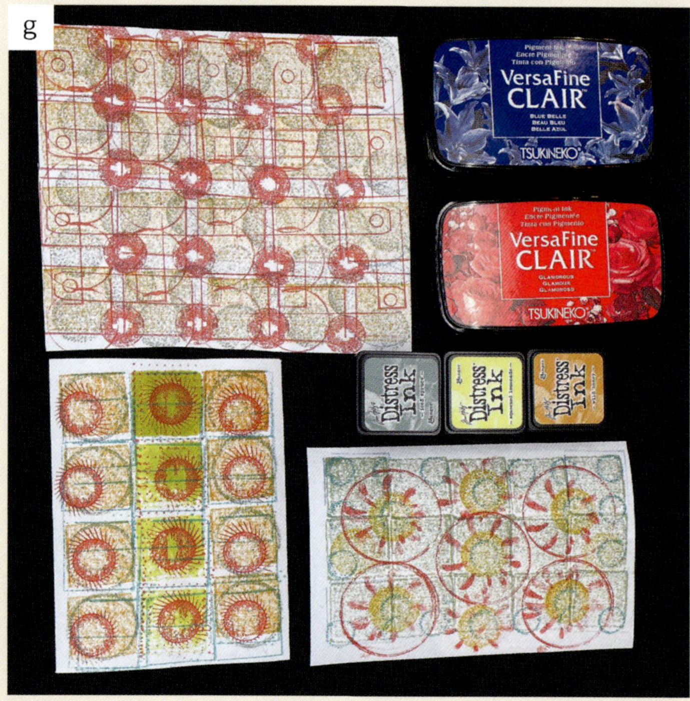

6. Create mark-making implements by wrapping string around a toilet roll tube or stretching rubber bands around a small block of wood (try to keep the wrapping as flat as possible). The string can be attached using double-sided tape. Apply the printing ink to the string or rubber bands with the roller or a sponge and print by rolling the tube across the paper or stamping the block on the paper. (e)

Build up a collection of interesting printed papers which can be used for collage or as backgrounds for development of pictures or journal pages. More creative ideas for using your printed papers can be found in Chapter 12 (see p.142).

7. Printing in layers creates interesting designs, limited only by your imagination. For flat-textured material (plastic meat trays, textured fabric, lace, corrugated card, bubble wrap, etc.) you can either use the ink pads to dab ink on to the surface, or roll printing ink over it. Then place your paper on the inked material and press firmly with your hands. (f)

8. Ink pads can be used either for printing with objects or for creating background colour by stamping the ink pads directly on to the paper – this gives you a head start and you can then print in one or more colours over the background using your objects. (g)

CLEANING UP

■ Use warm soapy water to wash the objects you have used and the inking tray/slab. Make sure the lids are firmly replaced on the ink pads to prevent them from drying out.

Monoprinting using a drawn image

This is a great way to create a monoprint image quickly when you have a layer of printing ink left on your inking plate after a linoprinting activity. Alternatively, you can start from scratch and roll out some ink especially for this process.

YOU WILL NEED
- printing paper to fit flat on the inking tray or slab (copy paper, sketchbook paper or cartridge paper)
- paper (with a simple design drawn or traced on it)
- scrap paper
- mount (optional)
- printing ink (Caligo Safe Wash)
- inking tray or slab
- roller (brayer)
- pencil
- washing-up bowl
- warm soapy water
- baby wipes or a damp cloth for cleaning up

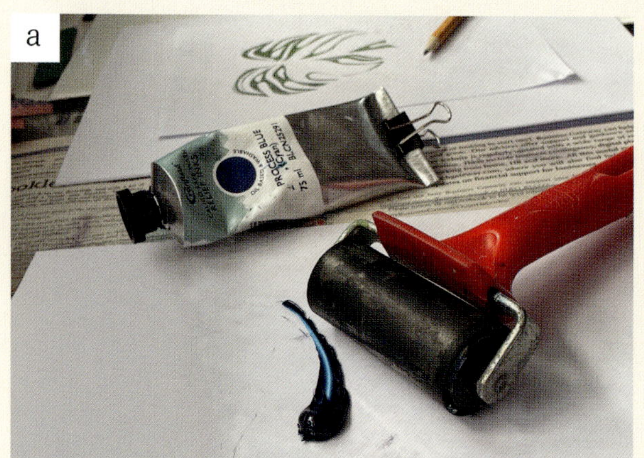

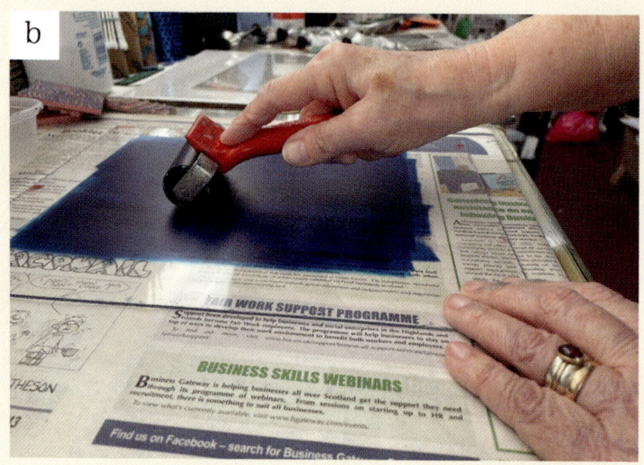

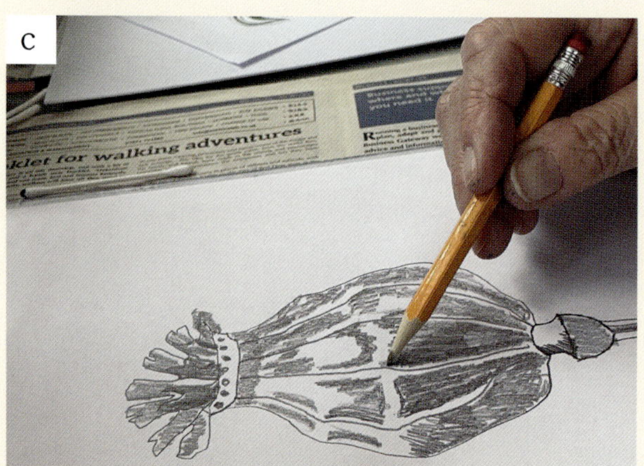

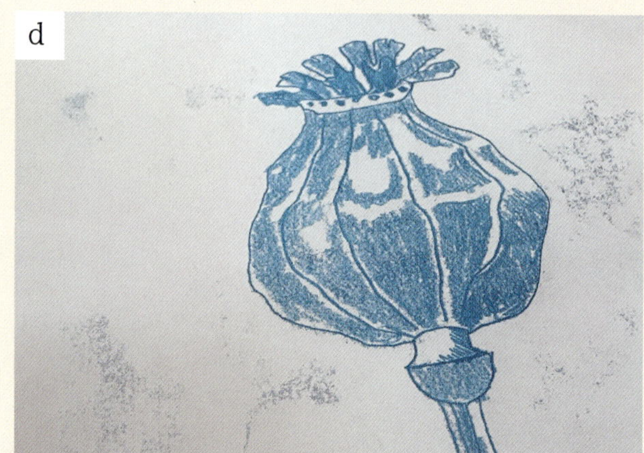

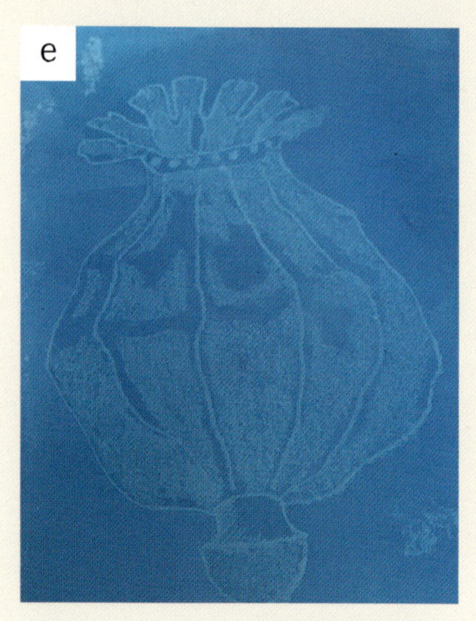

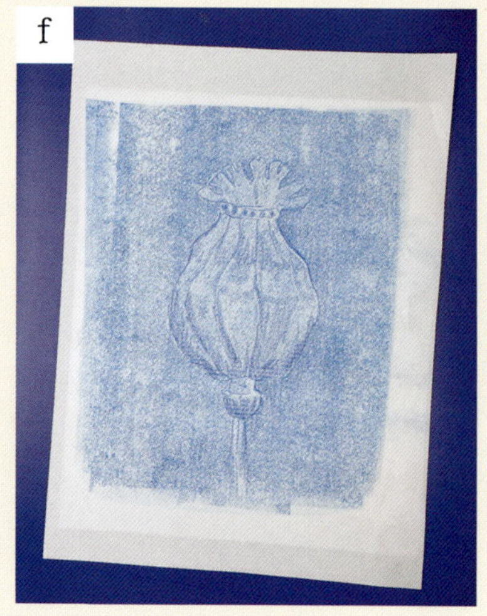

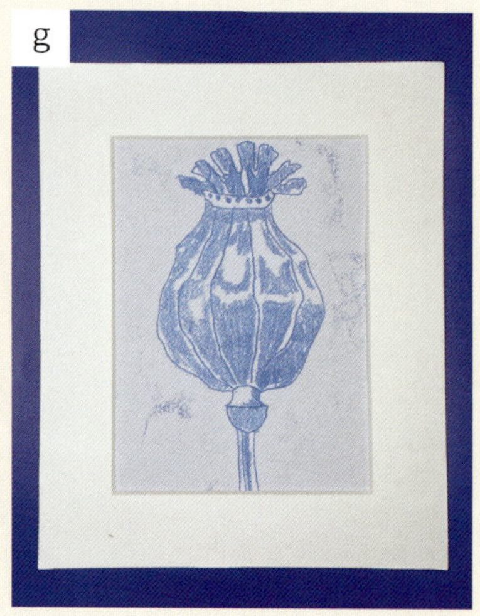

1. Squeeze a small amount of ink on to your inking tray or slab. (a)

2. Roll a thin layer evenly over the surface – it needs to be thin but evenly spread. (b)

3. Lay the printing paper carefully over the inked plate and then place the drawing face up on top of the printing paper.

4. Draw over the image with a pencil, without resting your hands on the paper. Press down firmly with the pencil. (c)

5. Lift the paper to reveal your print. There will be some background texture as well as the drawn image. You will see the drawn lines in the ink left on the plate. (d) (e)

6. Press a second piece of paper over the inked plate and rub the surface with your fingers, smoothing the paper so it makes good contact with the ink on the plate.

7. Lift to reveal the fainter 'ghost' version of your print. (f)

8. A mount around your print sets it off well. (g)

CLEANING UP

■ Clean the roller and inking tray/slab by rolling excess ink on to scrap paper and wiping ink from the inking try with paper or a baby wipe. Then wash with warm soapy water.

Monoprinting with a gel plate

You can use a variety of surfaces as the base for your printing plate – glass, an acrylic sheet, foil or even a tabletop – but a gel plate is an ideal surface to experiment with. A gel plate is a reusable printing plate that allows you to make monoprints without a printing press. Gel plates come in a range of sizes and are durable and long-lasting if cared for and stored properly. (Keep the acrylic sheets and clam-shell packaging your gel plate came in for storage.) A gel plate has a soft surface and is made with a mineral-based glycerine which gives the plate a soft, bouncy surface on which you can spread paints, add textures and make an infinite variety of prints using many different techniques. Gel plates are commercially available (see p.172) or can be handmade (see p.170).

Here are a few ways of using a gel plate for monoprinting, to get you started.

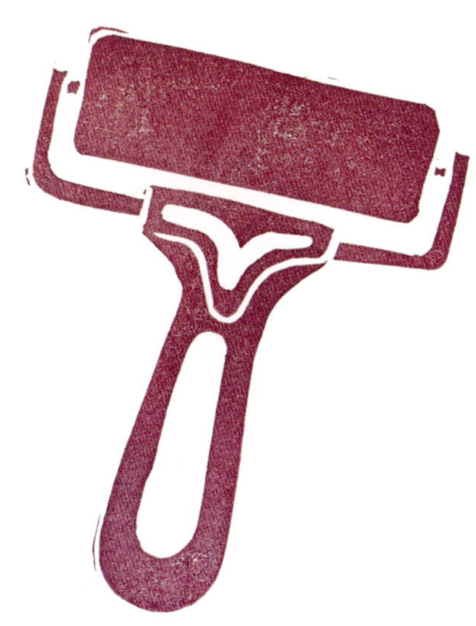

LAYERED BOTANICAL MONOPRINTS (TWO WAYS)

The gel plate can be used to build up a print in layers. You can print one image and then print over it again with a different colour and image, creating a complex print. You can also build the layers on the gel plate itself, allowing each layer of paint to dry before adding the next. Acrylic paint dries fast so have everything ready to hand and lift your print while the paint is wet. Make sure you roll excess paint from the roller between each layer so the paint does not dry on the roller. When applying the paint with your roller, you only need a light touch – do not press too hard or the paint will not spread evenly, and you will leave marks on the surface. If you are rolling a second layer of paint over another on the gel plate, be gentle so you don't disturb the layer of paint beneath.

Right: A selection of monoprinted papers made using a gel plate and acrylic paint.

Method A: Dark to light

YOU WILL NEED

- gel plate
- leaves, grasses or flowers (fresh or dried/pressed)
- textured materials (bubble wrap, corrugated card, scrunched cellophane or tissue paper, paper doilies, etc.)
- printing paper (sketchbook paper, cartridge paper or any smooth paper)
- spare paper (e.g., a piece of A4 copy paper)
- copy paper (optional)
- acrylic sheet (that the gel plate comes packaged in)
- roller (brayer)
- acrylic paints (any brand) (white and a range of light and dark colours)
- masking tape
- dry cloth (optional)
- damp cloth or baby wipes
- warm soapy water
- sanitiser gel

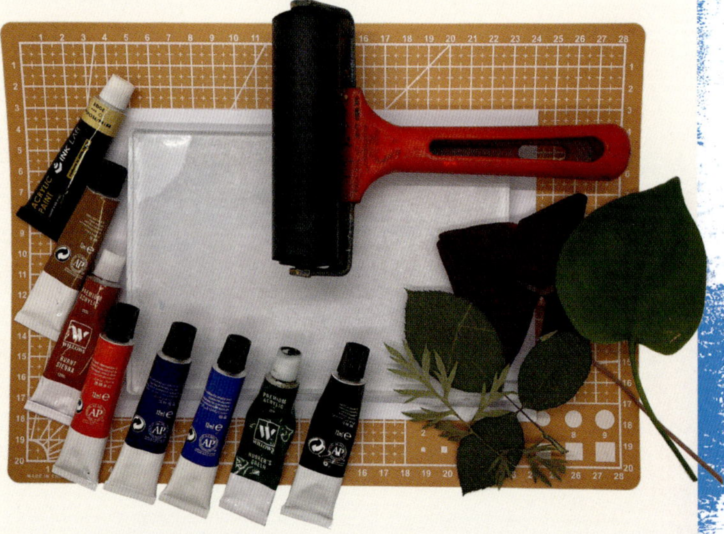

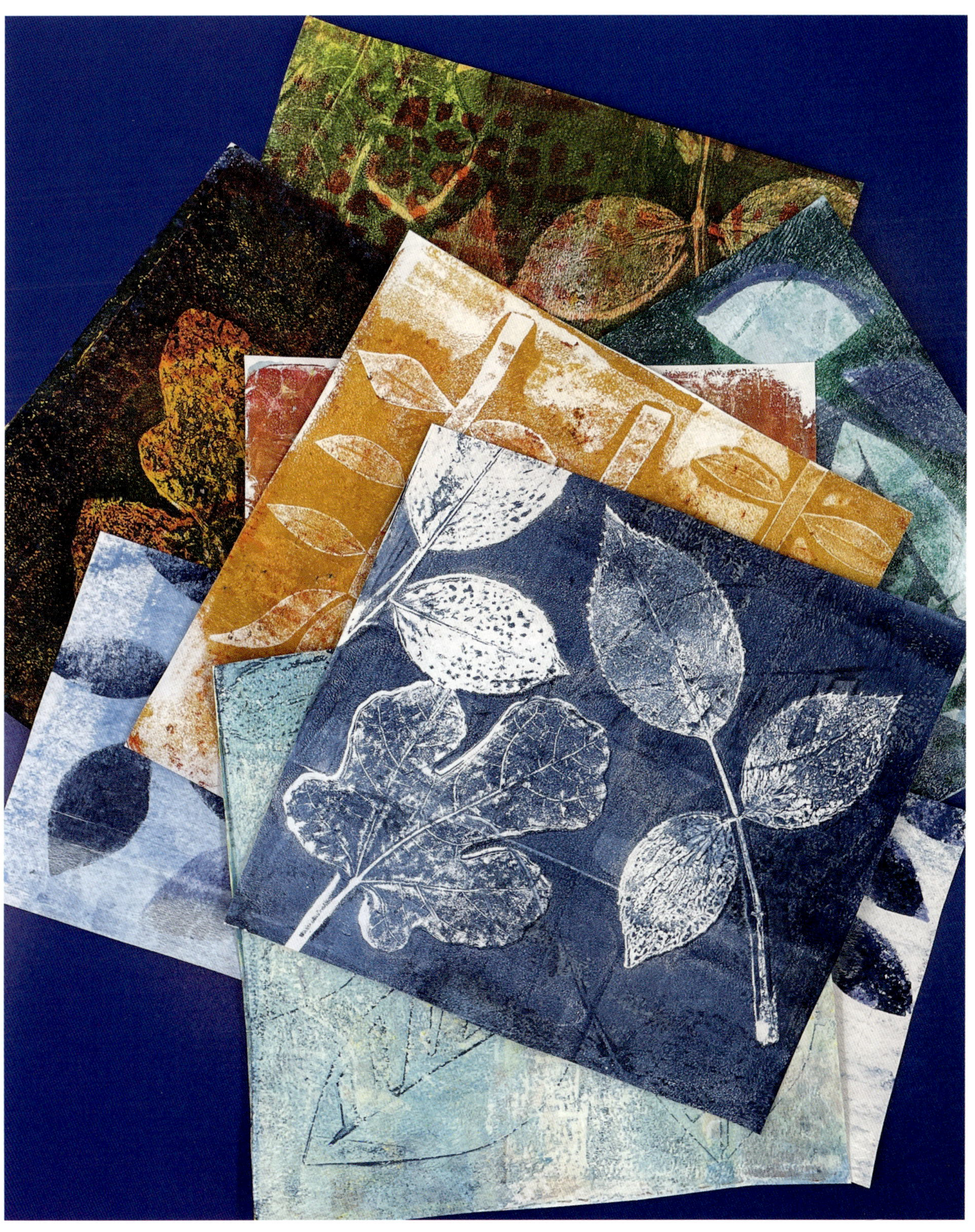

1. Place your gel plate on a firm wipeable surface – a sheet of acrylic is ideal. Copy paper or scrap paper on the tabletop is good too. Have some spare paper beside you to clean the roller in between layers (anything works for this except for newspaper as the print transfers to the gel plate). Using paper in this way stops the roller from becoming caked up with dried paint and difficult to clean. The 'clean-up' papers can become works of art in their own right and are great for collage.

2. Squeeze some small blobs of a dark paint (black, dark blue, dark green or brown) on the surface of the gel plate and spread an even, thin layer over the surface of the plate with the roller. (a)

3. Select some leaves or grasses, or a single large leaf. Arrange the foliage on the wet paint with the veiny side down. (b)

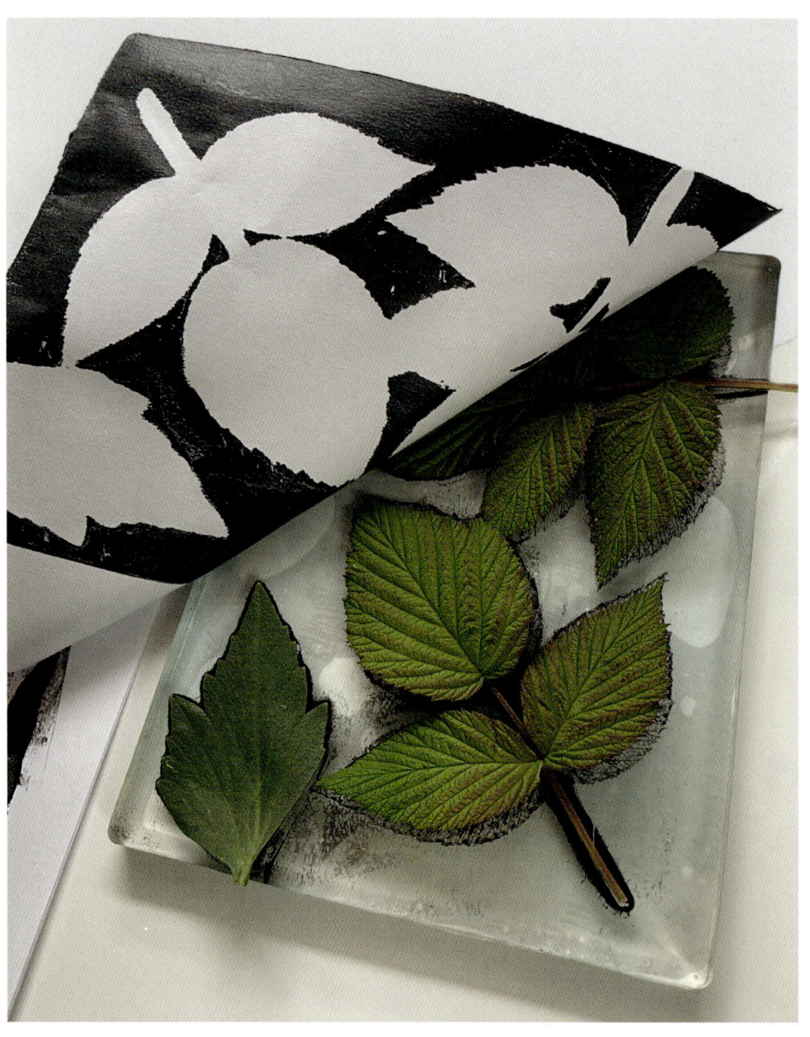

Left: **Pulling the first print from the gel plate. This removes the paint around the leaves. Once the leaves are lifted, a detailed image remains on the plate.**

4. Take a piece of printing paper and lay it over the leaves on the plate. Smooth the surface with your hands, making sure you press around the edges of the leaves carefully. (c)

5. Lift the paper from one edge, peeling it off. Remove the leaves, taking care not to leave fingerprints on the painted surface. The print on the paper will have white areas in the shape of the leaves. You could use this again and print over it. You now have a print with white leaf shapes on – these can be very dramatic. (d)

6. The imprint of the leaves will be left on the gel plate. Leave this imprint to dry for five to ten minutes before moving on to the next step. (e)

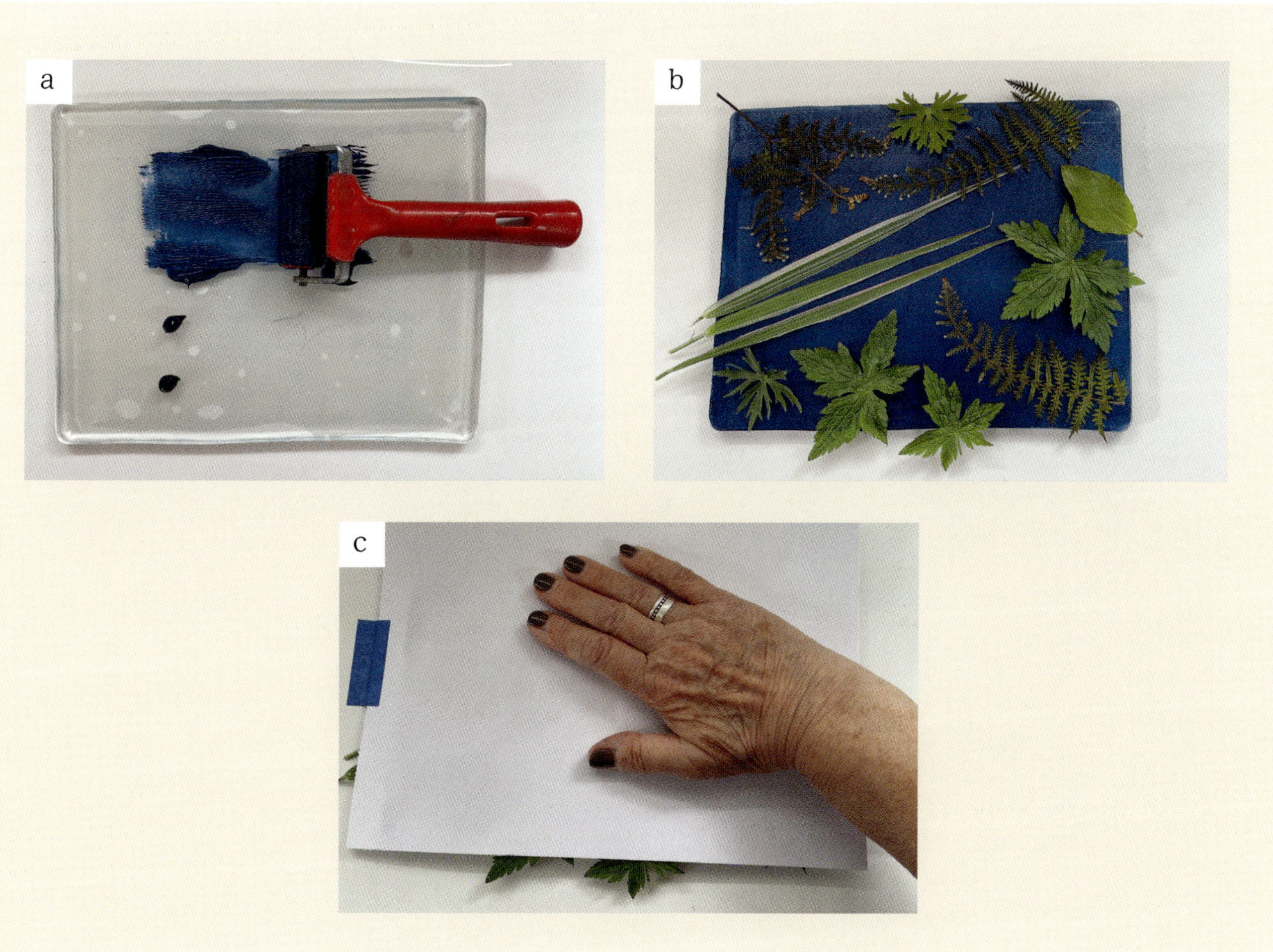

7. Once dry, apply some light-coloured paint to the gel plate, using the roller to spread a thin, even layer over the plate. (f)

8. Take a clean piece of paper and lay it over the plate. Rub firmly with your hands to ensure good contact and then peel away the paper. You will have a dark leaf print on a pale background. (g)

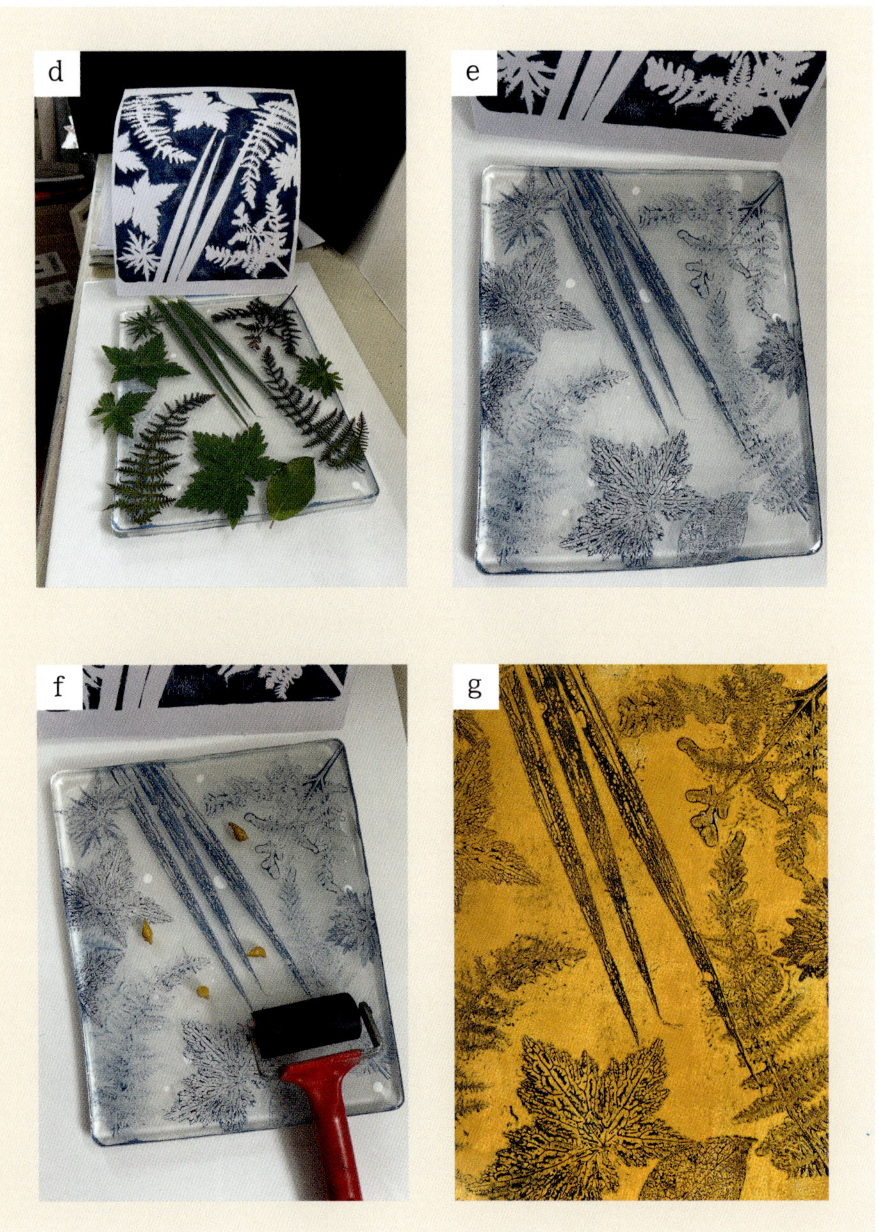

Method B: Light to dark

1. Place your gel plate on a firm, wipeable surface – a sheet of acrylic is ideal. Use a piece of spare paper as the clean-up paper for the roller.

2. Start with white and another light colour of acrylic paint and dab a few drops of paint on to the surface of the gel plate. Then gently roll the paint across the surface with the roller, blending the two colours to achieve a thin, even layer. Roll excess paint from your roller on to a spare piece of paper. (a)

3. Lay a piece of paper over the gel plate and use a piece of masking tape to fix the paper at the top. Gently but firmly, smooth the surface with your fingers. When you are satisfied that you have spread the paper right to the edges of the plate, lift the paper carefully, pulling it up from the lower edge and keeping the masking-tape 'hinge' intact. This is your base layer! Note that the paint will have transferred to the paper leaving the gel plate clean. If there is a small amount of paint remaining on the plate it does not matter. (b)

4. Roll a slightly darker layer of paint on to the plate. (c)

5. Add some texture to this second paint layer by pressing your chosen textured material into the wet paint and then carefully removing it. This will lift some of the paint, creating a pattern. (d) (e)

6. Fold the paper back over the gel plate and press down with your fingers to transfer the pattern on top of your first layer of paint.

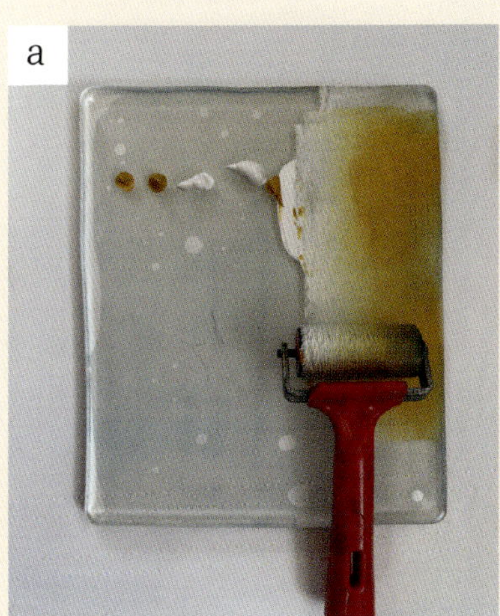

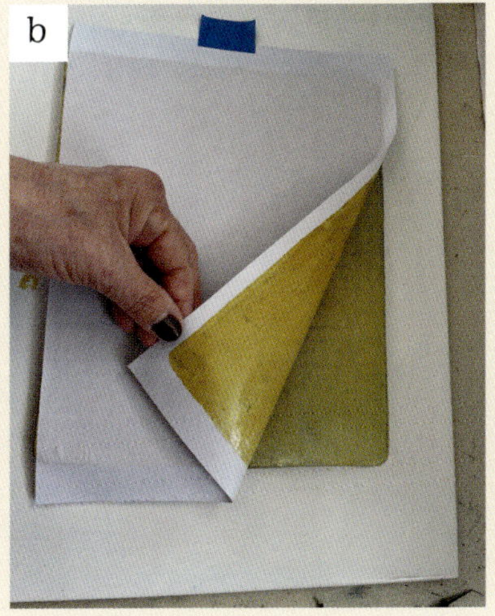

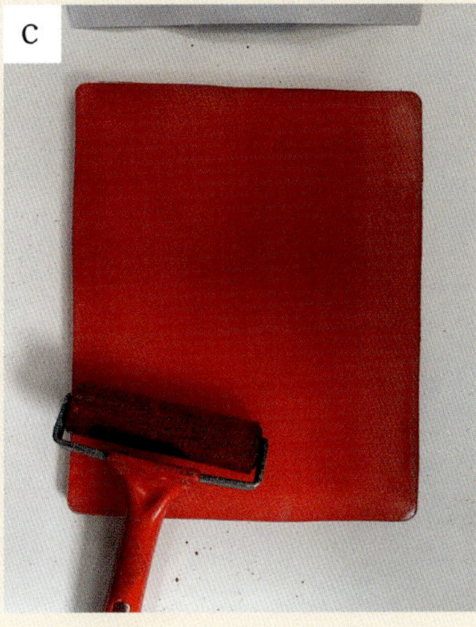

Carefully foid back the paper to reveal the combined layers. Clean the roller on your clean-up paper. (f)

7. Select a darker paint – green, dark blue or brown – and apply small blobs, spreading it to form a thin layer over the plate. (g)

8. Place some leaves and/or grasses carefully on the gel plate, with the veiny underside facing down. Fold your paper with the first two layers of paint back down on to the gel plate over the leaves and/or grasses. Firmly smooth the surface with your fingers, paying particular attention to the areas around the foliage to ensure they are flattened against the paint. (h) (i)

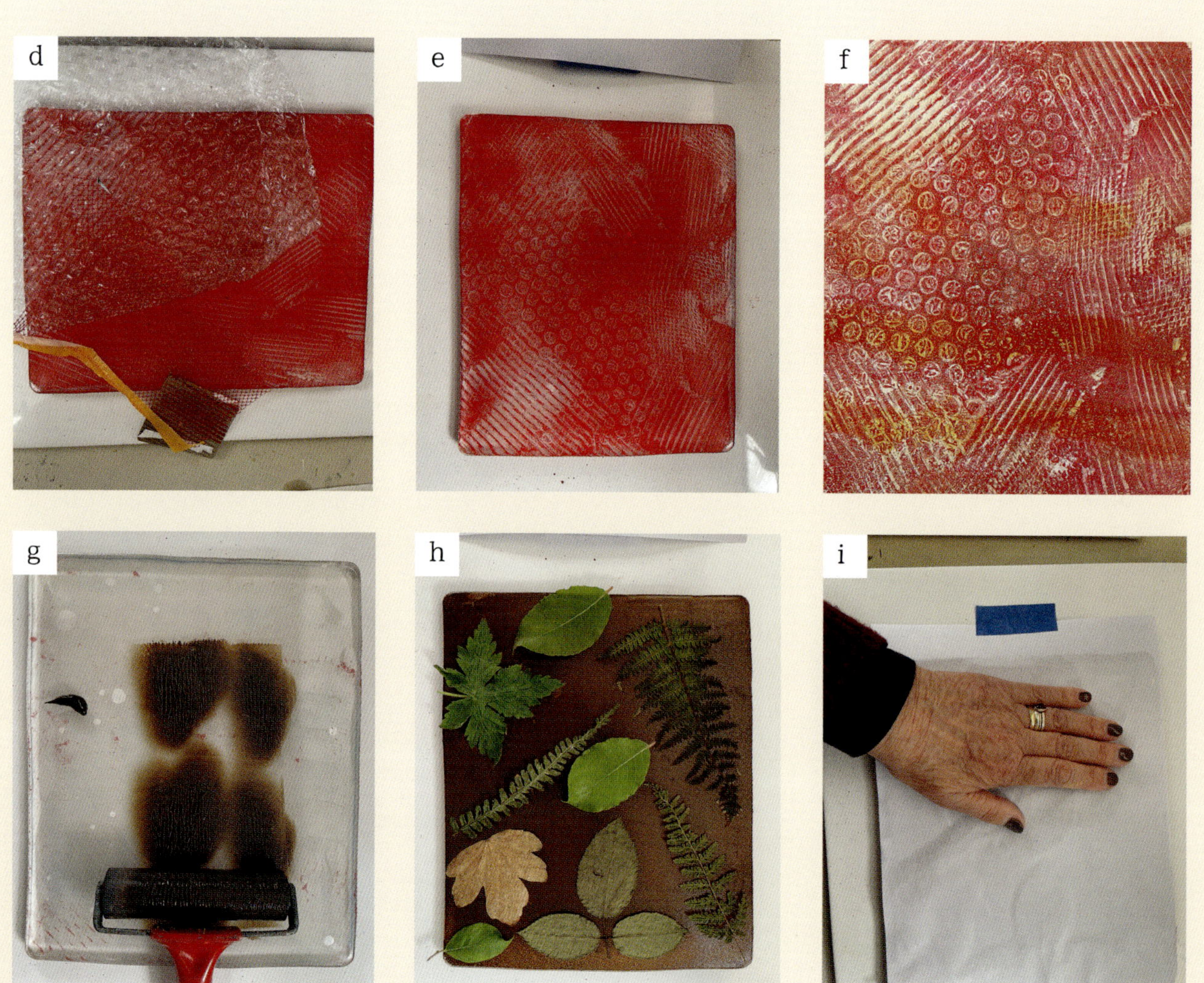

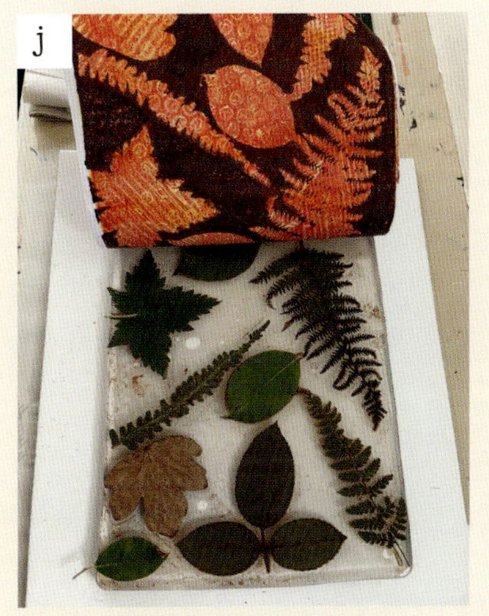

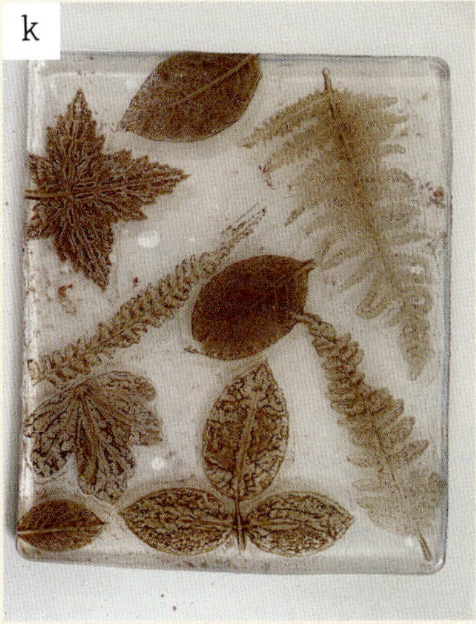

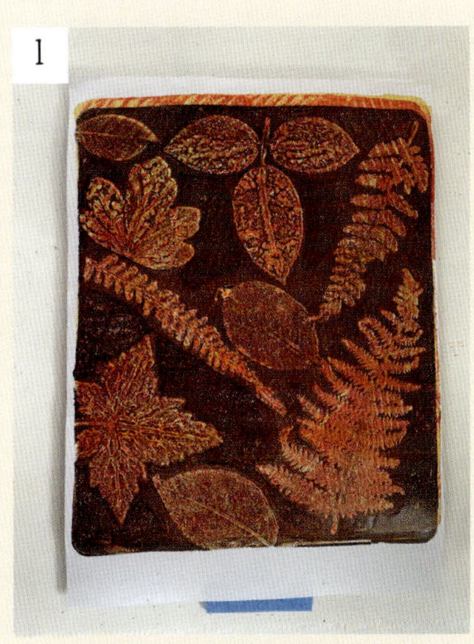

9. Lift the paper again. Remove the leaves and/or grasses. You should now see the textured background showing through the shapes of the leaves against a dark background. The image of the leaves will remain on the surface of the gel plate. (j)

10. While the paint on the plate is still wet, carefully fold the paper back over the gel plate to lift the impression left by the underside of the leaves. An image of the leaves will remain on the gel plate and this final print will have picked up the details from the leaves. (k) (l)

Cleaning up

- To clean your roller, roll any remaining paint on to the spare paper and then wash the roller in a bowl of warm soapy water. Rinse thoroughly and leave to dry.

- Wipe the gel plate with a damp cloth or baby wipe and then wash in warm soapy water, taking care not to damage the surface. Gently remove paint from the edges. Rinse and dry on a cloth or leave to air-dry. When dry, smear all over with a thin layer of sanitiser gel and place the original acrylic sheets (or plain paper) on each side. Gently press out any bubbles that form between the acrylic sheet and the surface of the gel plate, smoothing them to the edges. Pack in the clam-shell packaging the gel plate came in.

> Build up a collection of interesting printed papers which can be used for collage or as backgrounds for development of pictures or journal pages. More creative ideas for using your printed papers can be found in Chapter 12 (see p.142).

USING MASKS AND STENCILS

Stencils can be used to great effect to add pattern and texture. You can either buy these or make your own from thin card or plastic. Those made from paper or card tend to be more fragile than the ones cut from plastic material. Sheets of Tyvek® 'paper' are also useful for making stencils and can be obtained from craft suppliers.

Masks are shapes that are placed over the wet paint in places so that the paint does not transfer to the printing paper. You can use cut-outs from making stencils, torn or cut paper, or card shapes as masks. Similarly, adhesive craft foam shapes stuck to card can be pressed into the wet paint and then lifted to remove some of the paint in strategic areas.

YOU WILL NEED

- gel plate
- printing paper (copy paper, sketchbook paper, cartridge paper or any smooth paper)
- sketchbook paper, cartridge paper or spare paper
- thin card
- scissors or craft knife
- roller (brayer)
- acrylic paints
- masking tape
- dry cloth (optional)
- damp cloth or baby wipes
- warm soapy water
- sanitiser gel

1. Cut out some simple shapes from sketchbook paper, cartridge paper or thin card to create masks and a stencil. (a)

2. Put small blobs of a light-coloured paint on the gel plate and spread it using your roller, creating a thin layer of paint over the surface of the gel plate. You could experiment with using more than one colour to make a striped effect or just go with a single colour. (b) (c)

3. Place your printing paper over the gel plate and hinge it at the top with masking tape. Rub the surface of the paper with the flat of your hand and then fold the paper up. This is your base layer. If there is paint left on the surface of the gel plate you can leave it or use another piece of paper to lift the residue. (d)

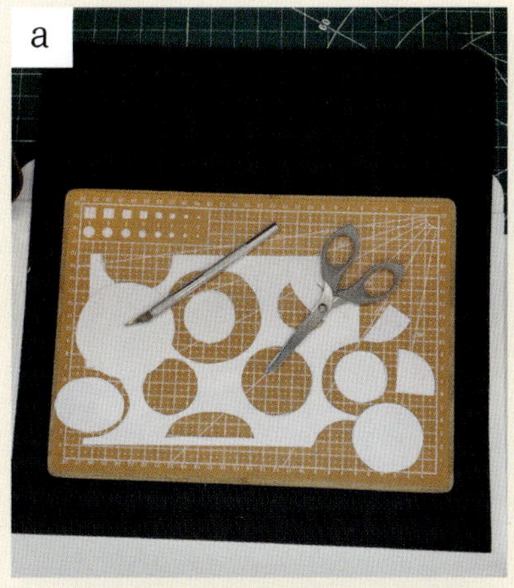
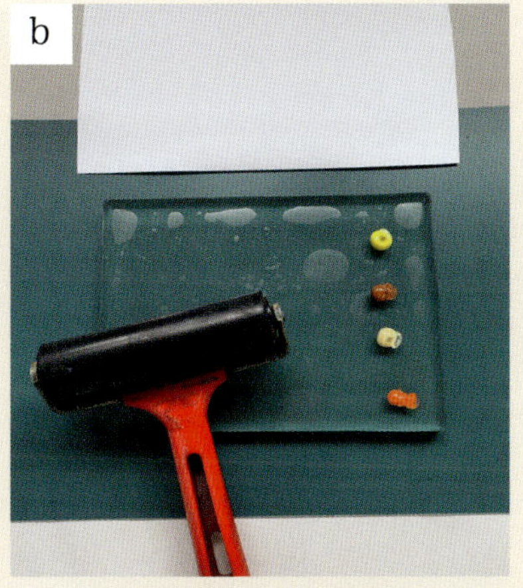
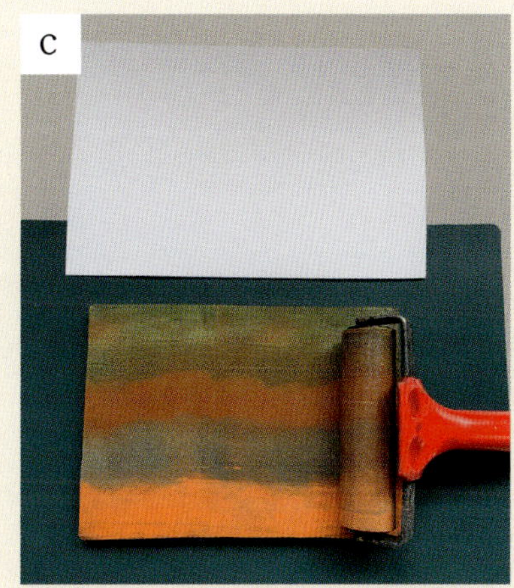
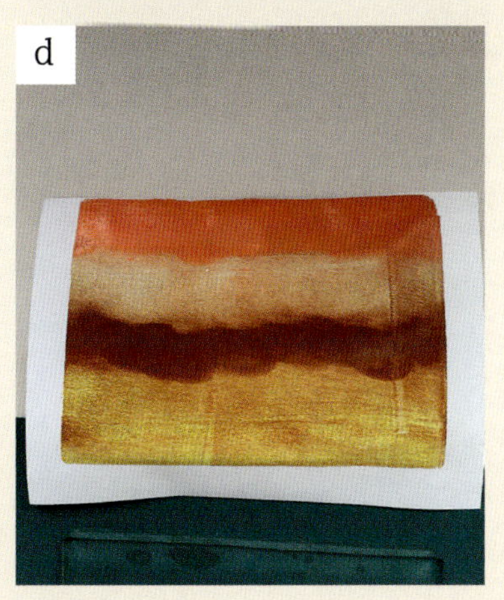
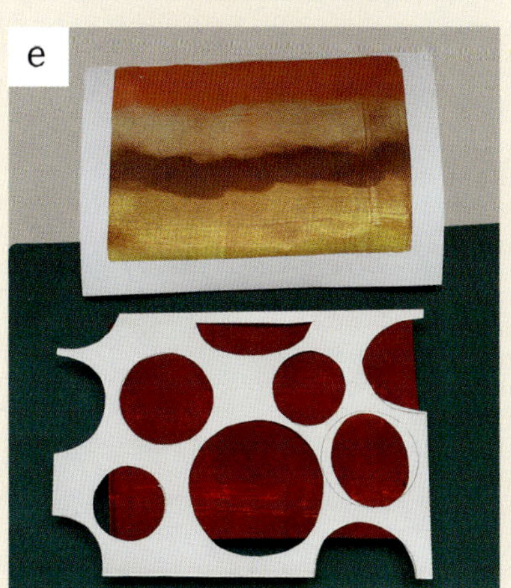
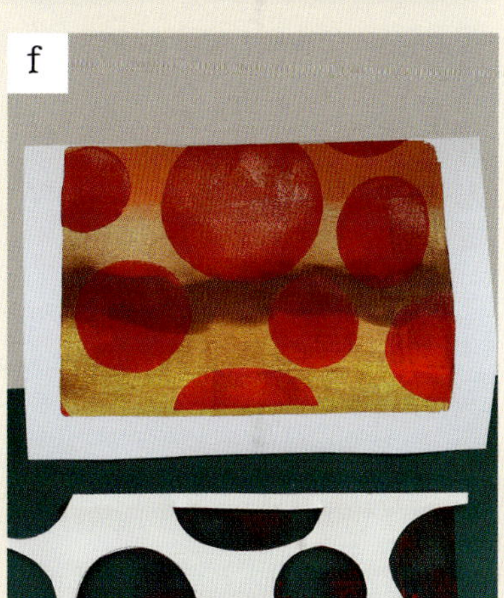

Play around with all manner of cut shapes and stencils to achieve different combinations of shape, texture and colour. Some will work brilliantly whilst others may be less successful, but even failed monoprints or your cleaning-off papers can be useful for collaged work (see Chapter 11, p.128).

4. Spread a thin layer of a darker paint over the plate with the roller and place your stencil gently on to the paint. (e)

5. Fold the printing paper back down, rubbing firmly all over the surface with the flat of your hand. Lift the paper and fold back. Remove the stencil. This is your second layer. (f)

6. Spread a contrasting, darker layer of paint on the plate and place some of the cut shapes on the surface in a pattern. Fold the paper back down and rub with your hands. (g)

7. Lift the paper to reveal your layered print. (h)

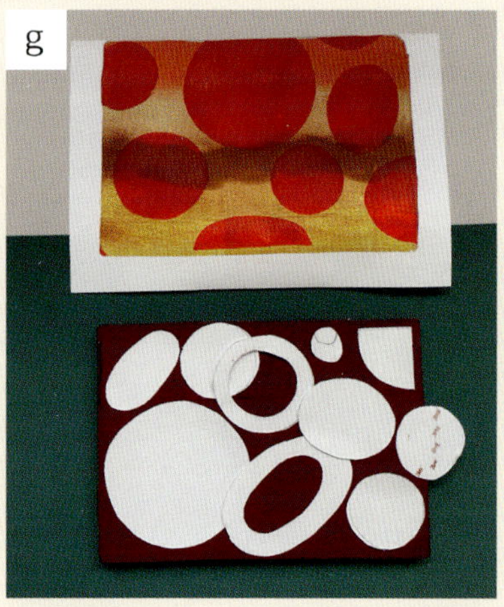

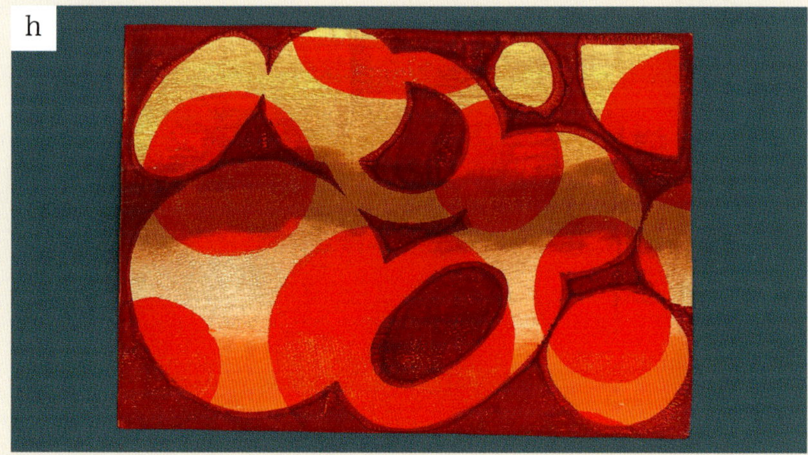

Cleaning up

- Stencils made from paper, card or Tyvek® can be left to dry; they become firmer with layers of dried acrylic paint on them.

- Clean the paint from your roller by rolling it on the spare paper and then wash with warm soapy water. Make sure the sides of the roller are free of paint. Rinse thoroughly and leave to dry.

- Wipe the gel plate with a damp cloth or baby wipe and then washing in warm soapy water, rinse and dry on a cloth or leave to air-dry.

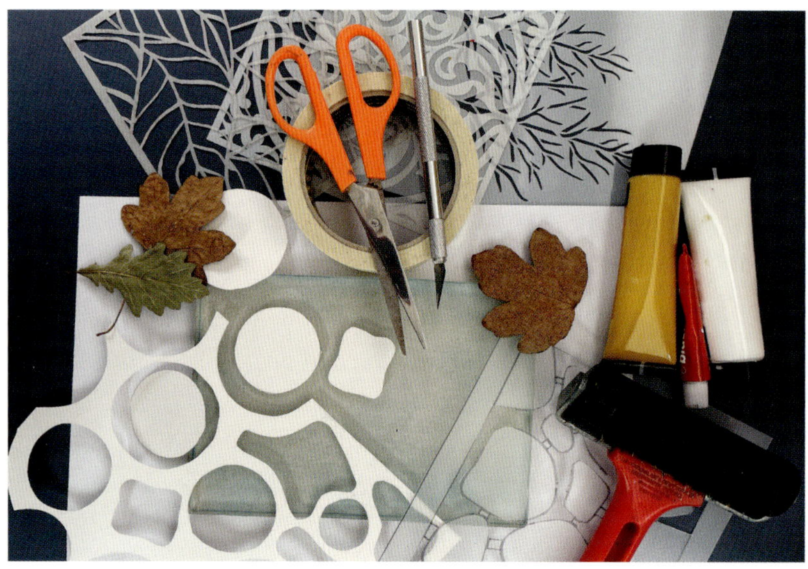

When dry, smear all over with a thin layer of sanitiser gel and place the original acrylic sheets on each side, gently smoothing out any bubbles that form between the acrylic sheet and the surface of the gel plate. Pack in the clam-shell packaging it came in.

CREATING TEXTURE

One of the exciting features of monoprinting with a gel plate is that you can use such a wide variety of found materials to produce unusual and intriguing textured prints. Something as simple as a piece of netting from a bag of oranges, a section of bubble wrap or some crumpled kitchen foil works a treat when gently pressed into the wet paint.

Try using bought stencils, layering one over the other or using them only in parts of the plate. Press down and use scrap paper to remove some of the paint from the cut apertures in the stencil. Lift the stencil and take a print — work fast before the paint dries. If it dries, spread a thin layer of a contrasting paint and take a print while this is wet.

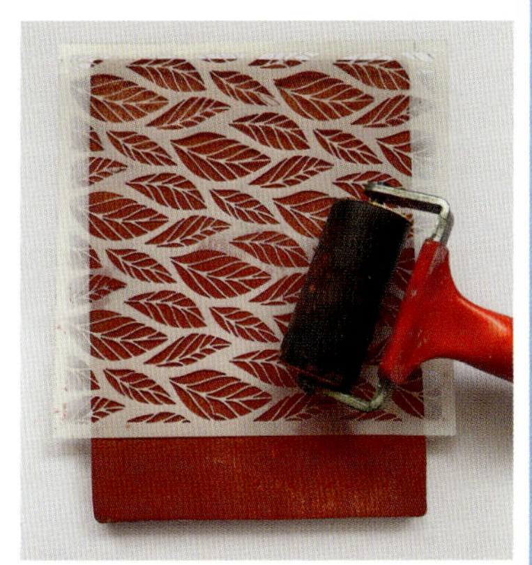

Experiment with craft foam shapes stuck to a piece of card to lift the paint in specific areas before taking a print.

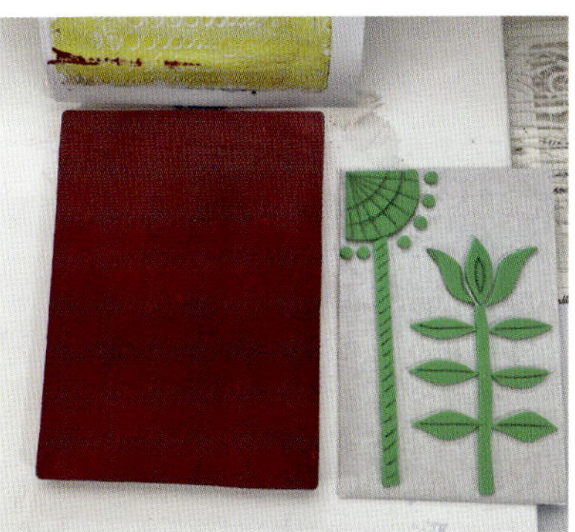

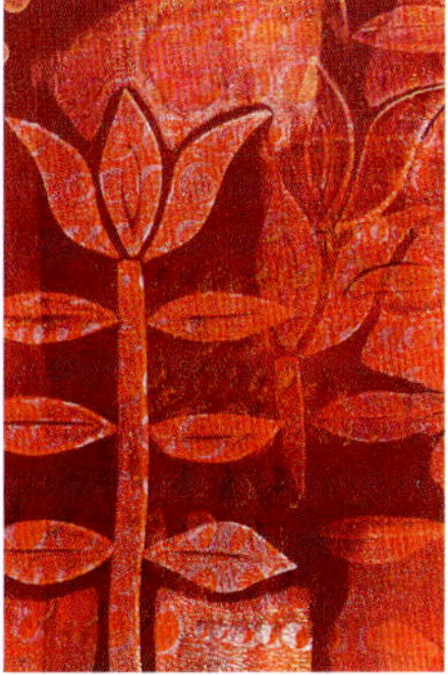

YOU WILL NEED

- gel plate
- printing paper (copy paper, sketchbook paper, cartridge paper or any smooth paper)
- sketchbook paper, cartridge paper or spare paper
- thin card
- scissors or craft knife
- roller (brayer)
- acrylic paints
- masking tape
- dry cloth (optional)
- damp cloth or baby wipes
- warm soapy water
- sanitiser gel

1. Start by finding useful mark-making objects around the house that have interesting shapes or textures. Cut or tear some random strips of paper or textured wallpaper. Have these and some textured materials ready to use.

2. Place your gel plate on a firm, wipeable surface. Have a piece of spare paper beside you as the clean-up paper for the roller.

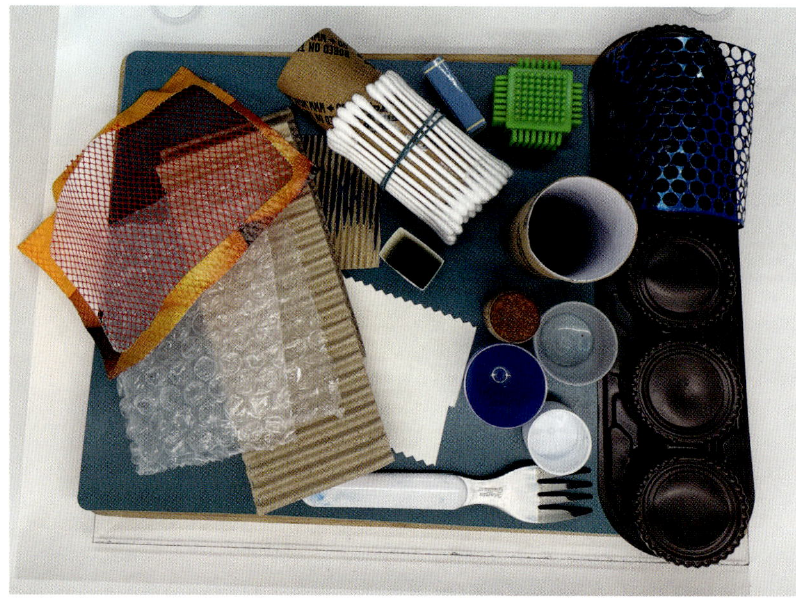

Left: A variety of materials that can be found around the home for creating texture in your printmaking.

3. Start with white and another light colour of acrylic paint and dab a few drops of paint on to the surface of the gel plate. Then gently roll the paint across the surface with the roller, blending the two colours to achieve a thin, even layer. (Alternatively, you could mix your white and coloured paints on a mixing tray or paper plate to achieve a smooth blend of colour and then transfer to the plate with your roller.) Roll excess paint on to a spare piece of paper to clean your roller between each layer (keep clean-up papers as collage material). (a) (b)

4. Use some of your mark-making materials to create an abstract pattern in the paint. Take care not to damage the surface of the plate when pressing objects into the paint and then removing them. Work quickly so the paint does not dry before you get to lift a print. Place a clean sheet of printing paper over the plate, attach it with masking tape like a hinge at the top and rub firmly over the surface with the flats of your hands. Peel the paper off gently to reveal the first of your layers. (c) (d) (e)

5. Repeat step 4 using a slightly darker paint layer. Use different materials to create texture — corrugated card for stripes, crumpled cling film or foil, strips of torn paper or textured wallpaper pressed into the paint and then removed. (You might get a print from these on your clean-off paper if the paint is wet enough.) (f)

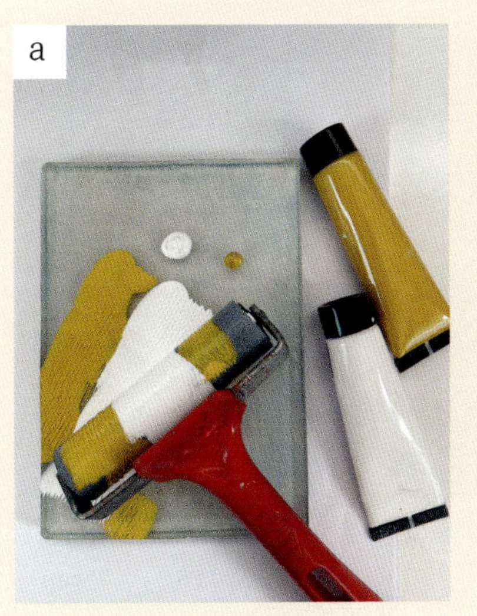

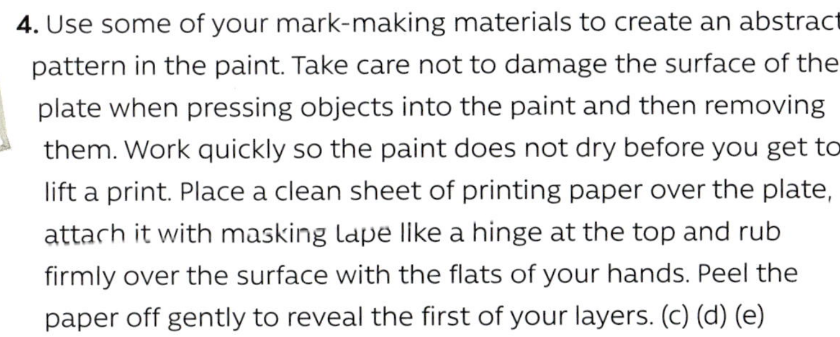

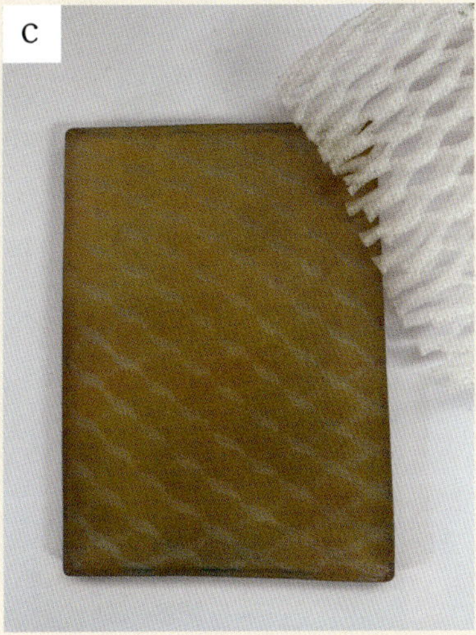

a

b

c

6. Fold the paper back over the plate and rub with your hands. Peel off to reveal the second layer printed over the first. (g) (h)

Cleaning up

■ Clean the paint from your roller by rolling it on the spare paper and then washing with warm soapy water. Make sure the sides of the roller are free of paint. Rinse thoroughly and leave to dry.

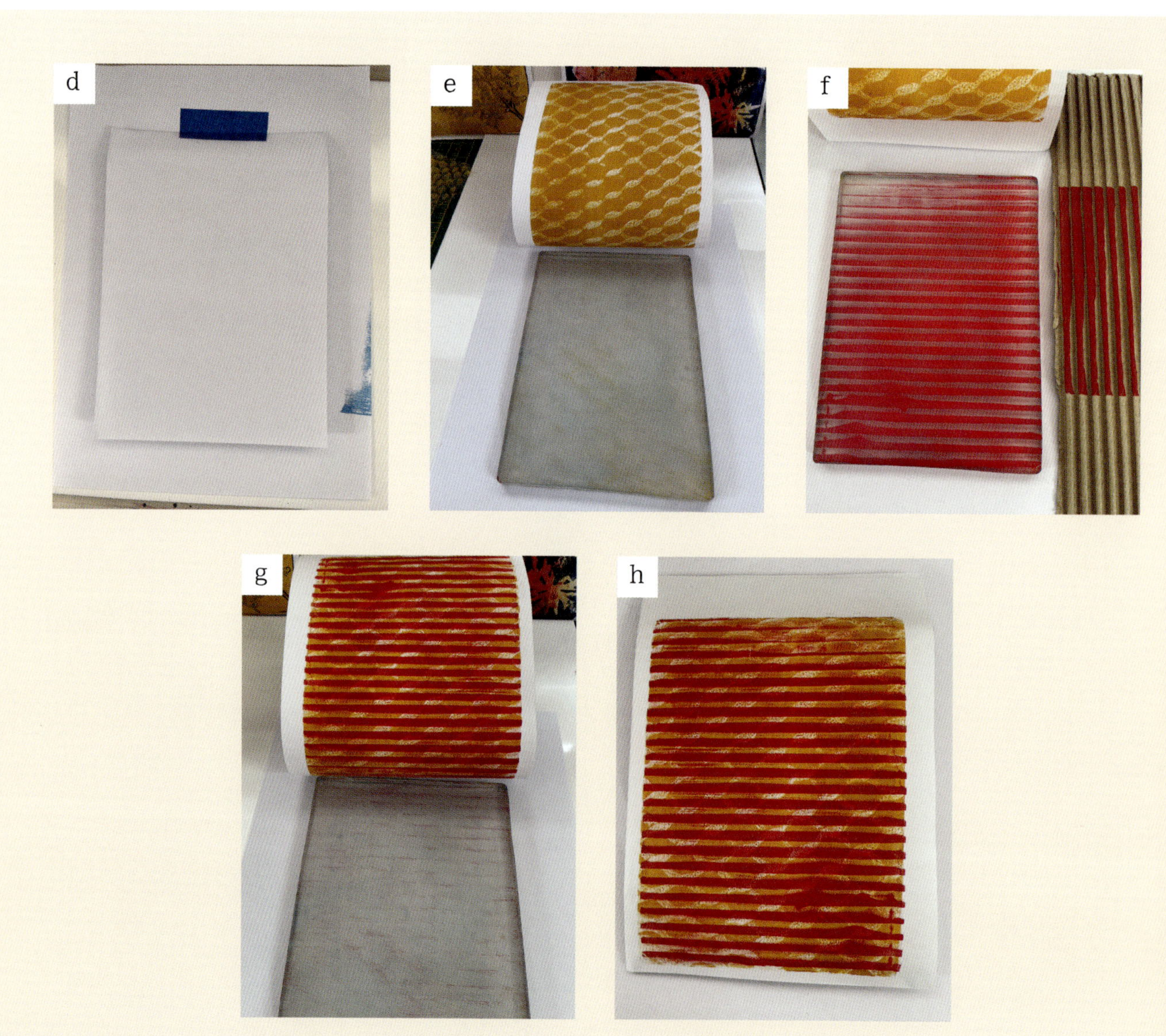

Add a third layer of paint if you like, although having two is enough to create an interesting textured print. It is worth playing with different combinations of textured materials and mark-making objects to print a range of varied and useful papers. These could be used as images or backgrounds or for collage work (see Chapter 11, p.128).

■ Wipe the gel plate with a damp cloth or baby wipe and then wash in warm soapy water, rinse and dry on a cloth or leave to air-dry. When dry, smear all over with a thin layer of sanitiser gel and place the original acrylic sheets on each side, gently smoothing out any bubbles that form between the acrylic sheet and the surface of the gel plate. Pack in the clam-shell packaging it came in.

LIFTING ALL THE LAYERS IN ONE 'PULL'

This is a slightly different method of creating layered prints that can be used to great effect. You just need a bit of patience while waiting for the layers to dry. You can use the three-layer method I have shown here, but there are other variations that you can try.

YOU WILL NEED
- gel plate
- textured materials (bubble wrap, corrugated card, scrunched cellophane or tissue paper, textured wallpaper samples, stencils, plastic netting from supermarket fruit, etc.)
- printing paper (copy paper, sketchbook paper, cartridge paper or any smooth paper)
- spare paper
- stencils (bought or handmade)
- scissors or craft knife
- roller (brayer)
- acrylic paints
- masking tape
- dry cloth (optional)
- toothbrush or foam dish scrubber
- damp cloth or baby wipes
- warm soapy water
- sanitiser gel

1. Spread a layer of dark paint evenly over the surface of the gel plate, clean your roller on a spare sheet of paper and then place some leaves over the paint. (a)

2. Gently press a piece of paper over the surface of the gel plate and rub with the flat of your hand, lifting the paint in the spaces. You will have a print with white spaces where the leaves masked the paint layer. You can print over it or paint into the shapes. (b) (c)

3. Carefully remove the leaves from the gel plate, leaving their pattern in the paint. Now wait five to ten minutes for the paint to dry on the gel plate. (d)

4. Once the first layer is dry, roll a lighter, contrasting layer of paint gently over the surface. Clean your roller on a spare sheet of paper. (e)

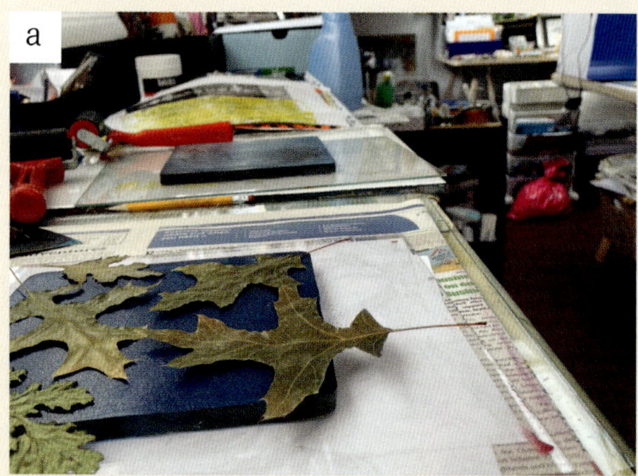

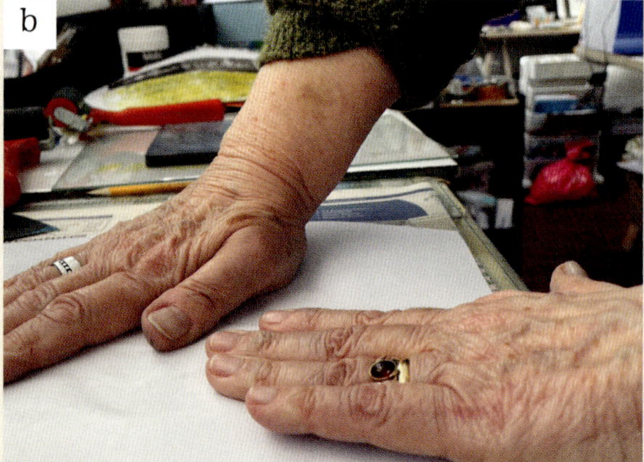

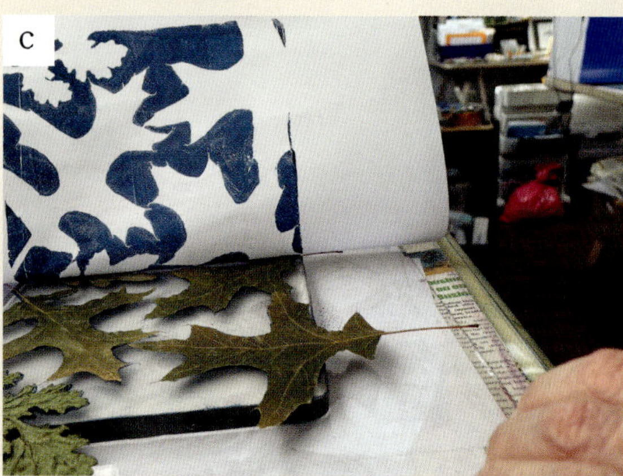

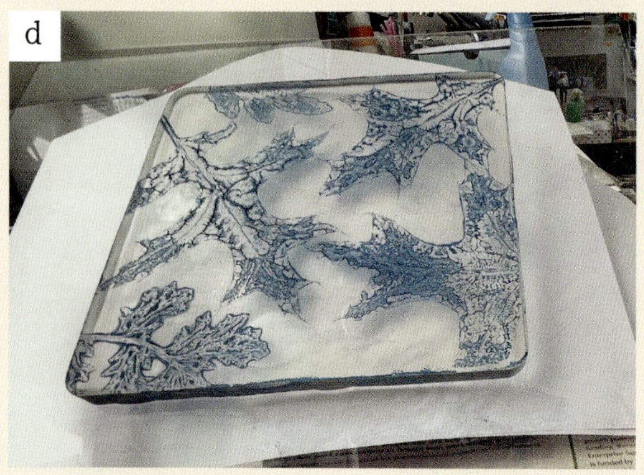

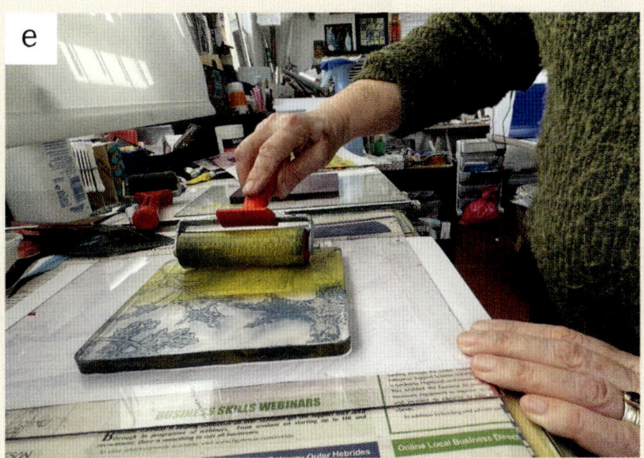

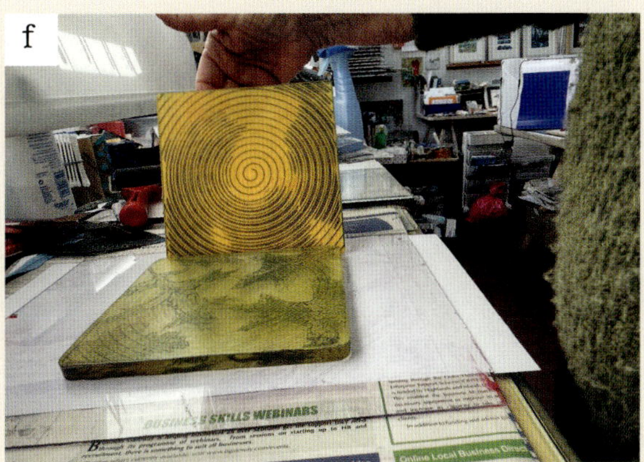

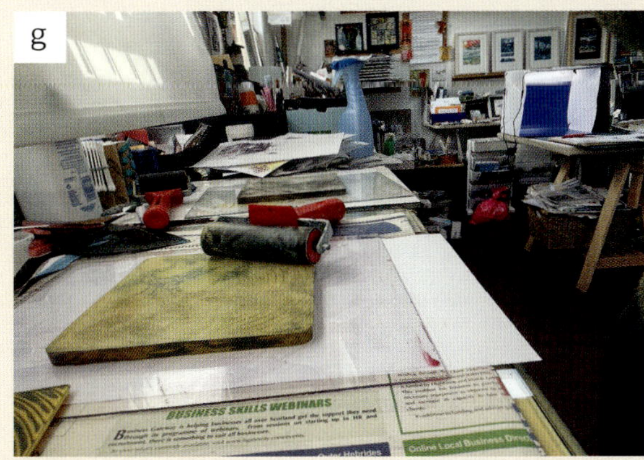

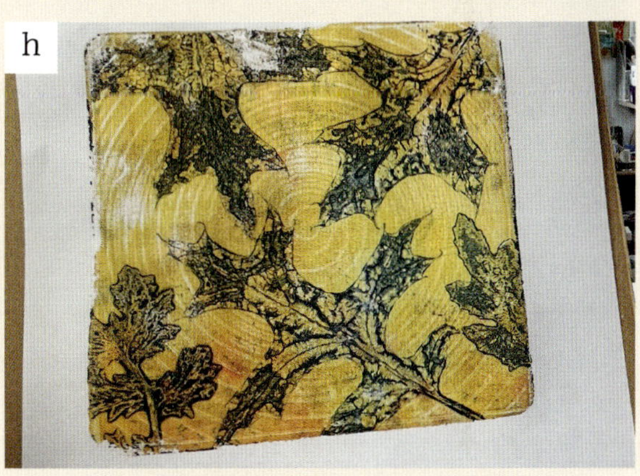

You could place cut shapes or a stencil on the gel plate instead of leaves in step 1.

5. Press some textured material into the wet paint — this could be corrugated card, bubble wrap or textured paper. I have used a plastic plate with a pattern on it. Clean your roller on a spare sheet of paper. A handmade stencil or some cut-out paper shapes could be used to mask areas of layer 1. Leave this second layer to dry. (f)

6. Roll a very thin layer of white paint over the surface and, while the paint is still wet, place a clean piece of paper over the gel plate and rub firmly all over the surface. (g)

7. Lift the paper and you should find all three layers printed together on the paper with the first, dark layer of leaf prints on top, then the texture behind them and the white layer as background. (h)

8. You may find some of the first two layers are left on the surface of the gel plate. Roll some more white paint over the plate, and lift it while the paint is wet — you might get a pale but interesting 'ghost' print.

Cleaning up

- Remove any remaining paint from your roller by rolling on the spare paper, then wash in warm soapy water. If the paint has dried on the surface of the roller, let it soak for a while and then use a toothbrush or foam pan scrubber to help lift the paint. Make sure the sides of the roller are free of paint as a build-up can prevent it moving smoothly. Rinse and leave to dry, resting the roller on its ledge so the roller is not touching any surface.

- Wipe the gel plate with a damp cloth or baby wipe and then wash in warm soapy water, rinse and dry on a cloth or leave to air-dry. When dry, smear all over with a thin layer of sanitiser gel and place the original acrylic sheets on each side, gently smoothing out any bubbles that form between the acrylic sheet and the surface of the gel plate. Pack in the clam-shell packaging it came in.

- If you have used plastic stencils they can be washed in warm soapy water.

Another way of using a stencil is to place it on the gel plate before adding the paint. Then use a sponge to dab paint into the cut holes in the stencil. Lift the stencil and leave the dark pattern to dry before adding layer 2.

EXPERIMENTING USING THE GEL PLATE

Now you have some idea of how the gel plate can be used, you can begin experimenting and trying different ways of creating monoprints. The more you play around with layers and materials, the more confident you will become. It can be very addictive and you will quickly build up lots of great printed papers. Here are some tips:

- Try using only black and white paints for a dramatic effect.

- Spread some paint over the gel plate and draw into the surface with a cotton bud before taking a print.

- If you get distracted mid-printing and your paint dries on the gel plate, don't worry — roll a new layer of paint over the plate in white or a pale colour and then lift your print while this layer is still wet. This can produce an unexpected and interesting version of the print you were planning!

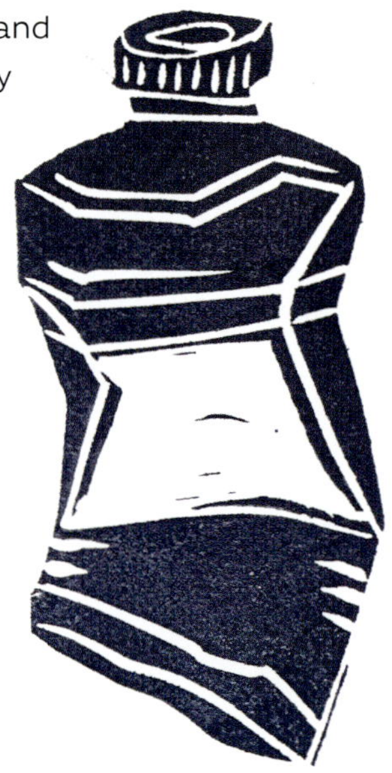

5

RELIEF PRINTING – AN INTRODUCTION

Relief printing is a form of printmaking where areas of the printing surface are cut away to leave raised parts of the printing block. When ink is applied to the printing block, these raised areas become covered with a layer of ink, whilst the areas that have been carved away remain free of ink. When the block is printed, the inked areas are in contact with the paper and transfer the image.

Relief printing can be done with a variety of printing materials – lino, rubber stamps, woodblocks, letterpress or even the cut surface of a potato.

An example of a composite relief print made using four Speedy Carve™ blocks.

Cutting tools

There are many different types of lino-cutting tools available to buy. If you are just starting out, I would suggest that you avoid the cheapest sets of tools and go for one of the mid-range sets which you can use on traditional lino, Japanese Vinyl or other types of printing blocks. If you decide to develop your practice, you can invest in some more expensive tools.

It takes a bit of practice to use the V- and U-shaped cutting tools effectively. (See also the safety tips on p.20.)

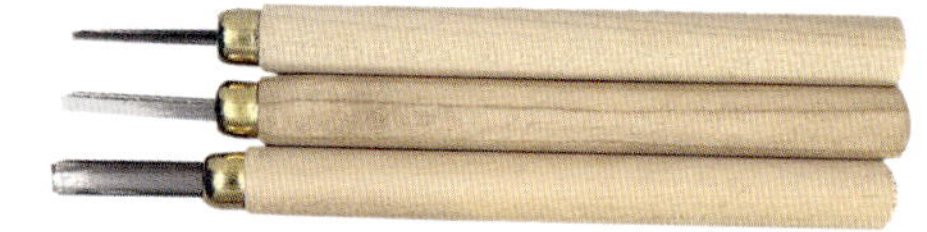

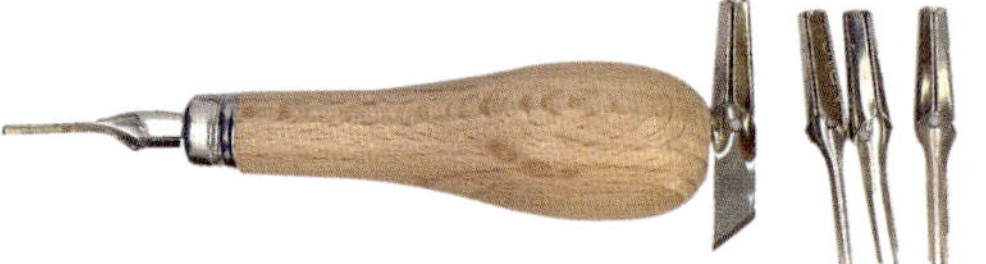

- V-tool: make sure that the point of the 'V' is down and in contact with the surface of your plate. You do not need to press down hard, just cut into the surface and let the blade glide around your drawn lines. If you're using one of the softer printing blocks, it is easy to cut into the surface. Using a V-shaped cutting tool with lino or Japanese Vinyl requires a more controlled cutting technique (see Chapter 6, p.64).

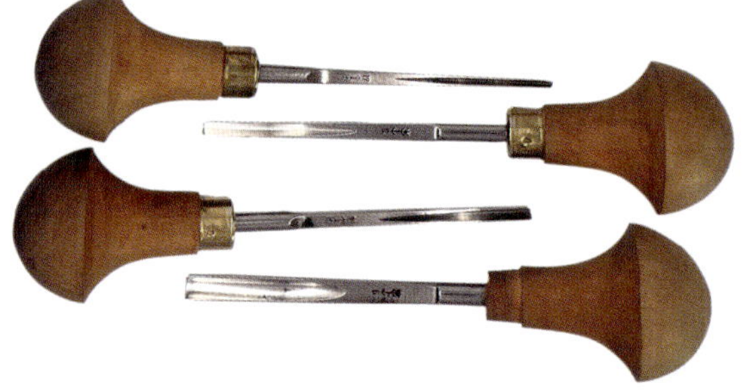

- U-tool: The U-shaped cutting tool removes a larger amount of the surface and is used to cut away background areas. A small U-shaped cutting tool can also make interesting marks or be used to make small circular holes.

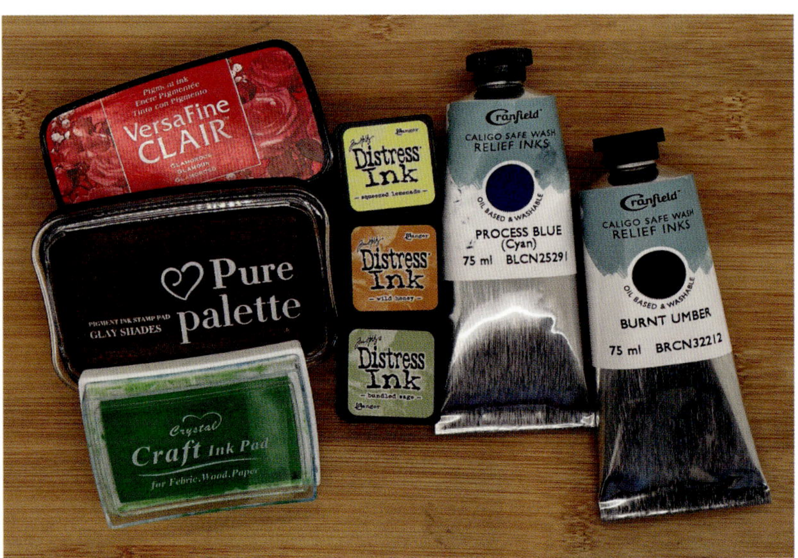

Inks

Inexpensive water-based printing inks do not always print evenly, so I use Caligo Safe Wash inks instead. The tubes come in a variety of colours, but start with black, white, red, blue and yellow, and you can mix a whole rainbow of colours. They are slower to dry than water-based inks so bear this in mind if you are making cards. The paper you print on affects the drying speed, and card is less absorbent than paper. You can also use ink pads as a quick and effective way of inking your printing block.

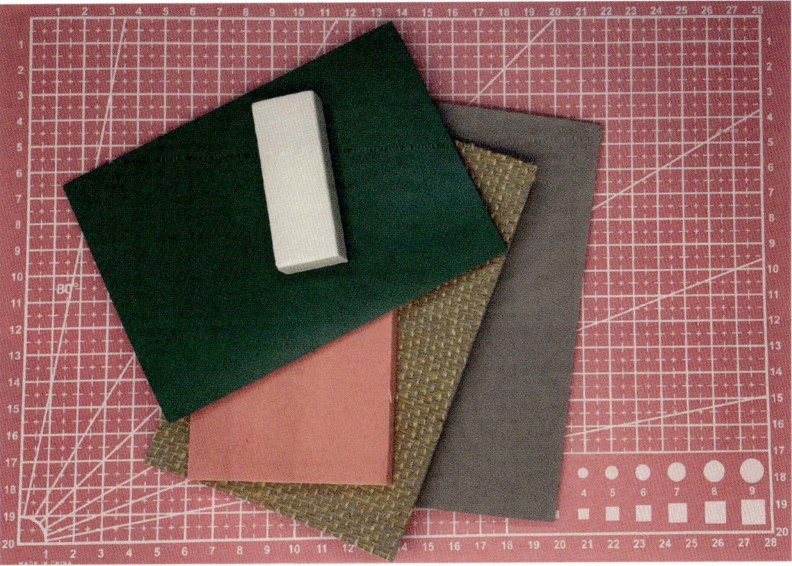

Right: **Materials that can be used for relief printing include erasers, Japanese Vinyl, pink Speedy Carve™ blocks and traditional lino with hessian backing.**

Materials

Traditional lino with hessian backing was originally used for relief printing and is used by many printmakers but there are now other options available from art shops and printmaking suppliers. Japanese Vinyl is my personal choice as it is easier to carve and does not dry out with age. There are various types of printing materials made from a flexible, rubbery substance which can be used for creating stamps or basic 'lino' prints — they are easier to carve than traditional lino or Japanese Vinyl but do not give the crisp outlines. Examples include Speedy Carve™ by Speedball® and SoftCut® by Essdee®. Other possible materials include carved erasers, craft foam, polystyrene sheets and even modelling clay, which can be pressed into interesting textured surfaces and then inked and printed on to paper. You can be very inventive once you start looking for materials to use.

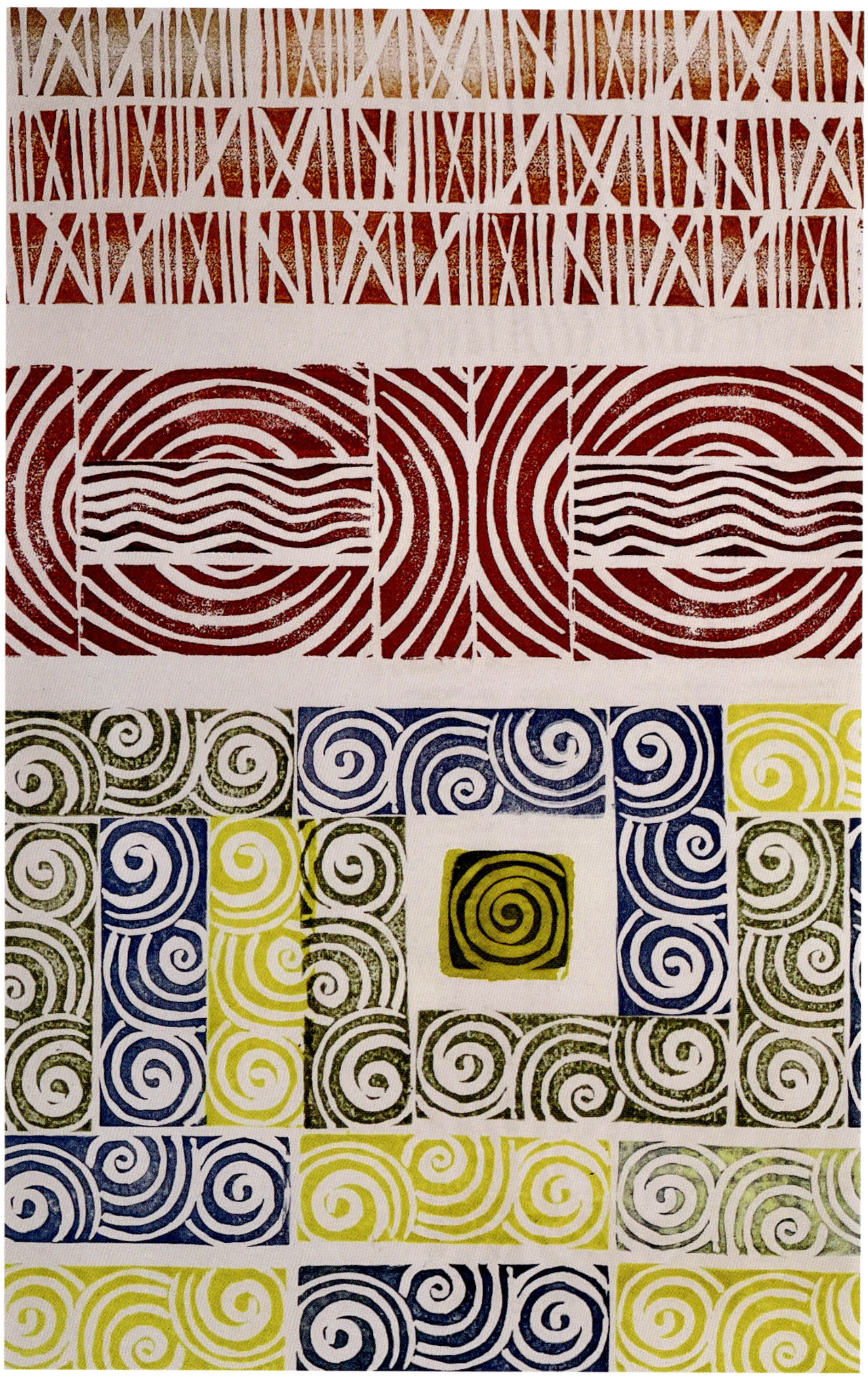

Above: An example of relief prints made from carved erasers.

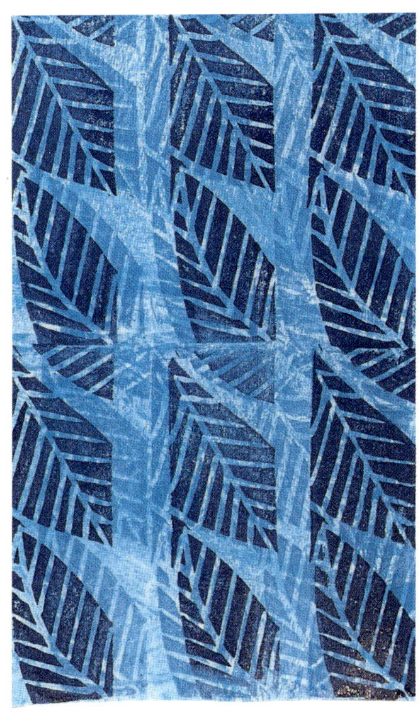

Here are two activities to introduce you to relief printing: the materials are easy to carve into and you will learn how to hold and use the cutting tools before moving on to lino or Japanese Vinyl.

Mini prints with erasers

Carving a simple image into a soft eraser is quick and easy. Ordinary erasers (rubbers) are available from stationers or supermarkets and come in a variety of shapes and sizes. The softer, rubbery ones work best, and you need erasers with a flat surface and right-angled corners. Here are a few tips:

- Keep your design very simple.

- Erasers make very small stamping blocks, so take care how you hold them when carving your design.

- Keep your fingers away from the lip of the cutting tool.

- Work on a non-slip mat.

- Use ink pads in different colours to create a variety of different repeat patterns.

YOU WILL NEED

- four erasers
- printing paper (copy paper, sketchbook paper, cartridge paper or any smooth paper – a smooth surface makes a crisper print)
- newspaper
- cutting mat
- non-slip mat
- cutting tools (V-shaped/ U-shaped)
- ink pads
- pencil
- warm soapy water

1. Draw around your erasers in your sketchbook and plan some designs in the outlines. Make them as big as possible so they will be easier to carve. You could draw a geometric shape, some lines or squiggles or a very simple object. Copy some of the designs to the largest surface of your erasers with a pencil. You can use both sides. (a)

2. Remember that the areas that you carve away will not receive any ink, so work out which parts of your image you want to transfer to the paper and cut away the rest. Use your V-tool to outline the image you have drawn. Then, carefully cut away the surface around the outer edge of the image using the U-shaped cutting tool. Do not cut too deeply into the surface. When you have completed your mini stamping block, move on to the next eraser until you have carved a design into each one. (b)

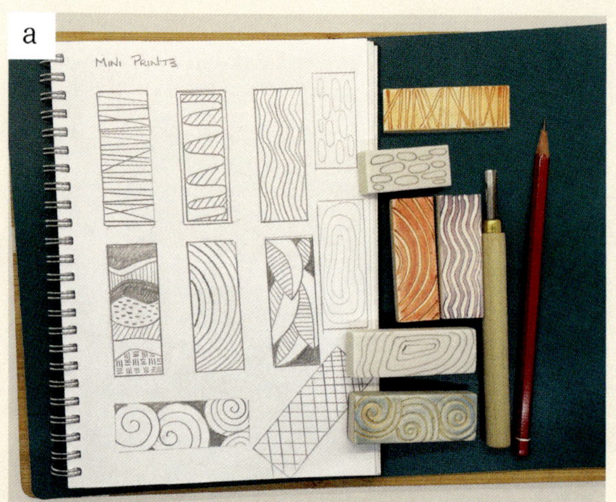

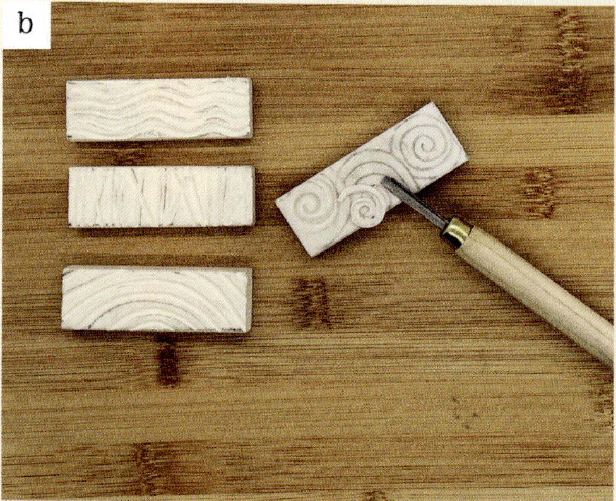

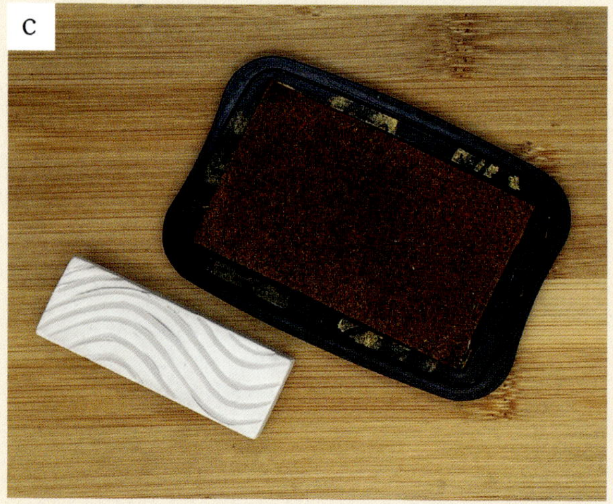

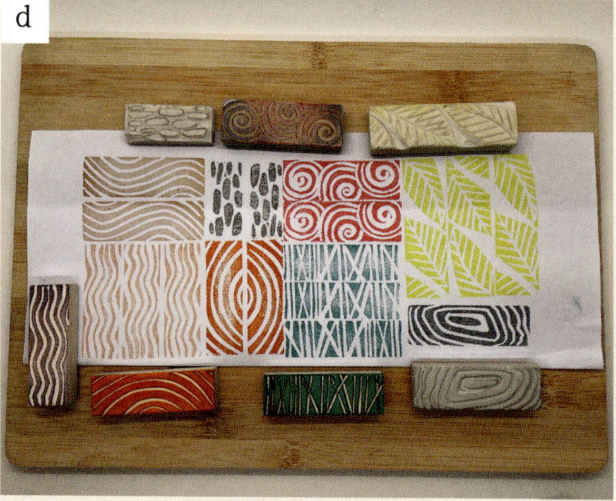

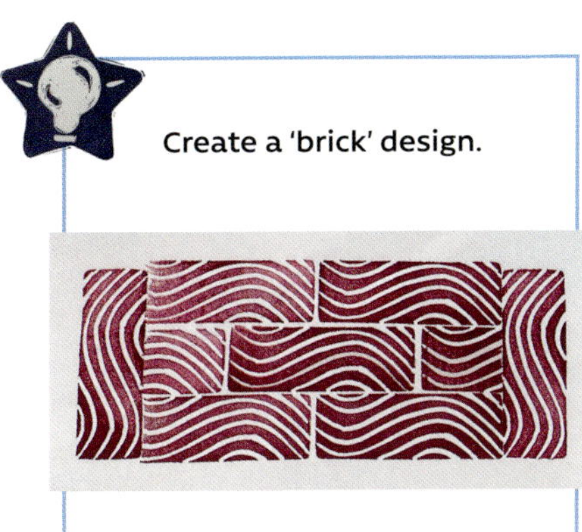

Create a 'brick' design.

3. Clear the small crumbs of rubber away so that you have a clean workspace for doing the inking and printing. Get your ink pads and paper ready. You may wish to use newspaper to protect your work surface. Place an eraser, carved side up, and ink it up by dabbing the foamy surface of the ink pad on to the surface until you have a good covering of ink. (c)

4. Pick up the eraser and press the inked surface on to the paper. Take care not to let it slide on the paper or your print will be blurred. Try printing each eraser individually and then you can have fun combining the prints in different ways. (d)

Once you have carved a few stamping blocks, you can produce patterns and simple images quickly. Try using the stamps to embellish cards, gift tags and envelopes. For creative ways of using your mini prints, see Chapter 12 (p.142).

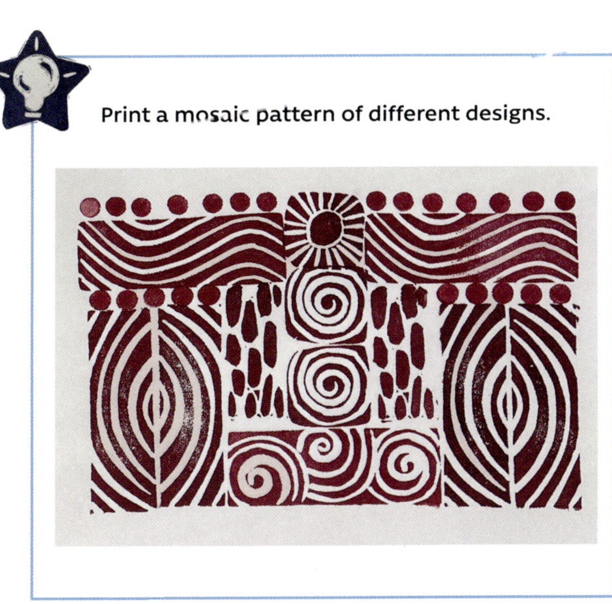

Print a mosaic pattern of different designs.

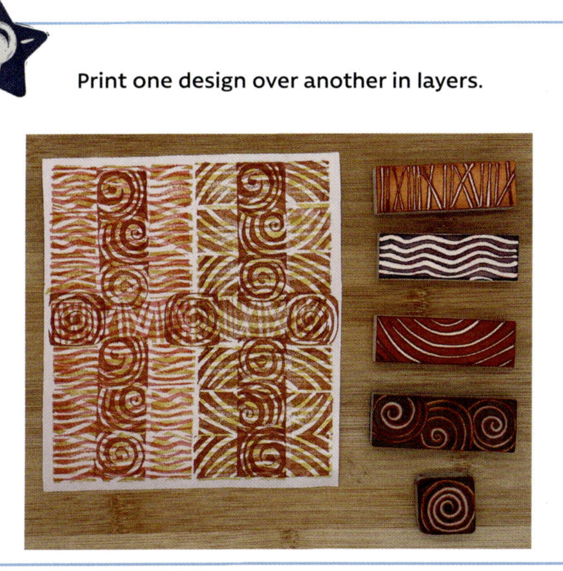

Print one design over another in layers.

CLEANING UP

■ Wash your erasers in warm soapy water and make sure they are thoroughly dry before changing to another ink colour.

■ I find that storing my ink pads upside down keeps the foam pad from drying out as fast. Make sure the plastic lid is on tightly. The cheaper ink pads don't last long so it is worth investing in the more expensive versions if you plan to take this print method further (see p.172).

Using soft printing blocks

Easy-carve blocks (the type I recommend is the pink Speedy Carve™ by Speedball®) are much easier to carve into than traditional lino or Japanese Vinyl, so go gently. You can use both sides of each block for carving (just flip it over), so, if you are careful, you can get a lot of prints and print variations from one block. You can buy other makes of similar block-printing material, but I recommend trying Speedy Carve™ first. It comes in small cut blocks or a larger piece that you can cut to blocks of a specific size. One 100 × 150 × 6 mm block will provide several pieces for you to use for the activity below.

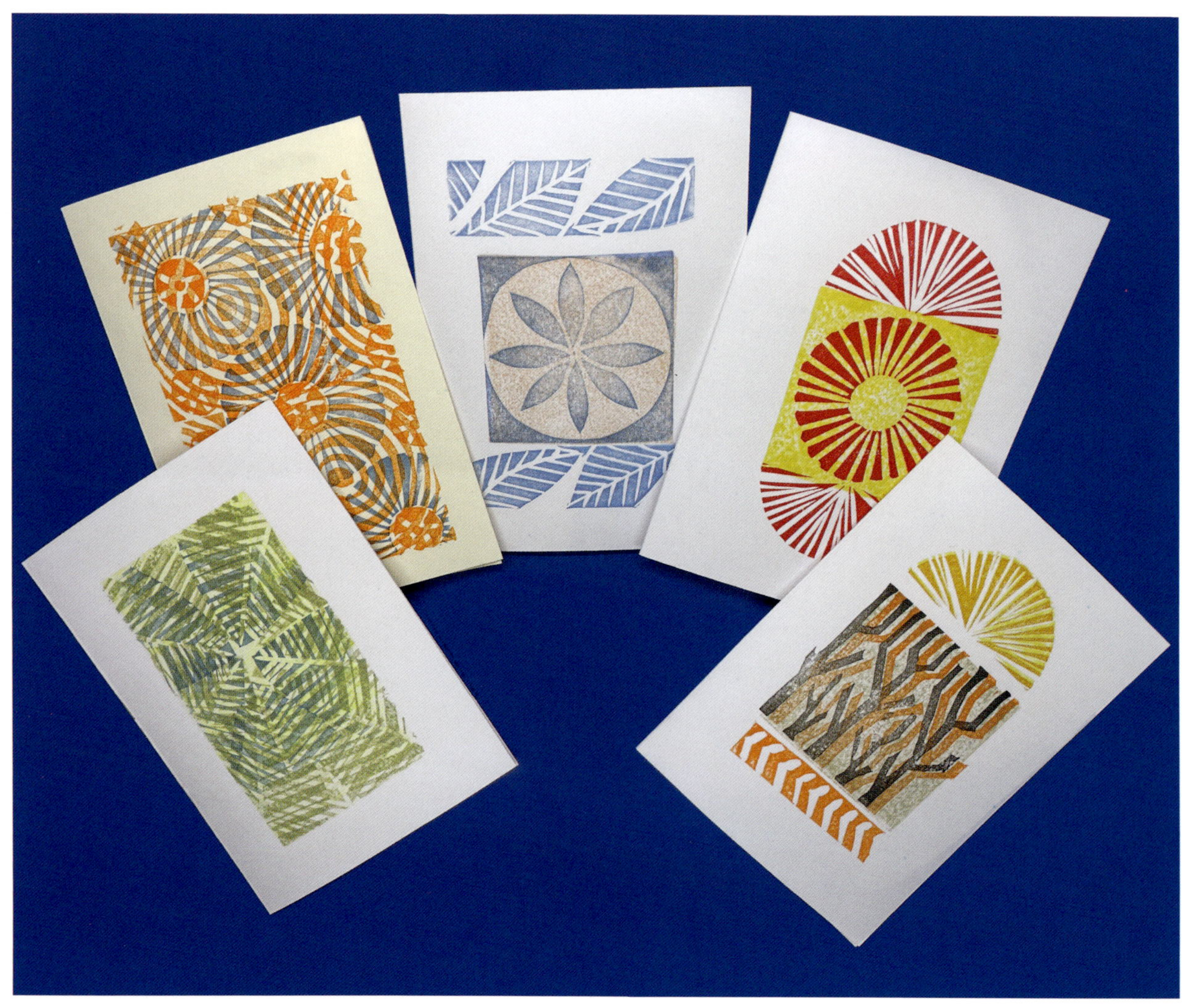

I will show you how to create stamps that can be used to print a variety of patterns on paper. (You can print on fabric too if you use fabric ink pads.) You can print using printing inks and a roller but for this activity I suggest ink pads as they are inexpensive, and quick and easy to use.

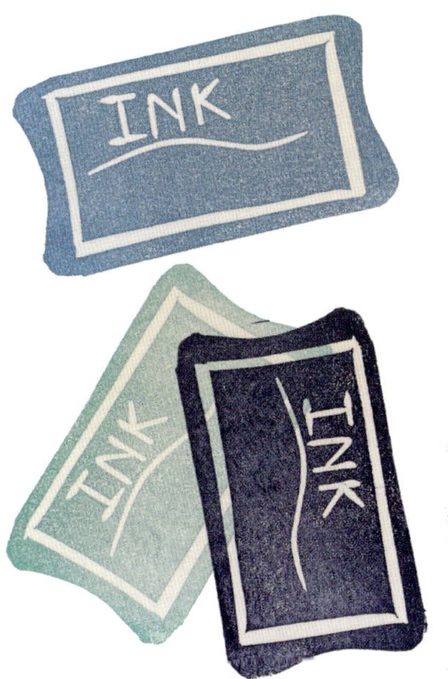

YOU WILL NEED

- Speedy Carve™ printing block (minimum 20 x 20 cm)
- printing paper (copy paper, sketchbook paper, cartridge paper or any smooth paper)
- newspaper
- cutting mat
- non-slip mat
- cutting tools (V-shaped/U-shaped)
- craft knife
- ink pads
- soft pencil
- ruler
- washing-up bowl
- warm soapy water

1. From a larger piece of Speedy Carve™, cut four 5 x 5 cm square pieces using a craft knife. It helps to draw these on to the material first using a pencil and ruler. (To save materials, you could cut just two 5 x 5 cm squares and carve designs on both surfaces, provided you don't cut too deep.) Any small pieces that you cut off can be trimmed and shaped with a craft knife to create additional stamps (circles, squares, stars, flowers, raindrops) to enhance your main design. Draw around the pink blocks on a piece of paper in your sketchbook to create several outlines. Design an image in each shape – these can be geometric or figurative designs. Keep it very simple. Now select four of your favourites to use on your blocks. (a)

2. If you draw the image clearly on the paper, you can transfer it by placing it over the surface of the printing block, drawing side down, and scribbling over the back of the drawing. This will reverse the image on the block, but it will print as your original drawing. (b)

3. Work out which parts of your design you want to cut away and which areas you want to be inked. Use the V-shaped cutting tool to cut outlines around your shapes. Don't dig too deep into the surface or the tool will cut raggedly. To have greater control, hold the carving

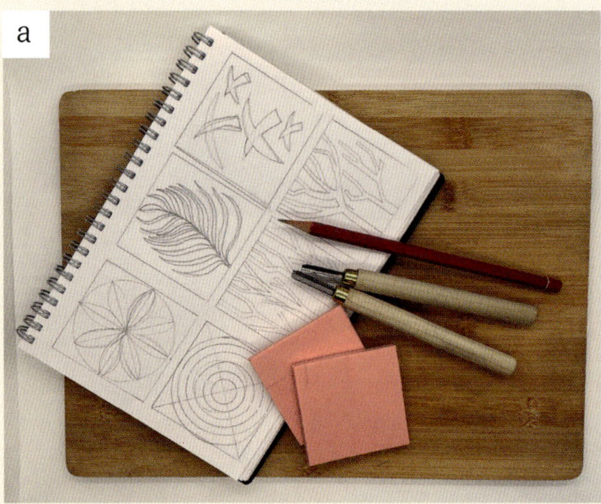

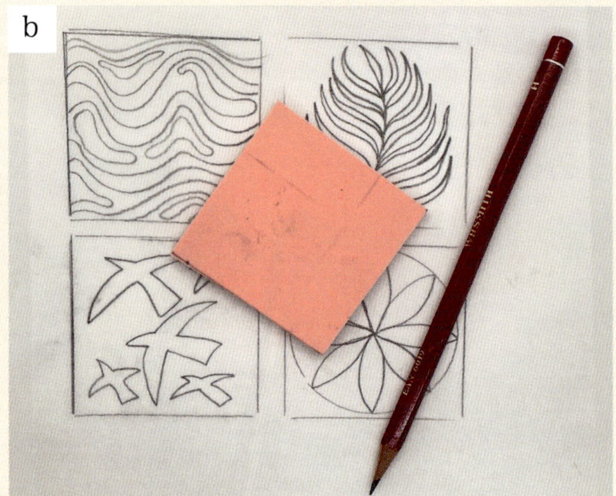

tool with your index finger on the top. With practice, you will find the best way to hold the carving tool that is comfortable for you. Use a U-tool or a large V-tool to remove any background areas. You can also cut around the shape to achieve a circular block or a specific shape. Use a craft knife to do this. (c)

4. Clear away all the bits of the printing block you have cut away, saving any larger pieces to use for carving blocks in your designs (e.g. simple shapes like stars, flowers, circles, squares). Open the ink pads and dab one all over the carved surface of your first stamp ensuring you get a good layer of ink. (I find it best to dab the ink pad on to the carved block rather than the other way around.) (d)

5. Press the stamp firmly on to the paper to take a print and lift it off, taking care not to smudge the ink. Print each block individually to see how it turns out. (e)

6. Develop the pattern by printing over the first layer. For your second layer, print in a different colour or use a different stamping block. (f)

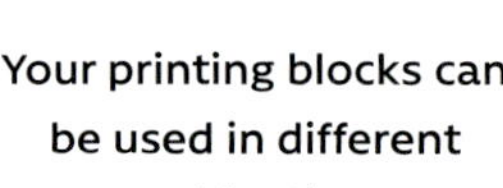

Your printing blocks can be used in different combinations:

Make a pattern with one block, turning it a quarter (90°) each time.

Printing a repeat pattern using two or more stamp designs alternately.

Print over paper that already has a pattern on it e.g. wrapping paper or wallpaper.

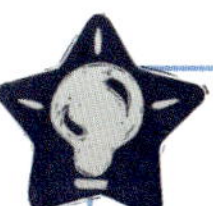

Use your printing blocks over and over again, combining them in different ways. These stamping blocks are great for making cards, embellishing envelopes, packages or notepaper, or for creating a unique picture. For creative ways of using your prints, see Chapter 12 (p.142).

CLEANING UP

- Wash your printing blocks in warm soapy water, rinse and dry. Store flat.

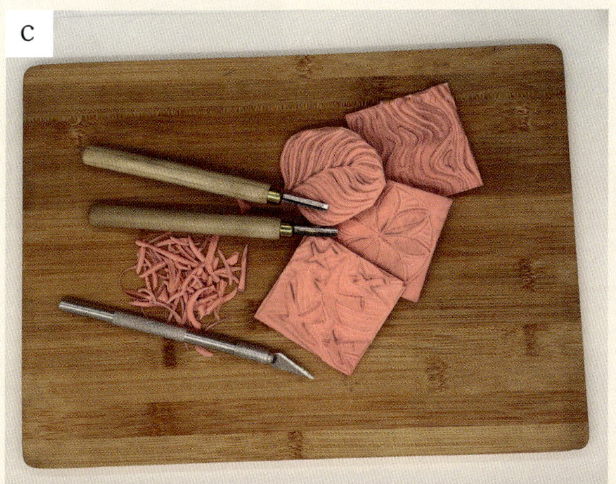

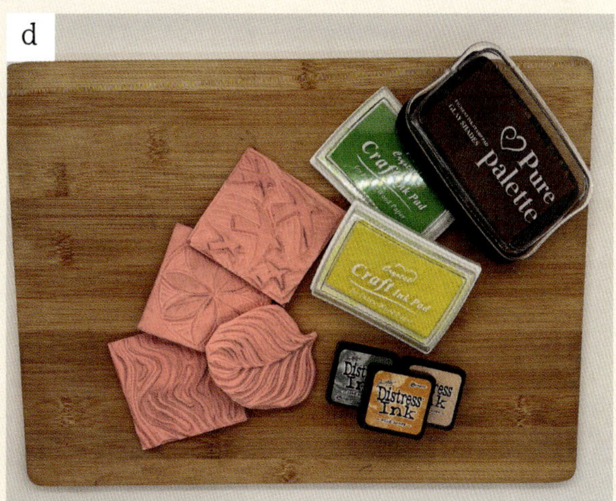

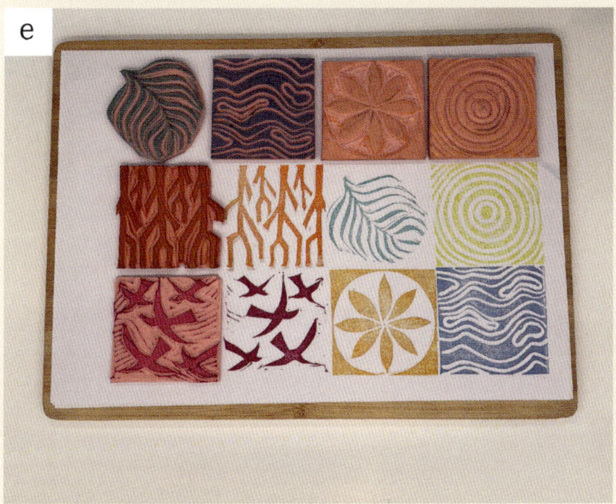

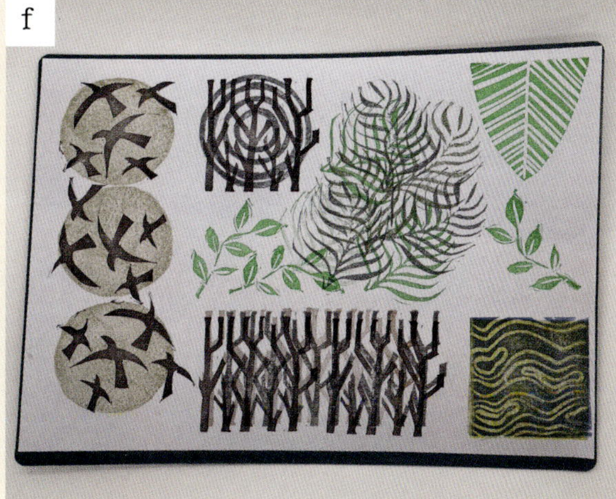

Right: Relief print using stamping blocks.

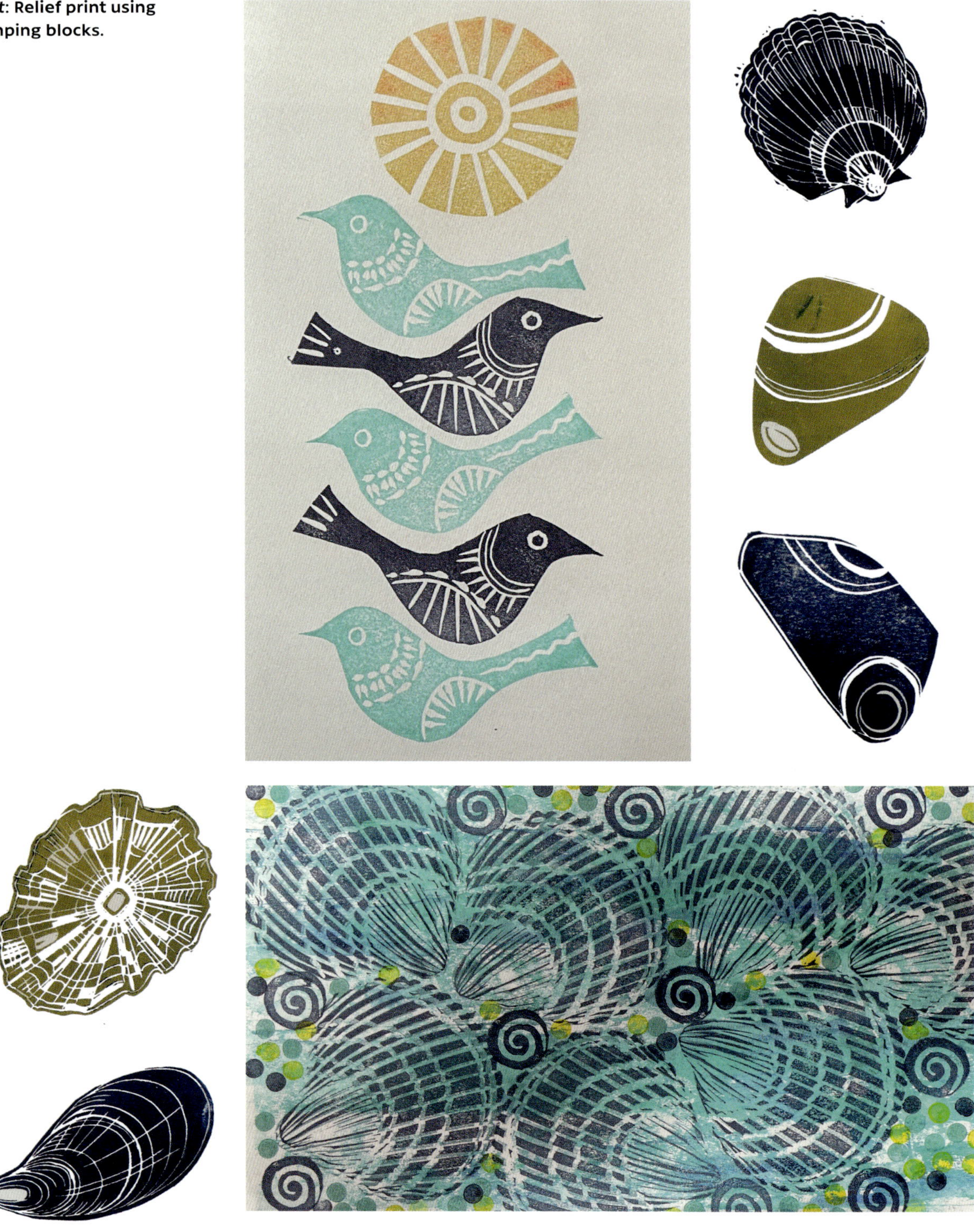

Above: A pattern on a gel plate background using a printing plate with a shell design. The small carved spirals and circles are printed with the eraser on the end of a pencil.

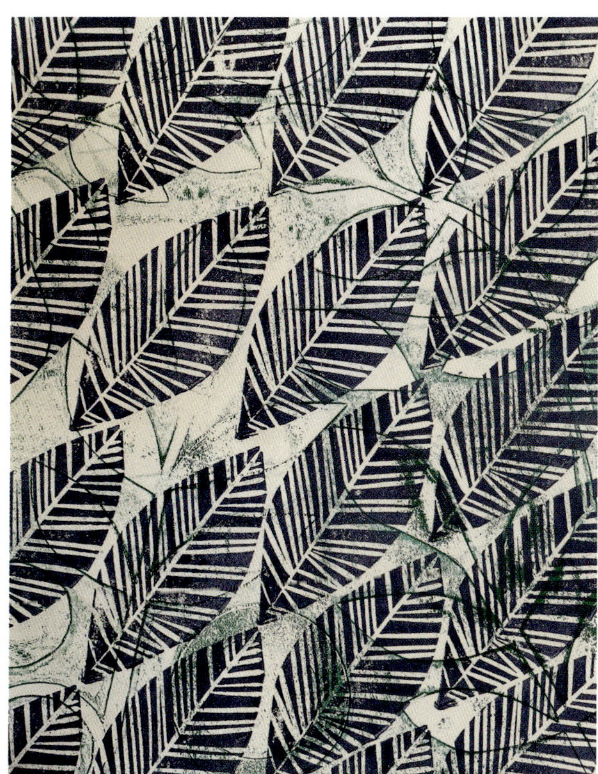

Left: Relief print of a leaf in blue over a green background.

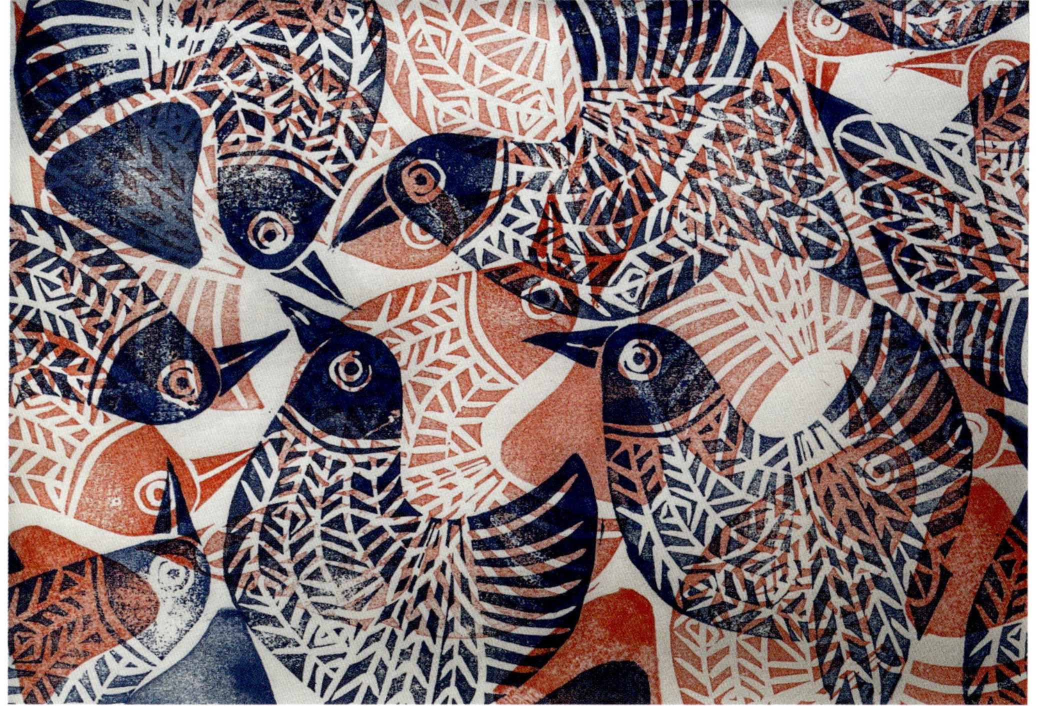

Above: Bird printing plate used with two colours in a random, overlapping pattern.

6

RELIEF PRINTING – LINOCUT

When people think of printmaking, this is usually what they think of (who remembers doing simple potato prints at school?). Linocut is, however, a very versatile printmaking technique and can be used in a variety of ways. It can be used for simple prints in one colour or for intricate, layered images that need a practised hand.

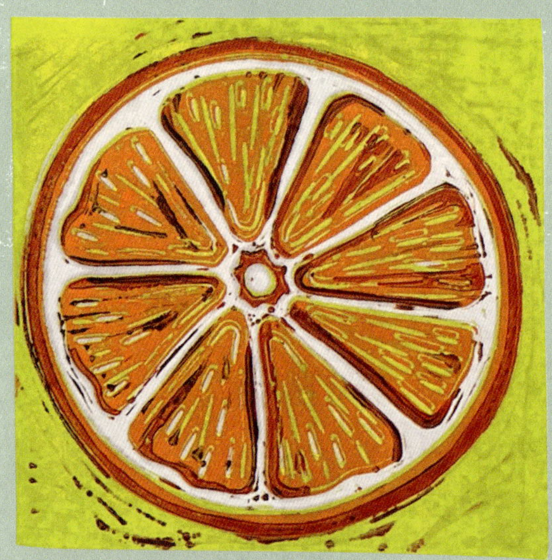

A reduction linoprint using three layers of colour.

Lino (originally called 'linoleum') is the material traditionally used for relief printing. It was first invented as a floor covering made using cork, resin and linseed oil, with a hessian backing. With its smooth surface, lino is good for carving printing plates, provided it is fresh and warm; older lino can become hard and dry and difficult to carve into.

Right: Cutting tools, spoon and two types of baren.

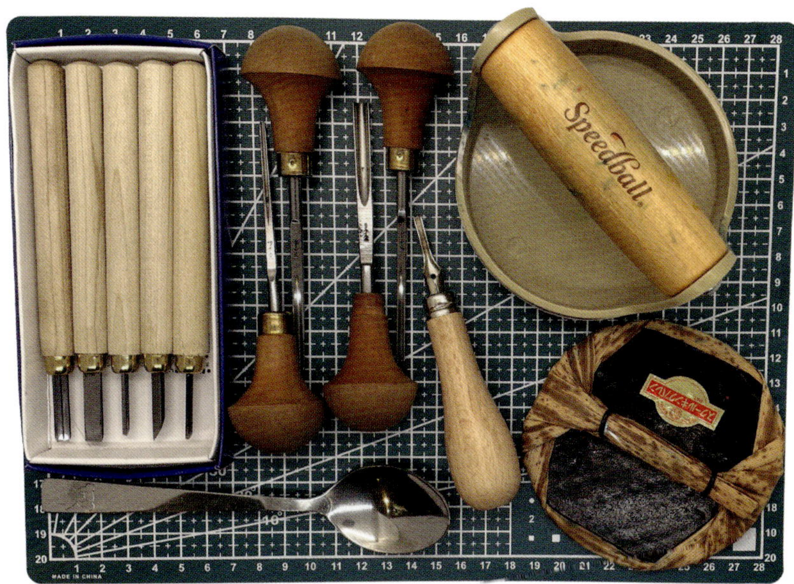

There are several alternatives to traditional lino available which you can use:

- Soft lino blocks can be used, but although easier to carve into, it is harder to achieve crisp, clean cutting lines. They are thinner than the pink Speedy Carve™ used in the previous chapter and tend to distort under pressure when you burnish it.

- Japanese Vinyl, which I use for my prints, gives a good, firm surface to carve and is firmer than SoftCut® lino. It is green on one side, blue on the other and the core is black, which helps you to see where you have carved. I will refer to it as 'lino' in this section of the book.

Here are a few reminders about working with lino and cutting tools:

- Use a cutting mat or a layer or two of newspaper to protect the surface of your table.

- Lay out your tools and materials ready for use.

- Always cut in a direction that is away from your free hand and the rest of your body.

- When you put your tools down after using, place them away from your immediate work area.

- Set up your 'inking' area away from your 'carving' area, if space allows. This way you do not risk getting the carved bits of lino mixed with your ink, which can create problems when making your print.

- Store cutting tools in a rack or a box, so the sharp points do not get damaged. Soft foam or corks can be used to protect the points.

Getting started – making marks

Carving a sample block with different marks will help you to get used to handling the cutting tools and to the variety of cuts that you can make in the surface of your block. Different tools can be used to outline shapes, create a range of different marks – for example, fine or wide, short or long, circles, spirals, cross-hatching, dots – or to clear away an area around a shape. This will be very useful when you plan your future designs and will give you the confidence to try more complicated linoprints. Copy paper is ideal for taking your first print. Other papers such as cartridge paper, mixed-media paper or Japanese rice paper can also be used, or you could print directly on to blank card.

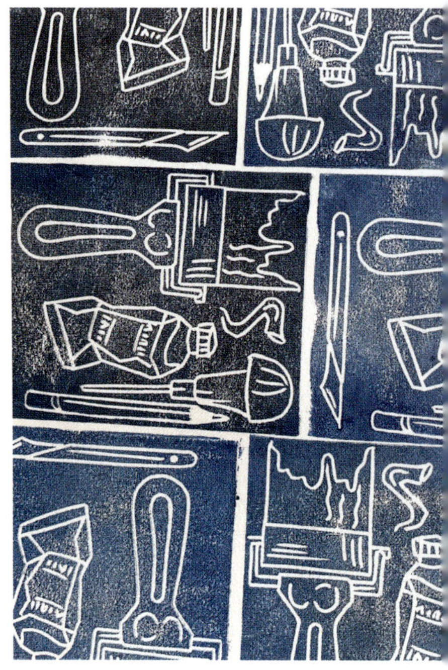

YOU WILL NEED
- piece of lino or Japanese Vinyl (100 × 150 mm)
- printing paper (copy paper, sketchbook paper, cartridge paper or any smooth paper)
- cutting tools (small and large V-shaped/U-shaped)
- printing ink (Caligo Safe Wash)
- disposable gloves (optional)
- stiff paintbrush or toothbrush for removing small carved bits from the plate
- spare paper
- newspaper squares
- cutting mat
- non-slip mat
- inking tray or slab
- roller (brayer)
- spoon or baren
- pencil
- ruler
- rags
- clean cloths
- soft toothbrush for cleaning the plate
- washing-up bowl
- warm soapy water

MARK MAKING

1. On a spare piece of paper or in your sketchbook, draw a range of simple marks and patterns that you can refer to when cutting into the lino, such as straight lines, curved lines, irregular shapes, crosshatched lines, short marks and longer marks. (a)

2. With a pencil and ruler, divide your piece of lino into squares. Use a small or large V-shaped cutting tool to carve straight lines over your pencil marks, forming a grid. Try out your tools, making different marks in each separate square on the lino. (If you are using traditional lino, it helps to warm it up before starting to carve. Place on a radiator or a heat pad, or even sit on it while you do your planning.)

This is a practice exercise, so take it slowly and experiment with making marks, getting a comfortable holding grip on your tools and familiarising yourself with how to use them. Note that you do not need to dig the sharp end of the tool into the surface too deeply. Every mark you make in the surface of the lino or vinyl will show on the print. Marks you can try include straight lines, zigzag lines, wavy lines, parallel lines, circles, 's' shapes, big and small dots, dashes, cross-hatching and teardrop shapes. You might want to do another sample piece and use different marks. (b)

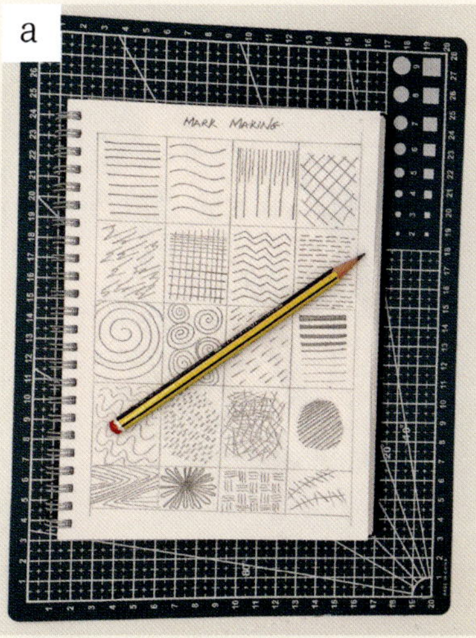
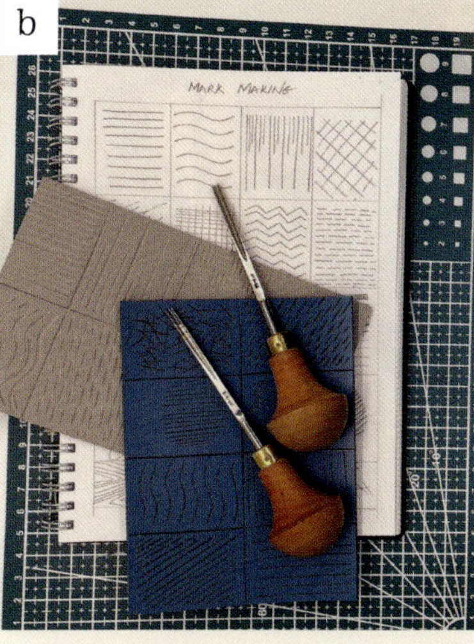
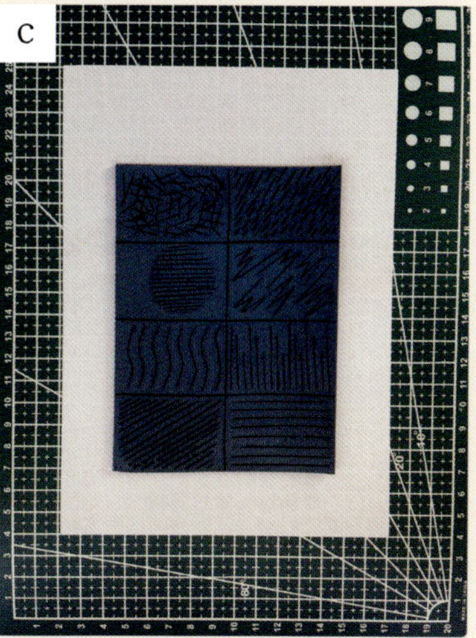

Tips for mark-making:

- When carving a line, flick the tool up to end the cutting neatly.

- Use a V-shaped cutting tool to carve continuous lines — aim to get a straight, steady cut.

- A little pressure will produce a thin line and if you press harder the line will be deeper and wider.

- Use the large and small U-shaped cutting tools to carve wider lines and to make short dashes. The large U-shaped tool is also used to clear away larger areas.

- Use the large and small V-shaped cutting tools to carve straight lines, to outline a shape and to create dashes, criss-cross patterns or parallel line patterns.

- Use a small U-shaped cutting tool to carve out circles. Push the tool down into the vinyl and, holding it firmly in a vertical position, rotate the vinyl block round the tool to cut out a small circle. The circle will pop up from the surface. This needs a bit of practice but is quite easy.

- Dig in and flick up to make short dots and dashes.

- Use both V-shaped and U-shaped cutting tools to vary the marks.

After you have carved your marks, use a stiff brush (I use an old, clean toothbrush) to remove any tiny pieces of lino from your block. Clear away all the cut-out bits so they don't get stuck in the ink when you start printing.

3. Your carved block is now ready to be inked up and printed. (c)

INKING UP AND PRINTING YOUR LINO BLOCK

4. Move to a different area for inking up or else clear the decks of carving tools and debris from the lino. You will need several pieces of paper to print on that are slightly larger than the lino block and plenty of squares of newspaper or scrap paper to place your block on for inking up and printing. Squeeze a small amount of ink on to the tile or inking tray and use the roller, working it until you have a thin layer covering the roller surface. If the ink is too thick (the roller will make a squelchy noise), it will fill the carved lines on your block and spoil the print. To remove ink, roll the excess on to a piece of newspaper and discard. (d)

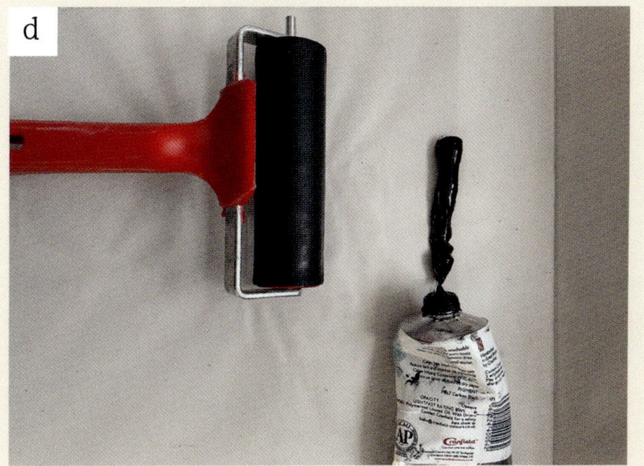

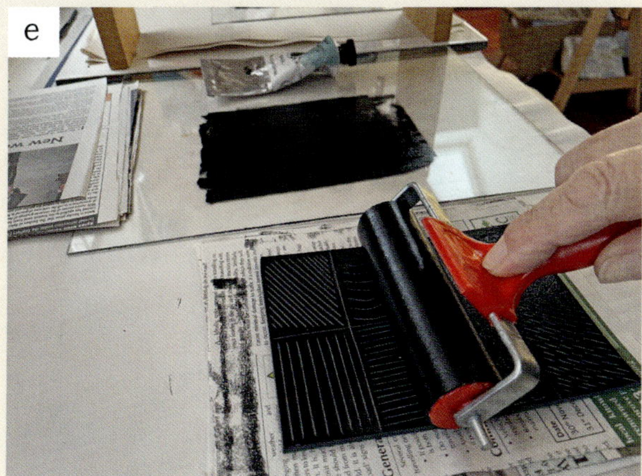

5. Place your carved lino block onto a square of newspaper and roll the ink over the surface of the block. Roll the ink slowly and carefully to ensure that every part of the surface has an even covering of ink. Try to roll in one direction rather than back and forth so that you don't remove the ink that you have just applied to the surface. Avoid applying too much ink, as that will flood your carved marks. You need a good layer that's even and smooth, without an 'orange peel' texture. Pay attention to the edges of the block as these are often missed. (e)

6. Put the roller down – most rollers have a protruding lip on one side, on which they can be rested. Lift the block carefully – without getting your fingers on the inked surface – and place it on a clean square of newspaper, inked side up. Carefully place the printing paper over the inked surface of your lino block. Smooth the surface with the flat of your hand. Now burnish your linoprint: using the smooth underside of the spoon or the flat surface of a baren, rub the back of the paper using circular movements. Ensure that you rub right up to the outer edges of the lino and take care not to let the paper slide on the lino. If your paper is thin, you will see the shape of the lino block through the paper as you burnish. (f)

7. Carefully lift the edge of the printing paper and peel it away from the block to reveal your print. (g) (h)

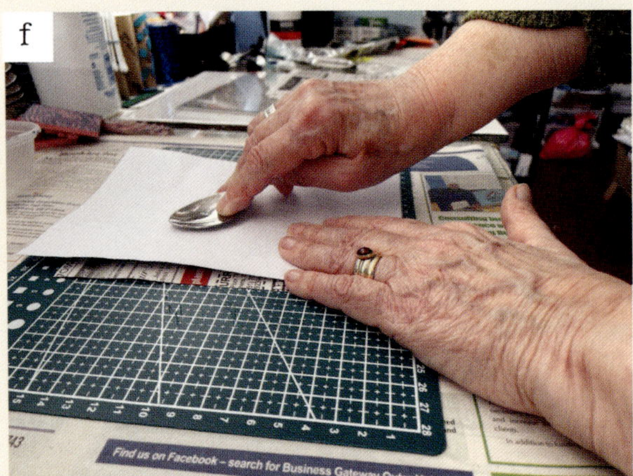

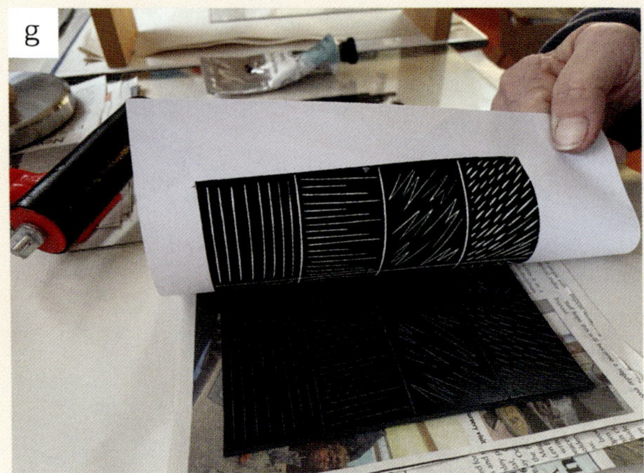

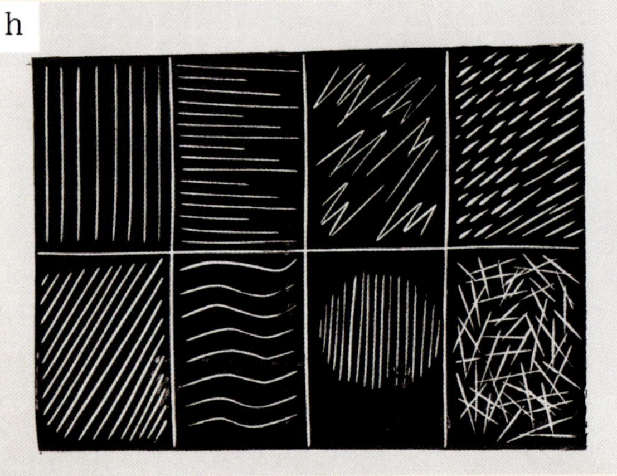

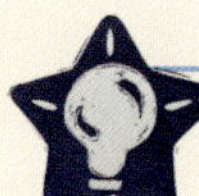

Keep one of your 'sampler' prints in your sketchbook. It is good to keep a record of your early prints to refer to as you progress. Make a few notes to remind you of the process and which tools made which marks. (h)

This may be your first attempt at linoprint so do not expect perfection!

■ Use this initial print to check if there is a good, even coverage of ink or whether the ink is patchy (too little ink) or blotchy and indistinct (too much ink).

■ If there are odd marks in the print, some tiny fragments of lino may have stuck in the ink or there may be whiskers of lino still attached. Try inking up your plate again, correcting what went wrong with the first print. Eventually you will get a print that you are pleased with.

Print your sample block on to a strip of coloured card. Leave to dry. Then cut it into strips to make bookmarks. Punch a hole at the top of each and thread a ribbon through.

■ If you stick to the same ink colour, there is no need to clean your lino and roller between prints. If, however, you need to make some carving adjustments to the lino block, you need to clean it first. If you want to try printing in a different colour, you will need to clean the block and the roller before inking up again.

■ The type of paper that you print on also makes a difference to the way the ink behaves. A smooth paper that is not too absorbent gives a crisp image, whereas a slight texture or softer paper can give a patchy print. Play around with different papers, different pressures and different types of baren.

CLEANING UP

■ When using the Caligo Safe Wash inks, you can clean up with soap and water. To clean your inking tray or slab and your roller, wipe excess ink off with a rag or newspaper and then clean with a cloth and soapy water. It is best to clear the ink up without delay; if left to dry out, this becomes more of a task. For this job, I wear disposable gloves to keep my fingers from staining. A soft toothbrush or cloth helps to clean ink from the lino and the edges of the roller. Rinse and dry. If you are using them again straight away, make sure you have dried them thoroughly. Otherwise, you can leave them to air-dry.

■ If you are using traditional lino with a hessian back, take care to store it flat to dry as it can curl a bit as the backing dries out.

■ Hanging the rollers on a rack is a good way of storing them between use. Don't leave them to dry with the rubber roller in contact with paper as it can stick and spoil the surface.

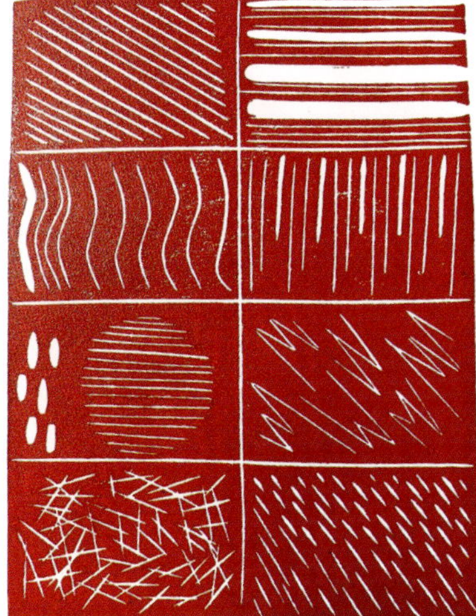

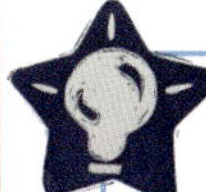

Print your sample block in different colours. Leave to dry. Cut out the individual squares of the printed sampler and reassemble them to collage designs. These could be used to make cards.

Carving a lino block four ways

Now that you have had a go at mark making, inking your lino block and pulling a print, you can start being creative with your designs. Understanding the principles of turning a drawing into a linoprint – including which areas to carve away and which to leave – takes a bit of practice. There are four main ways to go about carving a lino block: positive carving, negative carving, white-line carving and black-line carving. Once you have familiarised yourself with these methods, you will be able to design your own prints with greater confidence.

YOU WILL NEED

- four square pieces of lino (e.g. 10 × 10 cm) or a larger piece of lino to cut
- printing paper (copy paper, sketchbook paper, cartridge paper or any smooth paper)
- transfer paper (such as Tracedown®)
- tracing paper
- newspaper squares
- spare paper
- cutting mat
- non-slip mat
- cutting tools (small and large V-shaped/U-shaped)
- scissors or craft knife
- printing ink
- inking tray or slab
- roller (brayer)
- spoon or baren
- pencil
- metal ruler
- rags
- damp cloths or baby wipes
- washing-up bowl
- warm soapy water
- detergent

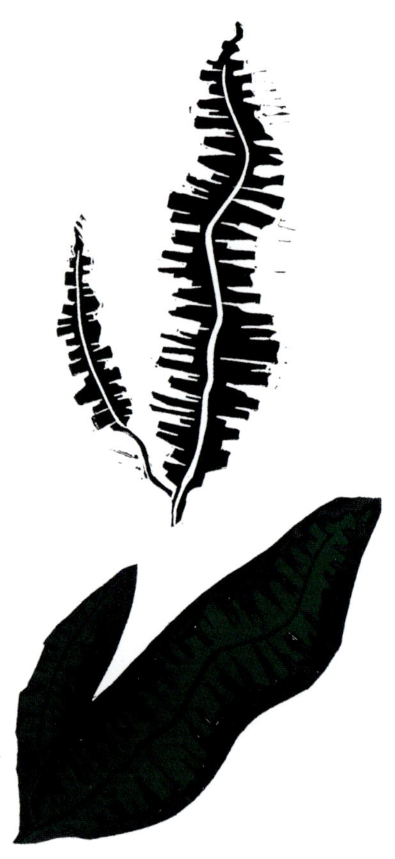

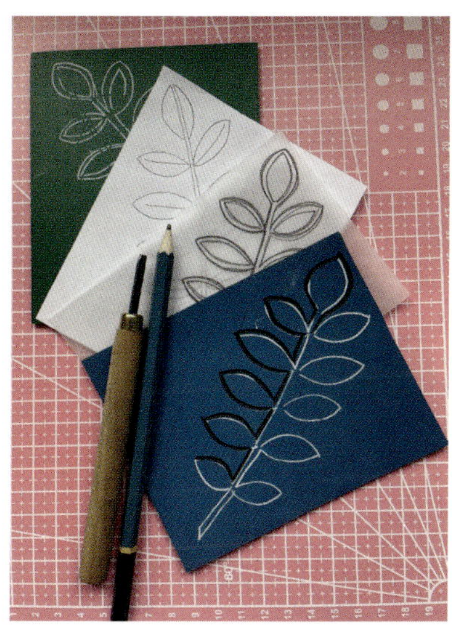

PREPARING YOUR LINO BLOCKS

1. If you are using a block of lino, cut four squares the same size – I suggest squares that are 10 × 10 cm.

2. Draw round one of the pieces of lino on a plain piece of paper.

3. Do a simple line drawing of a bird (or flower or other object) inside the drawn shape.

4. Trace your image using the tracing paper.

5. Cut a piece of the transfer paper the same size as the lino block and place it on the lino with the transfer side down. You will need to check which is the correct side as it isn't immediately obvious.

6. Place your tracing over the transfer paper, reversing the tracing paper. Use your pencil to go over the image so it is transferred clearly to the lino block.

7. Repeat this for each piece of lino, using the same bit of transfer paper and the same tracing. You should now have four identical images on the lino pieces. (a)

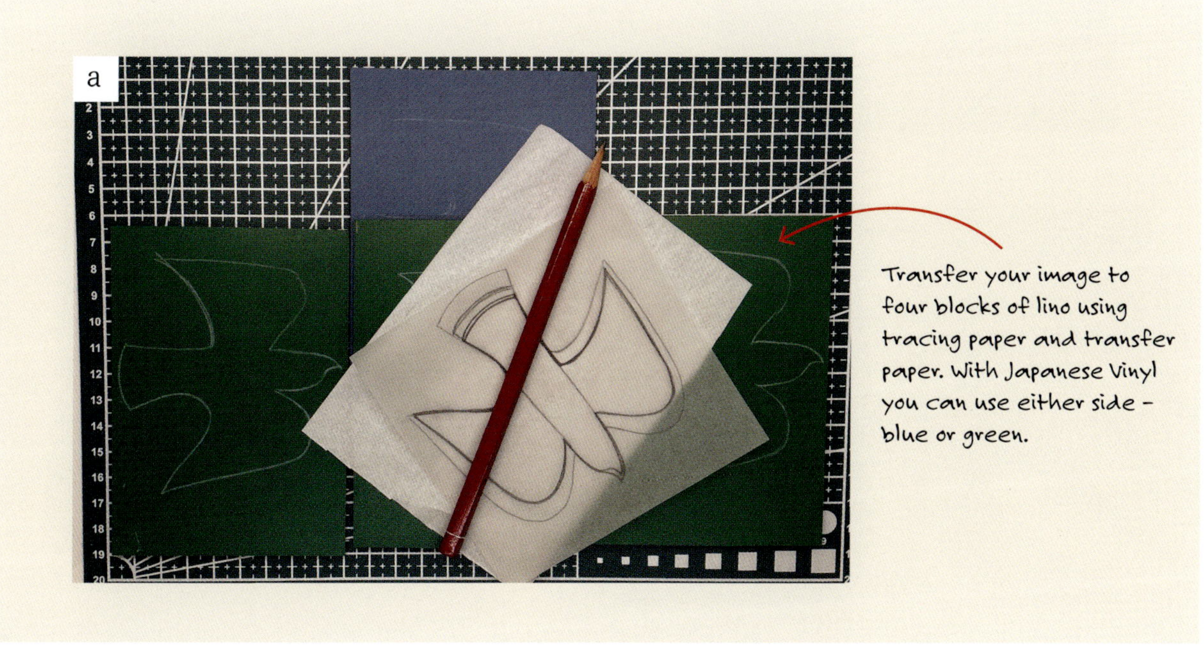

Transfer your image to four blocks of lino using tracing paper and transfer paper. With Japanese vinyl you can use either side – blue or green.

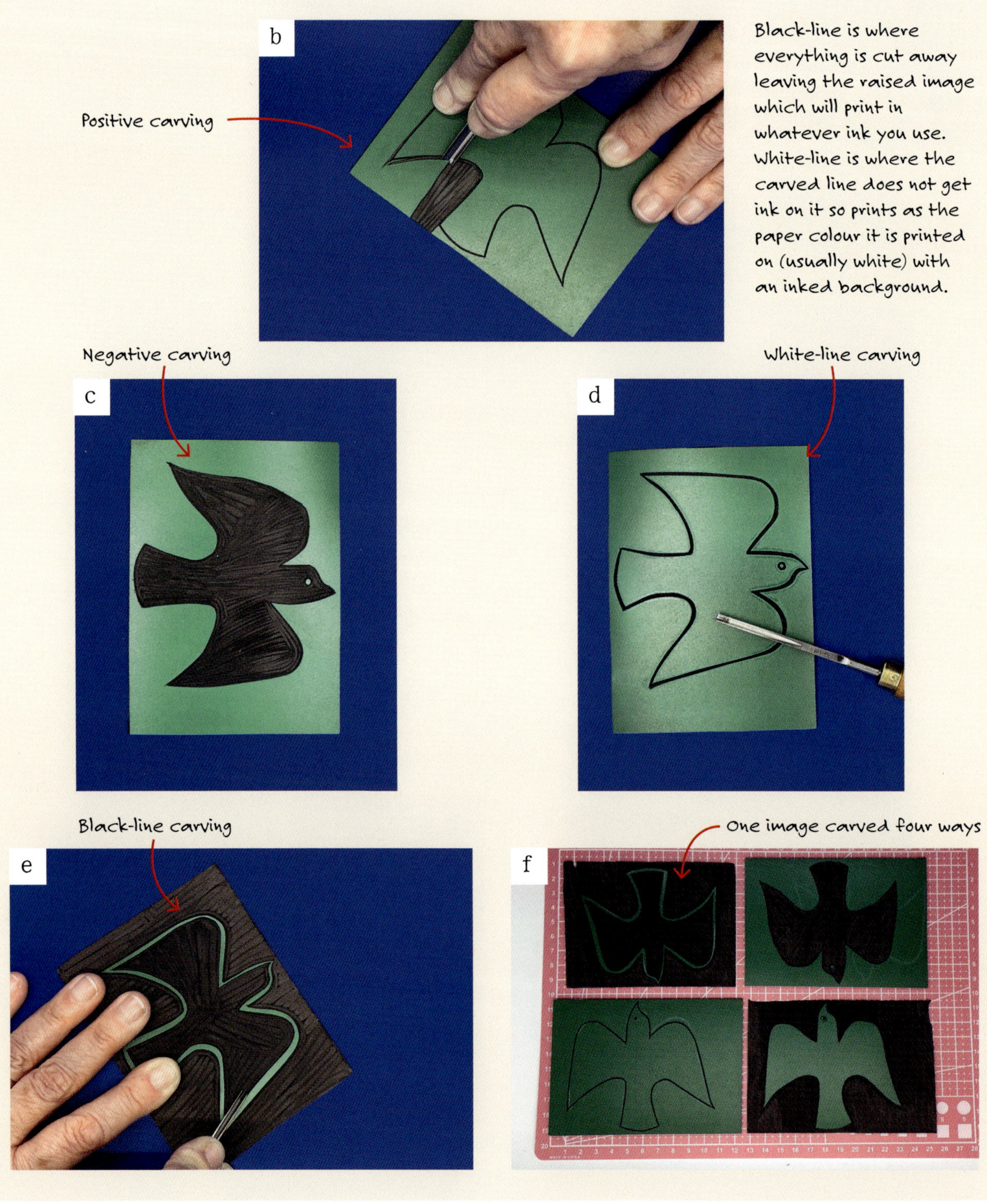

b
Positive carving
Black-line is where everything is cut away leaving the raised image which will print in whatever ink you use. White-line is where the carved line does not get ink on it so prints as the paper colour it is printed on (usually white) with an inked background.
Negative carving
c
White-line carving
d
Black-line carving
e
f
One image carved four ways

CARVING YOUR LINO BLOCKS

Positive carving

8. Take one of your lino pieces. Cut around the outline of your drawing with small V-shaped cutting tool, leaving the image intact. Use a large U-shaped cutting tool to clear the background, working out to the edges from your outline cut. You will have a positive image of the bird with the background completely removed. If you do not want the carving marks from the background to print, you could cut around the bird with a craft knife or scissors. You could also cut a paper mask to place over the lino when inking up. (b)

Negative carving

9. Cut around the outline of your drawing with a small V-shaped cutting tool. Cut away inside your drawing leaving the background intact. The background will print the colour of the ink and there will be a white silhouette of the bird. (c)

White-line carving

10. Cut around the outline of your drawing with a small U-shaped cutting tool. This will print as a white line drawing and the rest of the plate will be the colour of the ink. (d)

Black-line carving

11. This is fiddly to carve, and you need to cut slowly and accurately. Cut around either side of the outline of your drawing with a small V-shaped cutting tool, leaving the lines in relief (standing out). Use a large U-shaped cutting tool to carve the larger areas away both around the outside of the image and inside the image. This will result in a printed outline of the original image with no background. (e)

12. Your four pieces of lino are now ready for inking. (f)

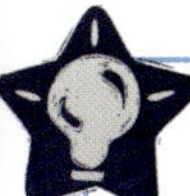

When the ink is dry, cut out the prints and stick them into your sketchbook with notes. This will serve as a reminder for future prints.

Print your different carved lino blocks on to a gel-plate printed background. This is particularly effective with negative and black-line lino blocks and will produce good images for cards.

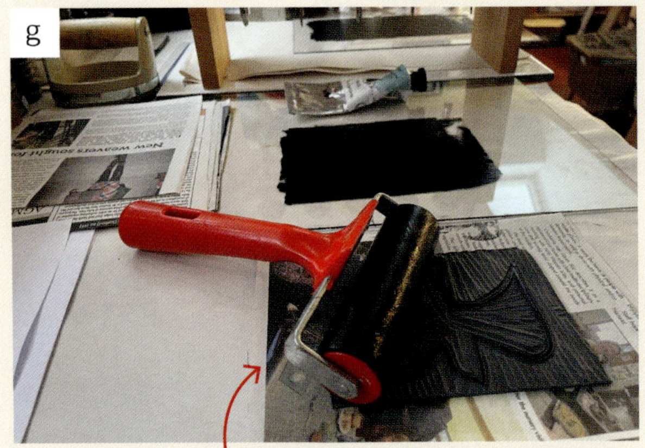

Inking the plate

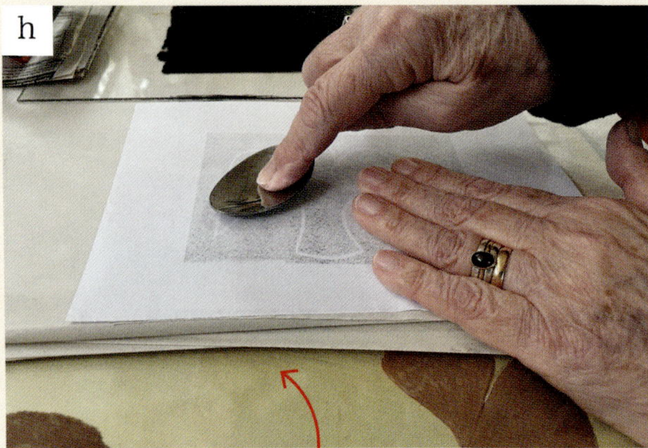

Burnishing the print

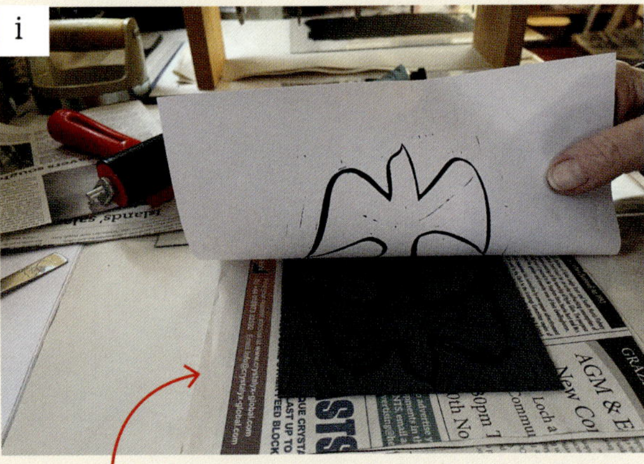

Revealing the print

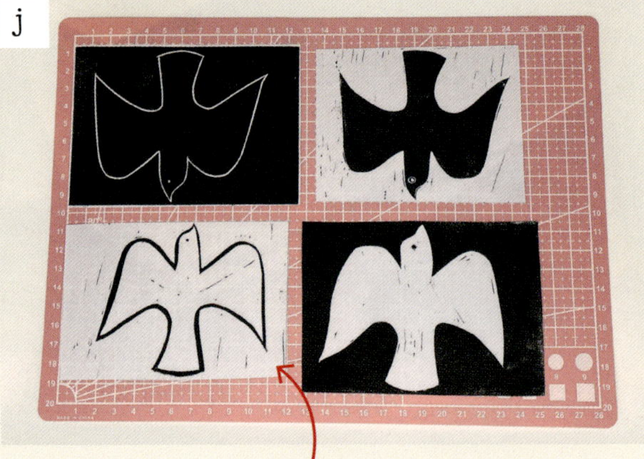

One image printed four ways

INKING UP AND PRINTING YOUR LINO BLOCKS

13. Ink each block up as before. (g)

14. Take each inked lino block in turn, position it on a clean piece of newspaper and place a piece of printing paper carefully over the block. Burnish the surface with a spoon. (h)

15. Lift the paper to reveal your print. (i)

16. Repeat this process with the other three blocks. You will see how each printed image is different, according to the way you have carved the block. (j)

CLEANING UP

- Roll excess ink from the roller on to a spare piece of paper, then clean it with warm soapy water, rinse thoroughly and leave to dry.

- To clean your inking tray or slab, remove excess ink with paper or a rag, then wash in warm soapy water, rinse and leave to drain and dry.

- Wash Japanese Vinyl in warm soapy water, rinse and lay on a flat surface to dry. If using traditional lino, it is best not to immerse it in water as it has a hessian backing. Clean the surface of the plate with a damp cloth and a small amount of detergent, then wipe with a cloth. Dry on a flat surface.

Using different marks to create tone

You can use the different marks you have practised to design a simple print with a range of tonal qualities. If you vary the size of your marks and how close they are to each other, you can produce a range of light and dark within the print. This technique is applicable for many images and can be used with a single colour or for some of the other inking styles such as a blended roll or a jigsaw print.

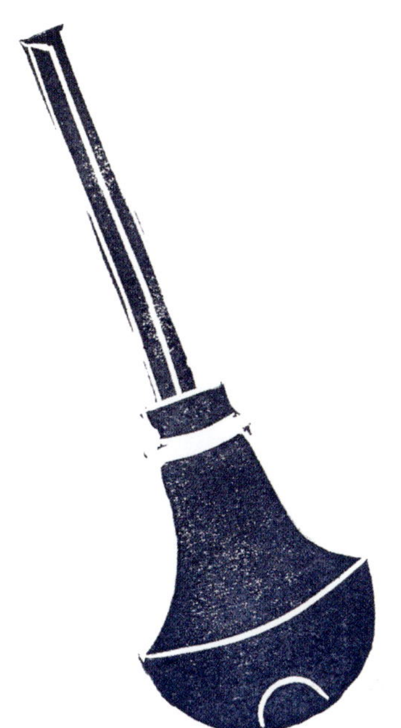

YOU WILL NEED

- piece of lino (approximately 10 × 14 cm)
- printing paper (copy paper, sketchbook paper, cartridge paper or any smooth paper)
- sketchbook or spare paper
- newspaper
- tracing paper
- transfer paper (such as Tracedown®)
- cutting tools (U-shaped/ V-shaped)
- printing ink (black or blue)
- spoon or baren
- pencil
- rags
- damp cloths or baby wipes
- washing-up bowl
- warm soapy water
- detergent

1. Take a piece of lino and draw around it in your sketchbook or on a piece of paper. Draw a simple landscape within the outline. This should just be simple lines dividing the space into defined areas. (a)

2. Fill each shape with a different pattern of marks. (b)

3. Trace the image using tracing paper and transfer it to your lino block by flipping the tracing paper and using a piece of transfer paper to give a clear picture on the surface.

4. Carve the design carefully, taking care with the marks in each different section. (c)

5. Ink it up in black or blue ink. (d)

6. Place your inked block on a clean piece of newspaper, put your printing paper carefully over the inked surface and burnish with a spoon or baren. (e)

7. Lift the paper to reveal the print. Note how the range of different marks has given varying tones to your printed image. (f)

CLEANING UP

- Roll excess ink from the roller on to a spare piece of paper, then clean it with warm soapy water, rinse thoroughly and leave to dry.

- To clean your inking tray or slab, remove excess ink with paper or a rag, then wash in warm soapy water, rinse and leave to drain and dry.

- Wash Japanese Vinyl in warm soapy water, rinse and lay on a flat surface to dry. If using traditional lino, it is best not to immerse it in water as it has a hessian backing. Clean the surface of the plate with a damp cloth and a small amount of detergent, then wipe with a cloth. Dry on a flat surface.

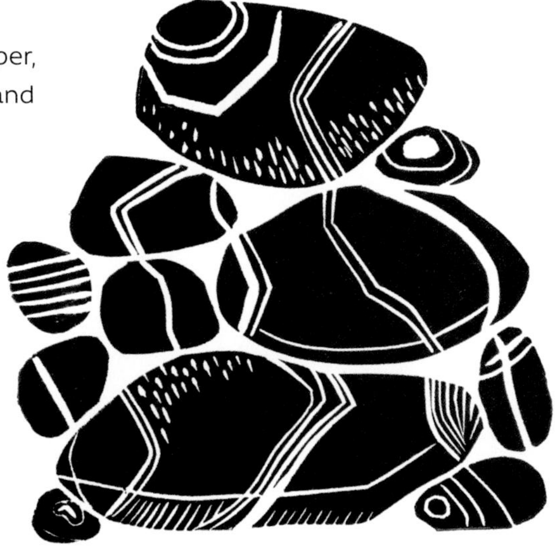

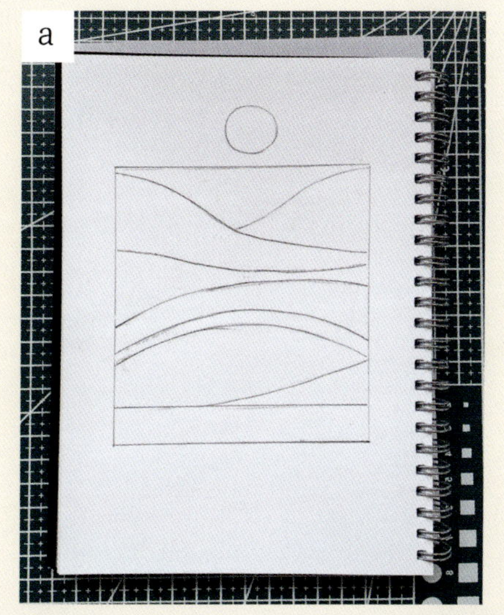

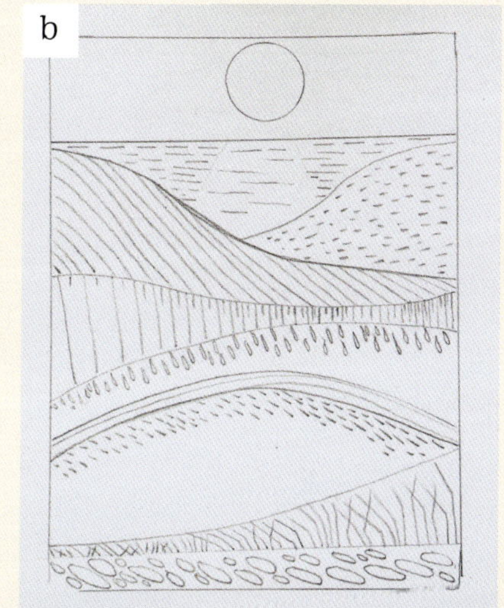

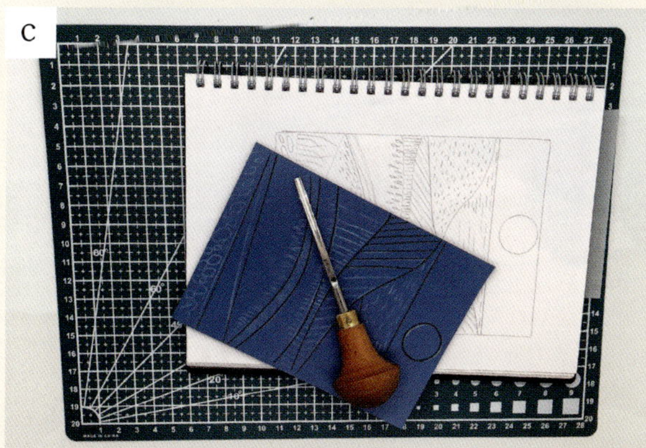

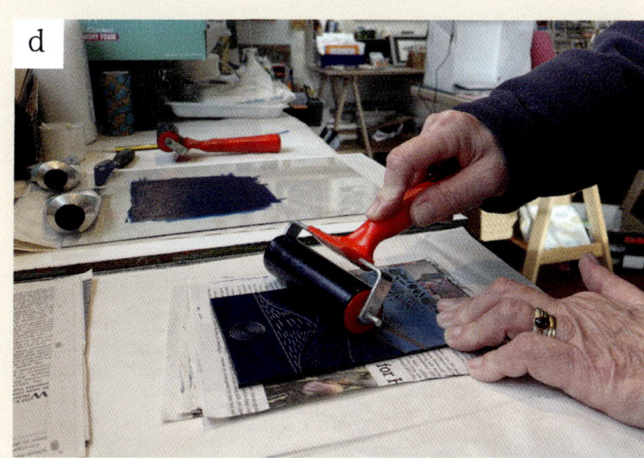

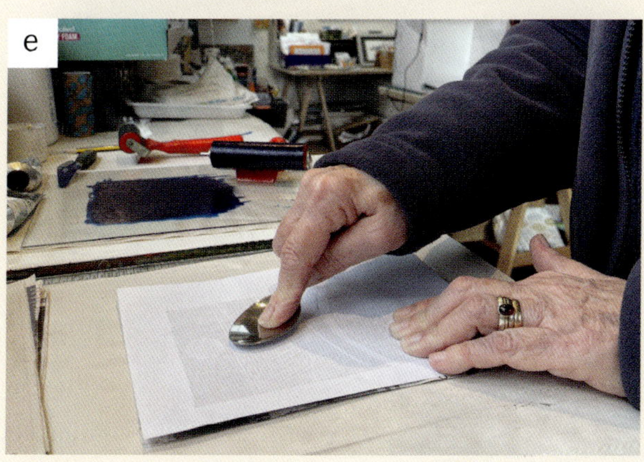

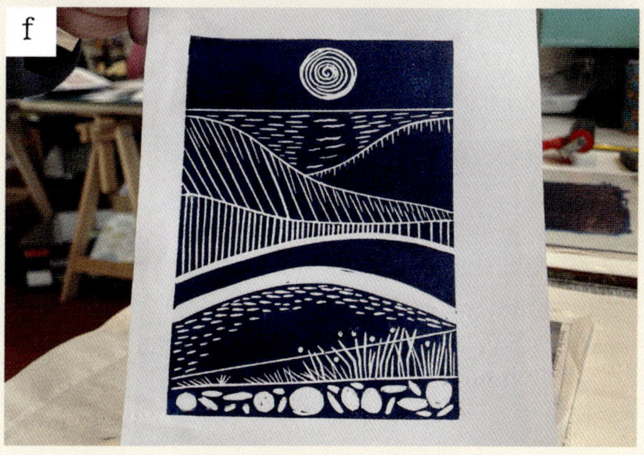

Printing in more than one colour

RAINBOW ROLL – USING MORE THAN ONE COLOUR ON ONE LINO BLOCK

This inking technique blends two or more colours on the same roller. It is a simple way of using more than one colour and can be very effective. The colours can be contrasting or tonal – a single colour blended from light to dark by adding a little white to the first colour and then a little more (good for printing a sky that lightens towards the horizon). This technique works best with a roller that is wide enough to take two or more colours.

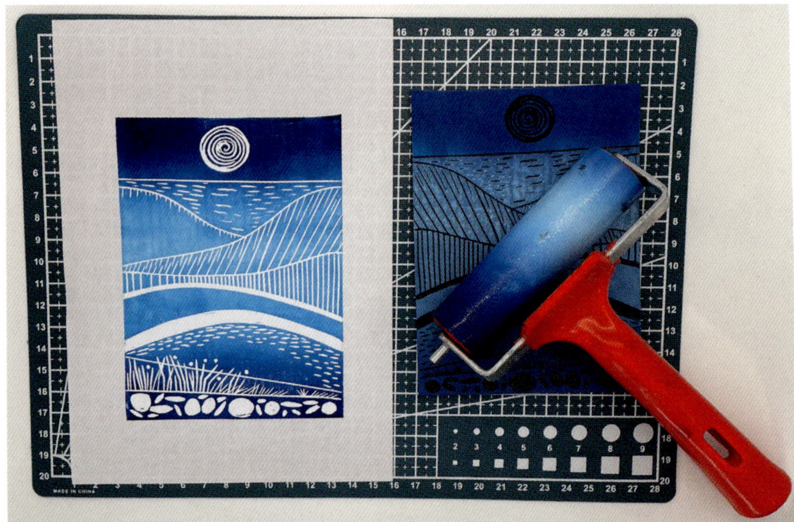

Left: A graduated 'rainbow roll' using blended colours of ink on the roller.

YOU WILL NEED

- linoprinting block (already carved)
- printing paper (copy paper, sketchbook paper, cartridge paper or any smooth paper)
- printing ink (two different colours)
- inking tray or slab
- roller (brayer)
- damp cloths or baby wipes
- washing-up bowl
- warm soapy water
- detergent

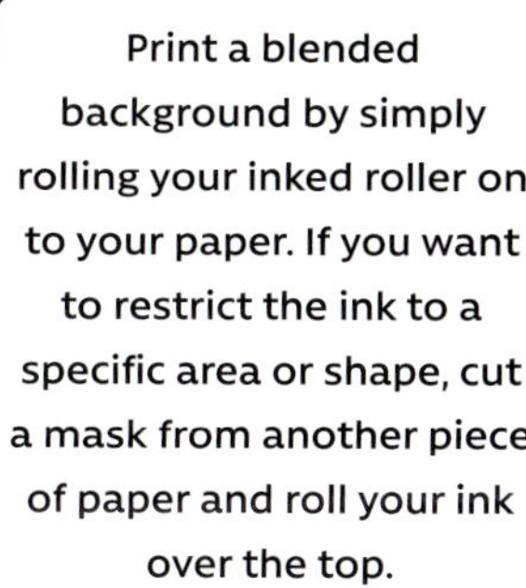

Print a blended background by simply rolling your inked roller on to your paper. If you want to restrict the ink to a specific area or shape, cut a mask from another piece of paper and roll your ink over the top.

1. Squeeze two blobs of different inks side by side on the inking slab. Use the roller to roll out the ink, moving the roller side to side a little so that the two colours merge together and blend. The roller should have a smooth, even coating of the mixed ink but with both colours distinct at each outer edge. (a)

2. Roll the ink on to your printing block in one direction only, taking care not to mix up the colours any further. I have used the landscape block from the previous exercise. I rolled the lower part first, with the dark blue ink at the bottom and the lighter blue in the centre; I then turned the roller for the upper section so that the darker blue was at the top. (b)

3. Print your image in the usual way. (c)

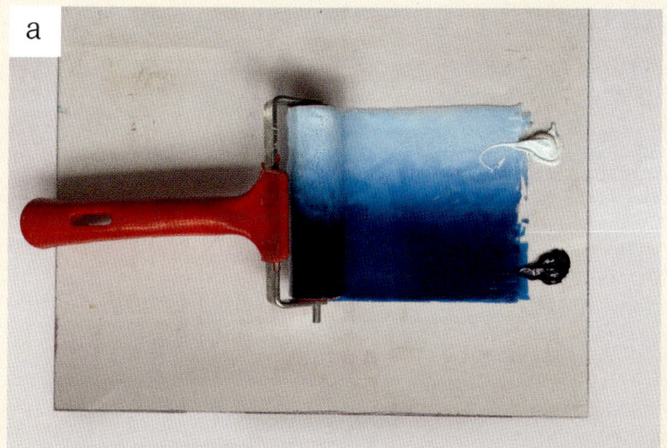

a

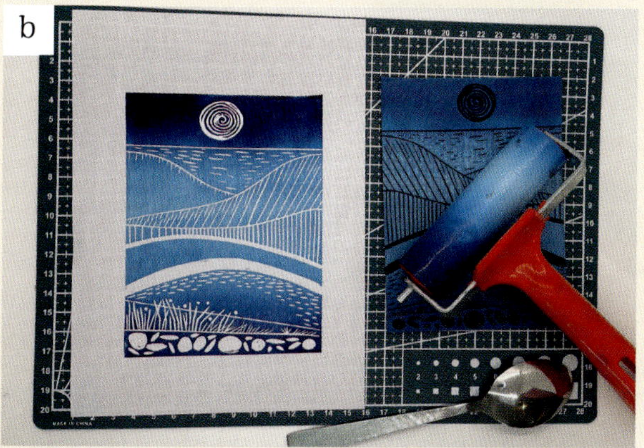

b

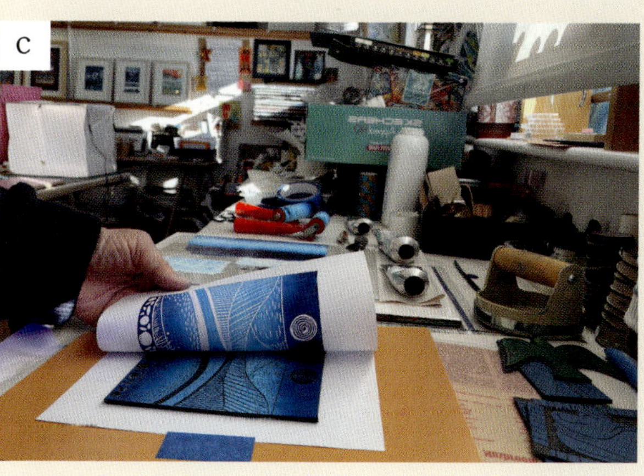

c

Use this method to print a background that you can then overprint with a different block — just roll your blended ink on to an uncarved piece of lino/vinyl and print. It is best to let this printed layer dry before adding the second print over it.

Cleaning up

- Roll excess ink from the roller on to a spare piece of paper, then clean it with warm soapy water, rinse thoroughly and leave to dry.

- To clean your inking tray or slab, remove excess ink with a damp cloth or baby wipe, then wash in warm soapy water, rinse and leave to drain and dry.

- Wash Japanese Vinyl in warm soapy water, rinse and lay on a flat surface to dry. If using traditional lino, it is best not to immerse it in water as it has a hessian backing. Clean the surface of the plate with a damp cloth and a small amount of detergent, then wipe with a cloth. Dry on a flat surface.

JIGSAW PRINT

This is a way of printing in more than one colour by cutting your block into pieces that can be inked up in different colours and then reassembled like a jigsaw. To start with, we will just use two jigsaw pieces, but once you have tried it you can be more adventurous. Just ensure that your initial design includes sections that can be easily cut into separate pieces and then put back together. If you do not cut the pieces accurately, you get a white line in your print where the pieces join up.

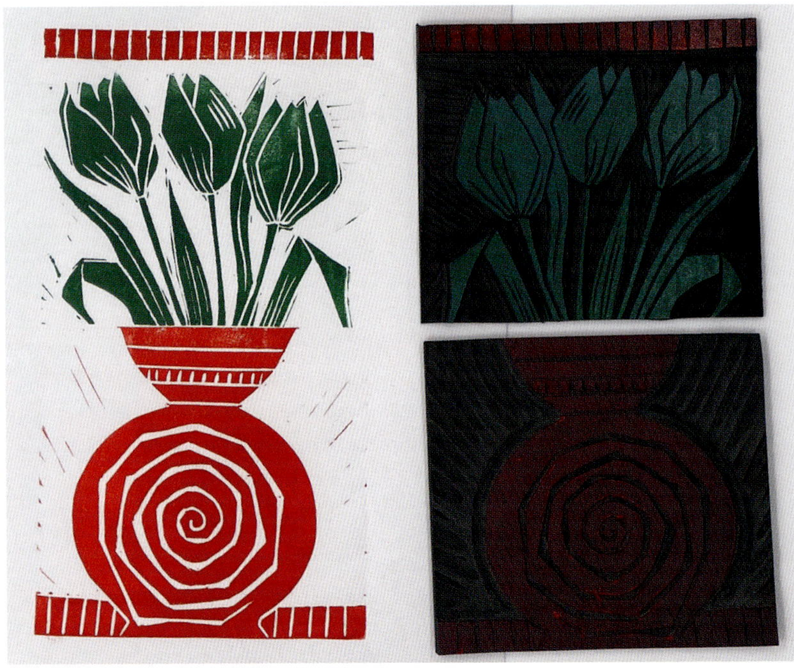

Left: **A jigsaw print made with two sections.**

YOU WILL NEED

- piece of lino (approximately 10 × 14 cm)
- printing paper (copy paper, sketchbook paper, cartridge paper or any smooth paper)
- spare paper
- tracing paper
- transfer paper (such as Tracedown®)
- cutting mat
- cutting tools (U-shaped/ V-shaped)
- craft knife
- printing ink (two different colours)
- spoon or baren
- pencil
- disposable gloves
- damp cloths or baby wipes
- washing-up bowl
- warm soapy water

1. Draw a simple design on a piece of spare paper that will fit on your block. It needs to have areas that you can then cut out individually. (a)

2. Trace the image on tracing paper and transfer it to your block using transfer paper. (b)

3. Carve your design.

4. Now you will need to cut the carved block into two separate sections that can be fitted back together once you have inked them up. Use a large V-shaped cutting tool to go neatly around the line where you are going to cut your plate, cutting deep. Then use a craft knife to cut the block in two. (c)

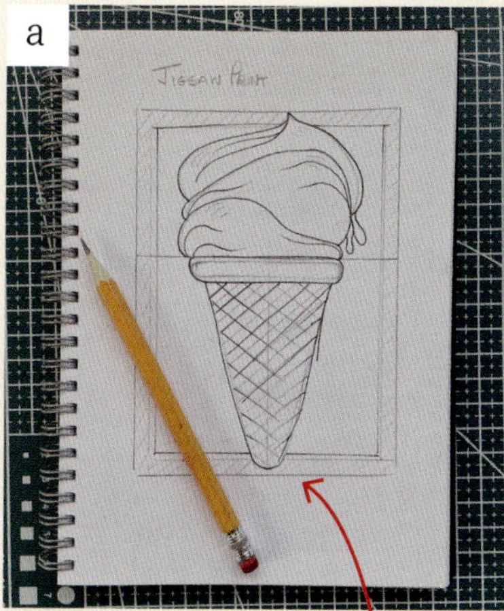

The image could be cut in two along the top of the ice cream cone

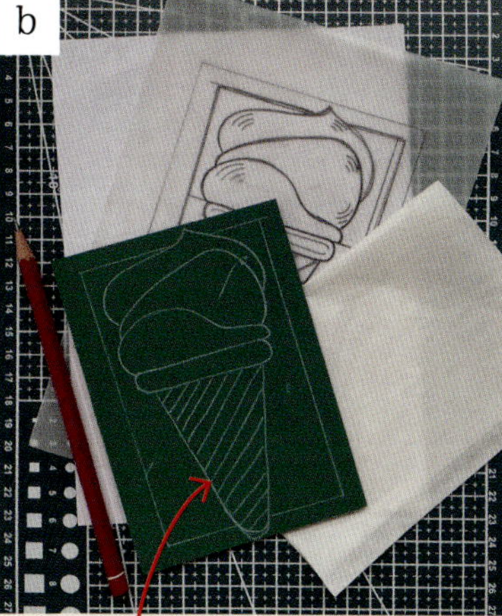

Transferring the image to your lino block

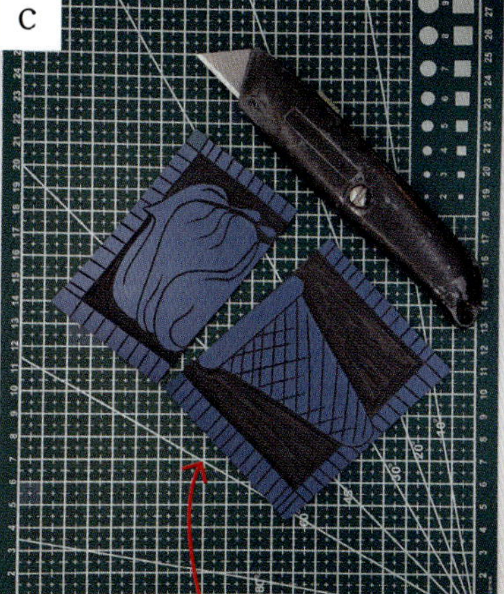

The carved block is cut in two using a craft knife

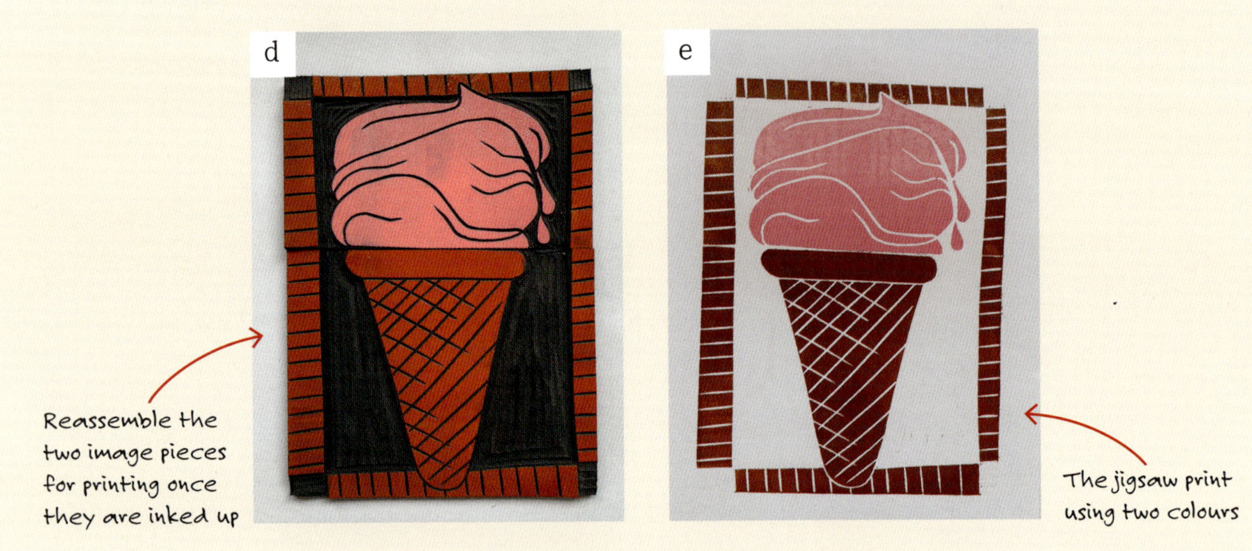

Reassemble the two image pieces for printing once they are inked up

The jigsaw print using two colours

5. Ink up both blocks, using different colours for each. I decided to ink the frame around both pieces in the same colour, which was relatively easy.

6. With clean hands, reassemble the image, cover with paper and rub with a spoon or baren. Take care not to push the two pieces apart as you burnish the paper. (d)

7. Reveal the print. (e)

Cleaning up

■ Roll excess ink from the roller on to a spare piece of paper, then clean it with warm soapy water, rinse thoroughly and leave to dry.

■ To clean your inking tray or slab, remove excess ink with paper or a damp cloth or baby wipe, then wash in warm soapy water, rinse and leave to drain and dry.

■ Wash Japanese Vinyl in warm soapy water, rinse and lay on a flat surface to dry. If using traditional lino, it is best not to immerse it in water as it has a hessian backing. Clean the surface of the plate with a damp cloth and a small amount of detergent, then wipe with a cloth. Dry on a flat surface.

Below: **Stamped print of puzzle pieces using a soft printing block.**

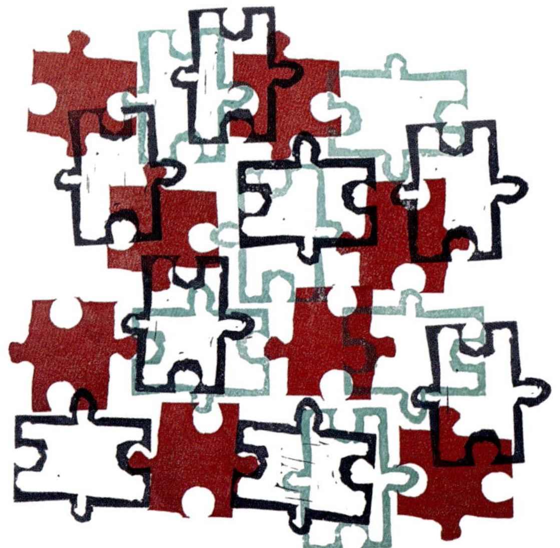

Reduction printing

This method of creating a print in several colours is perhaps one of the more complicated ways of working. The lino block is carved in progressive layers. For each layer of colour, more of the lino block is cut away, leaving very little of the block by the final layer. Start with a simple image so you can learn the process as you go through the sequence of stages. Once you have understood how it works, you can try a more detailed version. Do not rush the stages — it is a good idea to let the ink dry for at least 24 hours before you print the next layer.

You will need to register your prints very carefully with this method of printing so that, for each layer, the lino is positioned in exactly the same place and the paper is accurately lined up with the base paper.

YOU WILL NEED

- piece of lino (approximately 10 × 10 cm)
- printing paper (copy paper, sketchbook paper, cartridge paper or any smooth paper)
- tracing paper
- transfer paper (such as Tracedown®)
- spare paper or card (same size as printing paper)
- cutting mat
- cutting tools (U-shaped/V-shaped)
- printing ink
- inking tray or slab
- roller (brayer)
- spoon or baren
- crayons, felt pens or paint
- permanent black marker (optional)
- pencil
- disposable gloves
- rags
- damp cloths or baby wipes
- washing-up bowl
- warm soapy water
- detergent

Registration

1. Make a simple registration guide by using a piece of paper or card the size of your printing paper as the base. Place the lino block that you will use centrally on the paper and draw around it. This will be where you place the inked lino block when printing each layer. The printing paper will be aligned with the registration paper each time it is placed over the inked lino block. There are more sophisticated registration methods, but this works if you take care to place the lino block and the printing paper accurately. (a)

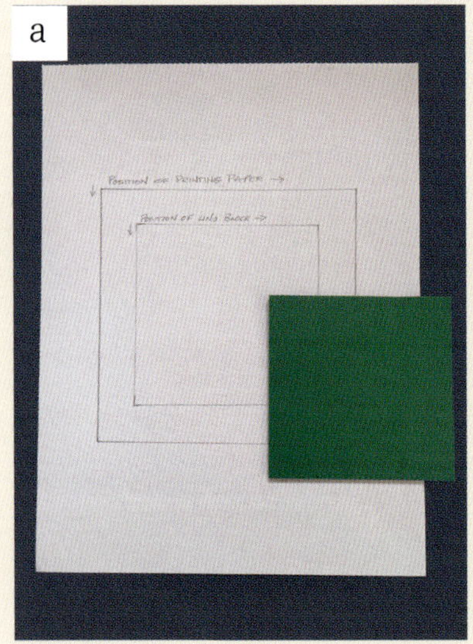

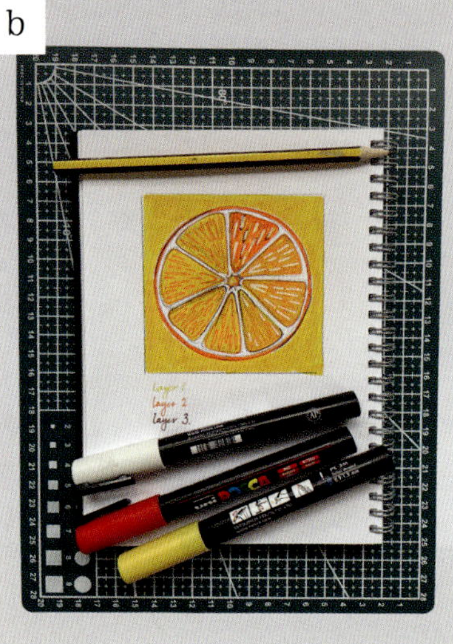

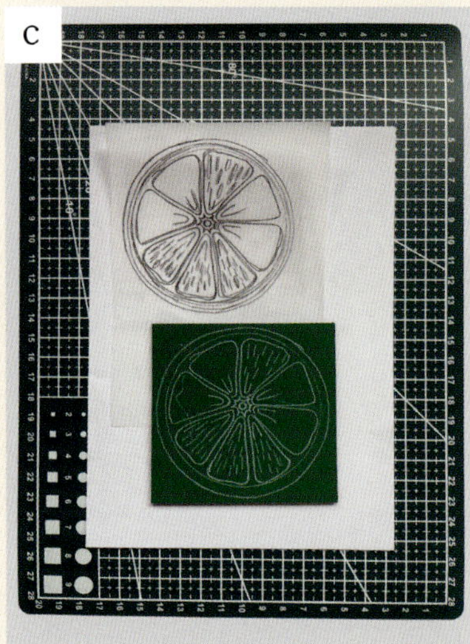

PLANNING YOUR REDUCTION PRINT

2. Decide which colours you are going to use. It helps if you draw your image on paper and then apply colour where you want it, including the background (using crayons, felt pens or paint). Leave some areas white to highlight specific parts of your picture — these will be made by the white of your printing paper. This coloured image will be your reference for carving. (b)

3. Trace your image and keep the tracing as you may need to reuse it if the image gets wiped from the lino.

4. Transfer your image from the tracing paper to the lino block using transfer paper. You could go over the white drawing with a permanent black marker, but you may find that this will transfer to your first layer. (This is not necessarily a problem and should not show on the finished print.) (c)

Layer 1

5. Carve out the areas that you want to stay white — the colour of your printing paper. This might be just a few carved marks or an outline. (d)

6. Ink the plate using the lightest colour and print it in the usual way. The print will look strange with a solid colour and a few white marks on it. (e)

7. The first layer shows the carved areas in white and the rest of the block in your first ink colour. I suggest printing three or four for your first attempt. These will be your 'print edition'. When you are familiar with the process you can print a larger edition of 10 or more. (f)

Layer 2

8. Clean your lino block and dry it. You should still see the drawing but if it has disappeared, place the transfer paper and tracing paper on the block and transfer the drawing again, taking care to match it accurately. If you used a permanent marker, the image should still be clear.

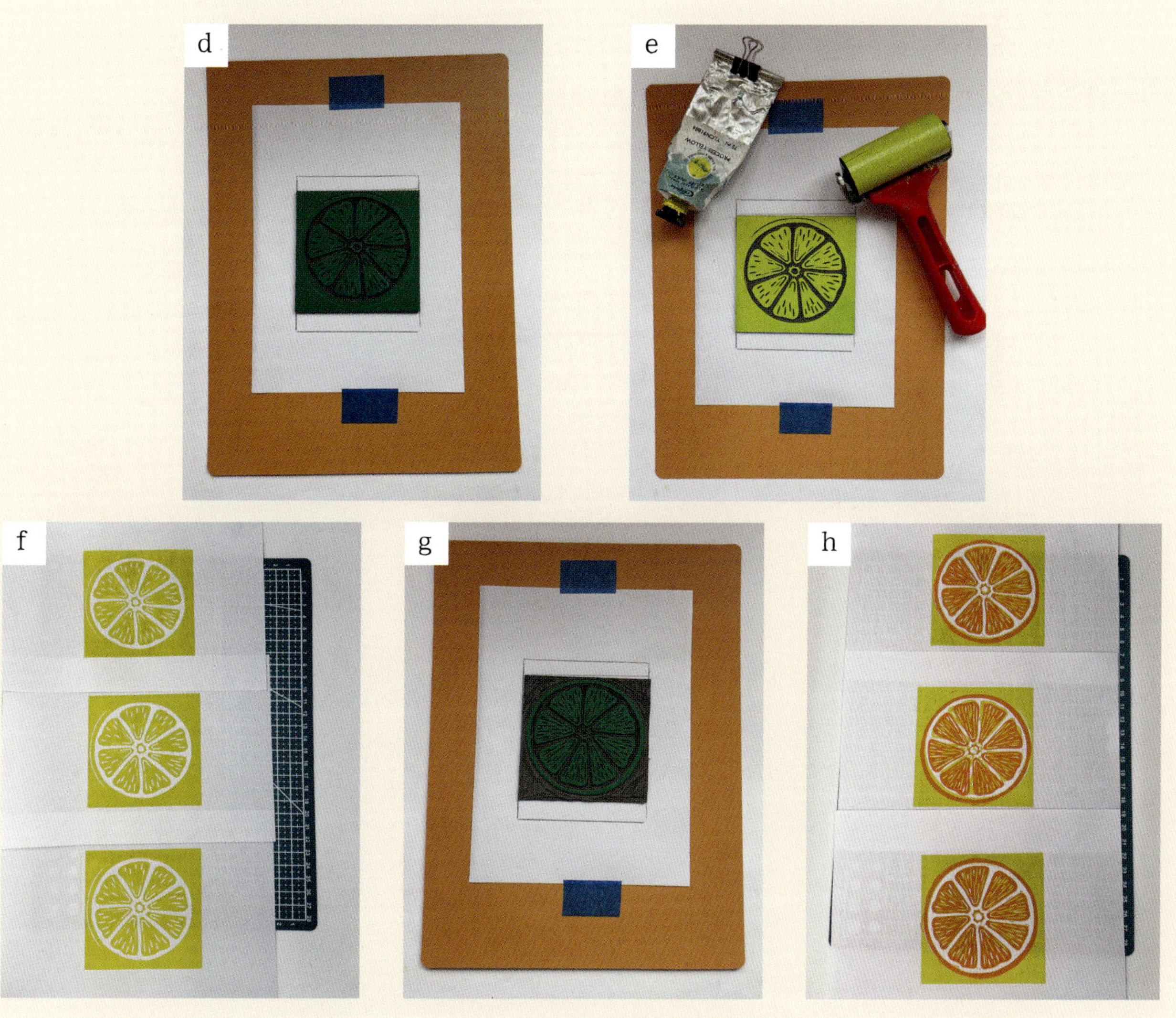

9. Look at your reference drawing and identify the areas that you want to be in the first colour that you used. Carve out the areas that you want to remain in this first colour. (In the example shown, the areas carved out at this step are those that need to remain yellow.) (g)

10. Ink the block using the second colour, taking care to place the block exactly on the marked shape and the paper with your first layer matching the base paper accurately. Burnish the paper and lift the print. Repeat this with the other printed papers in the edition. (h)

Layer 3

11. Clean your block as before. Refer to your original drawing and identify the areas that you want to be in the second colour. You may need to transfer the image again if it has disappeared. Carve out the areas that you want to remain in this second colour. (i)

12. Ink the block with your third colour of ink. Most of the surface of your block will now be carved away. Place the inked block exactly on the marked shape and match the printing paper with the base paper accurately. (j)

13. Burnish the paper and lift the print. Repeat this with the other printed papers in the edition. Your prints should now look complete. They may not be as perfect as you would like but remember that reduction printing is complicated, and it takes practice to master the technique.

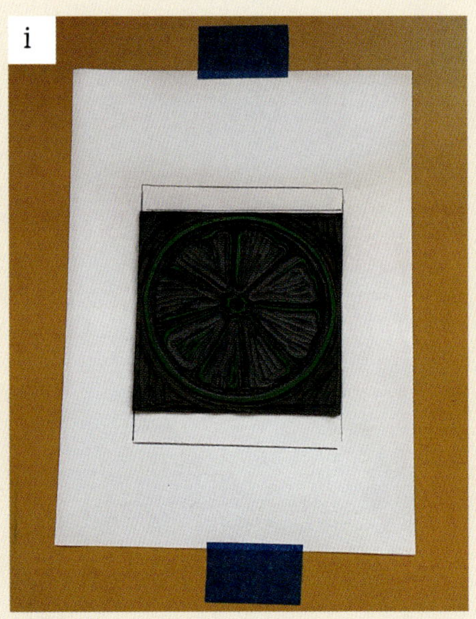

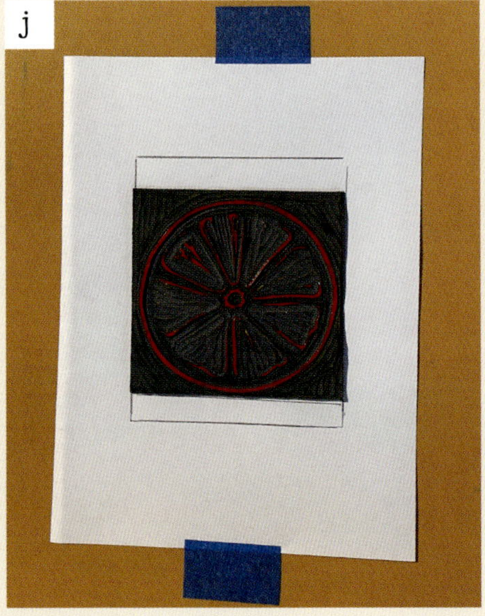

Right: **Three layers of a reduction print (yellow, orange, red).**

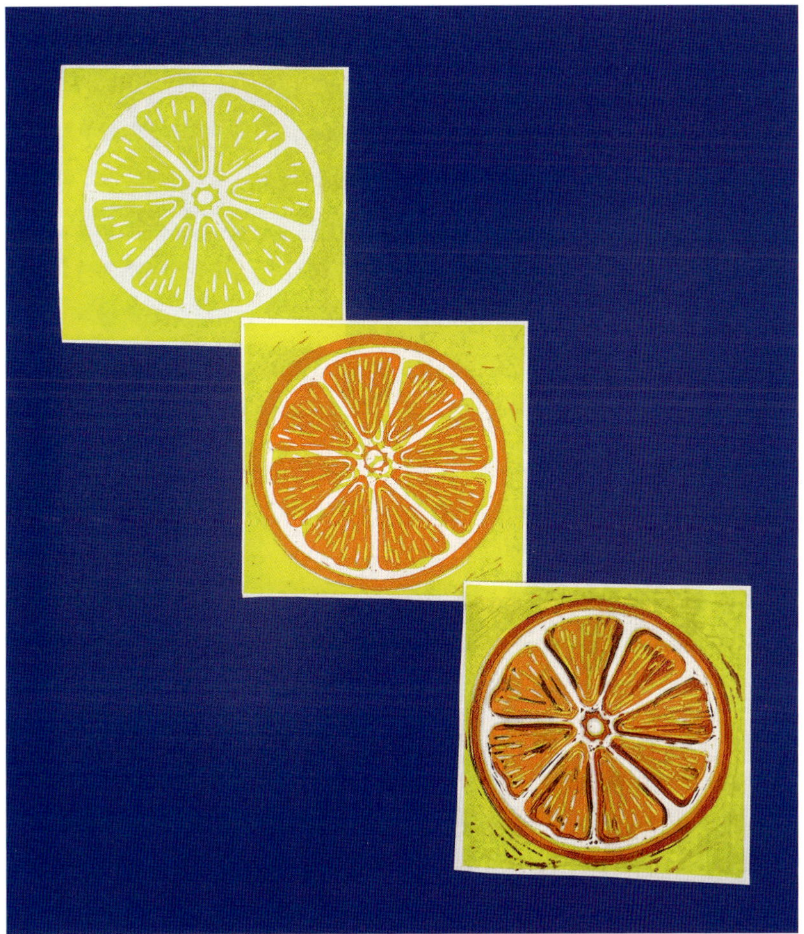

Cleaning up

- Roll excess ink from the roller on to a spare piece of paper, then clean it with warm soapy water, rinse thoroughly and leave to dry.

- To clean your inking tray or slab, remove excess ink with paper or a rag, then wash in warm soapy water, rinse and leave to drain and dry.

- Wash Japanese Vinyl in warm soapy water, rinse and lay on a flat surface to dry. If using traditional lino, it is best not to immerse it in water as it has a hessian backing. Clean the surface of the plate with a damp cloth and a small amount of detergent, then wipe with a cloth. Dry on a flat surface.

Printing on fabric and other materials

- There are many images that you can use to print on to fabric. Stamping blocks are ideal, or you can use linoprints. (a)

- Caligo Safe Wash relief printing ink can be used on fabric without any fixing but must be allowed to dry completely before being washed (about a week). You can buy ink pads (such as those made by VersaCraft), which are specially for using on fabric; the ink can be fixed with a hot iron to make the print permanent. There are also fabric printing inks available at craft shops.

- It is best to select smooth fabrics that are not heavily textured for printing on. Textured material such as linen needs a press to give a clear, crisp print.

- Place a smooth, hard surface under the fabric to help the transfer of ink. If printing on a T-shirt or a tote bag, place a piece of card or an acrylic sheet inside the shirt to avoid the ink transferring to the back.

- You need apply pressure to transfer the image, so it can help to put something heavy over the lino block. Fabric tends to stretch and move if the burnishing technique is used, which can result in a fuzzy print, so it is preferable to press down hard or weight the lino block.

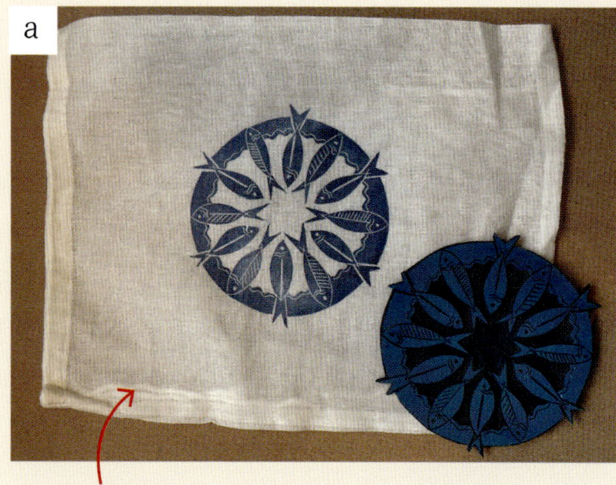

Linoprint on a calico drawstring bag

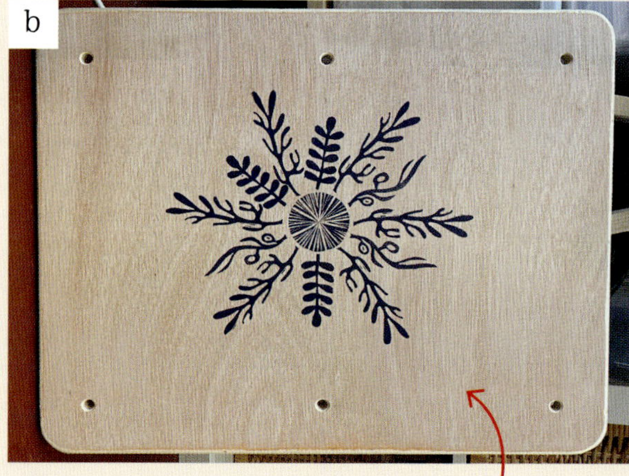

Linoprint motif on a wooden flower press

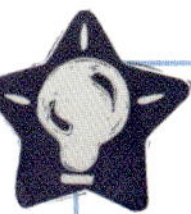

Print on fabric squares
and quilt them together
to make a cushion cover.

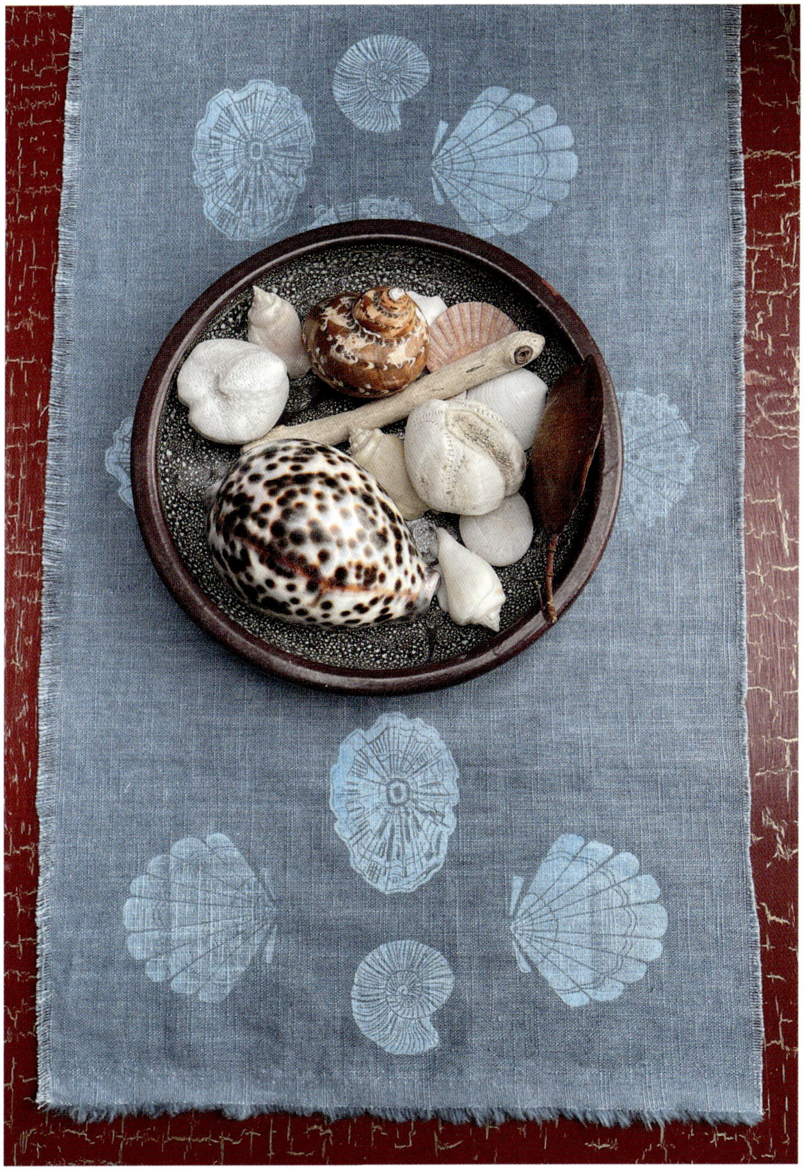

Right: Individual lino shells on a
blue linen table runner using
light blue Caligo Safe Wash ink.

■ It is best to experiment and do some test pieces to find out what
works. I have had success with tea-towels, napkins, aprons, T-shirts,
tote bags and table runners. I have also printed on wooden
coasters and a wooden flower press using Caligo Safe Wash inks. (b)

Printed T-shirts make great gifts for both children and adults.

Karen Komurcu aka Linocut Lassie — printmaker

'I have a background in design but have always been drawn to printmaking and started by buying some basic tools – an Abig wooden-handled tool with interchangeable blades, Speedy Carve™ and water-based inks. I started at my kitchen table, and it still serves me well. A large space is not a necessity: the access to a sink nearby was my main requirement. The first prints were basic, as I learned how the cuts I made translated onto paper, but I wanted to push myself into multiple plate and reduction printing to see where that could lead. It was lot of trial and error and discovery. This is what makes printmaking so enjoyable, I think.

'I soon started selling with a local art group in a pop-up shop and this quickly grew into joining Cowal Open Studios. I found it a good way to focus, meet other artists and find support and advice.

'Once I became more confident, I invested in some better tools, inks and paper. Finding good inks and a registration method that works was, for me, the biggest leap in creating better prints. Start with the basics and build your skill before investing.

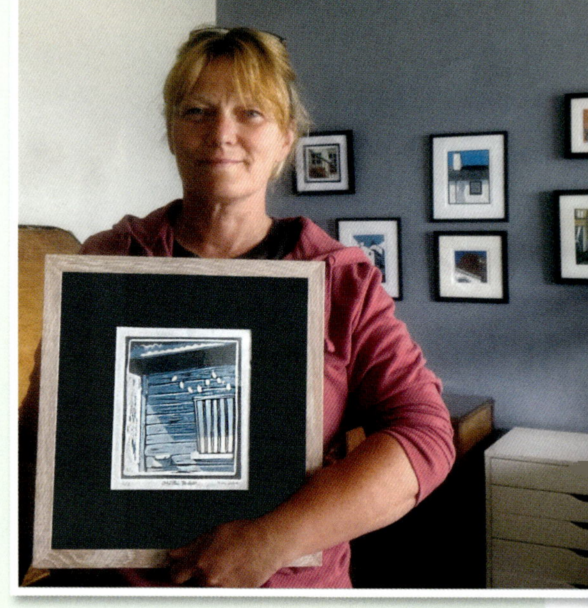

'My work always starts with observation; the things I find pleasing in my surroundings soon become a print idea. For me, it would be light and shadow, strong colour or a pleasing palette of colours that draws my attention. I work in a fairly small size and in low-numbered editions as my time is limited. The main thing I have learned is to experiment, to create things that may not make it to a final print, and learn from the process. You can draw directly on to the lino, which makes for a more fluid creative print, or

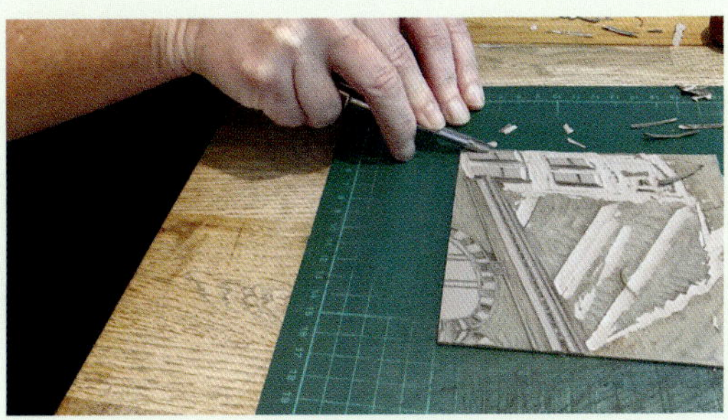

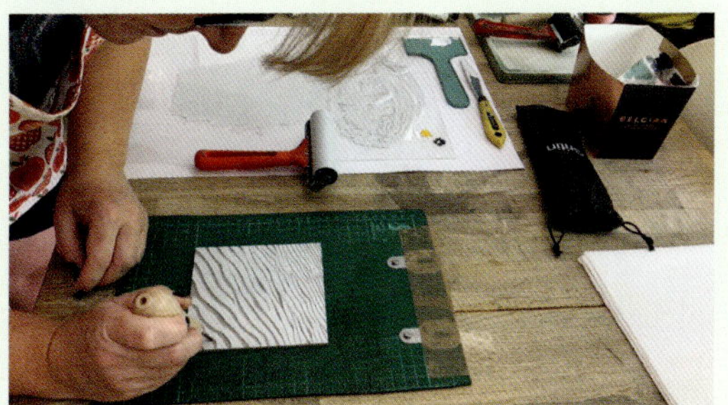

draw the image then reverse it on to the lino. Although there are basic techniques to follow, you can take your printing anywhere you wish – applying ink with brushes, using drills instead of gouges, creating collage with print pieces ... really, the list is endless.

'Joining online print groups is a great way to get advice and ideas, and visiting exhibitions of all kinds of printmaking is a learning tool. I've found other printmakers are very generous with advice and encouragement.

'For me, linocut is the ideal low-cost print method; it incorporates multiple skills – design, drawing, carving and colour mixing to name a few. Incidentally, I also find it very meditative and a good way to relax and focus the mind.'

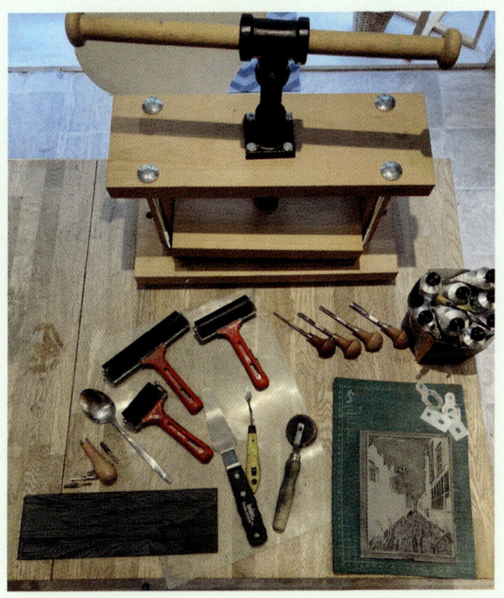

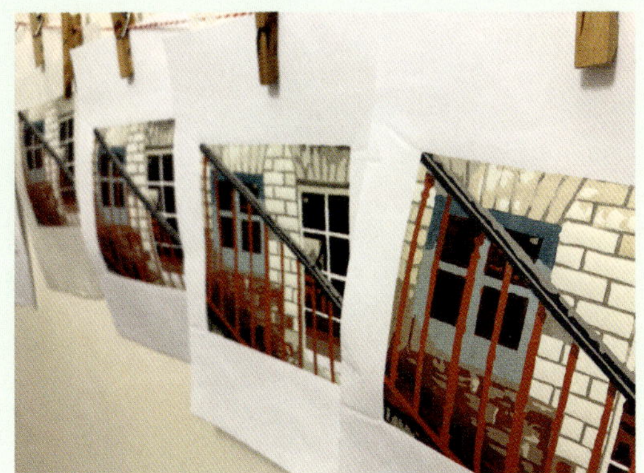

7

RELIEF PRINTING – COLLAGRAPHY

Collagraphy is a printmaking process in which materials are applied to a rigid base plate, such as mount board, acetate or wood. The word 'collagraph' is derived from the Greek words *kolla*, meaning 'glue', and *graphos*, meaning 'writing'. To create a collagraph print, you work the ink into the printing plate and then wipe the surface, leaving ink in the incised and textured areas. This method of inking is called 'intaglio'. The plate is then printed on damp paper using an etching press. A collagraph plate can, however, be used to make a relief print, without a press. Many subjects lend themselves to this way of printing, including landscapes, buildings, still-life compositions and abstract images.

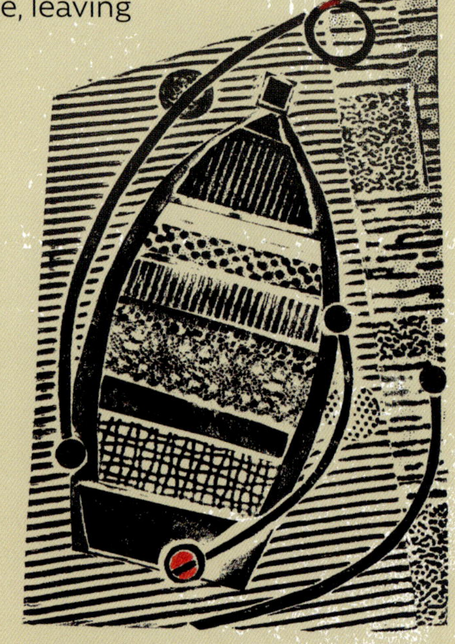

Collagraph printing without a press

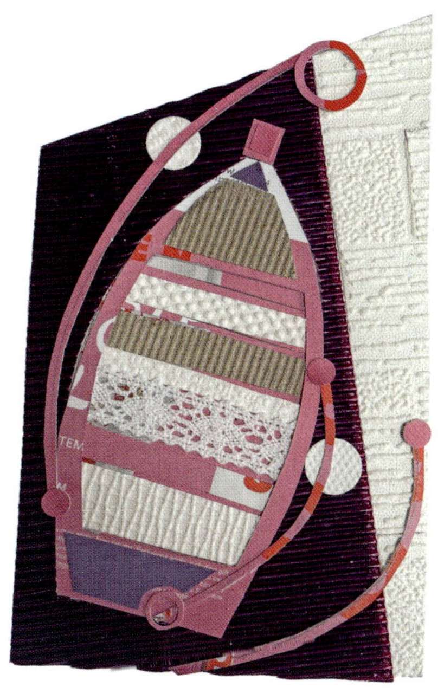

The basis of a collagraph printing plate is mount board, but it is possible to use cardboard packaging to great effect. A variety of materials can be glued to the base plate. The collaged materials must be well stuck down so that the plate can be inked without areas tearing off or ink becoming trapped under raised edges. Once you have built your collagraph plate, you apply the ink over the surface of the plate and print it using a spoon or baren, resulting in a uniquely textured print. If you are planning to print multiple versions, it is advisable to seal your printing plate with either a layer of PVA or shellac varnish (button polish) to make it more durable. Make sure it is completely dry before applying ink.

TEST PLATE

Creating a test plate is a chance to try out the process and see how different materials react when inked and printed. You will find that some materials work better than others.

YOU WILL NEED

- mountboard or packaging card (cereal box or similar) (approximately 10 × 30 cm)
- textured materials (cut shapes from thin card, textured wallpaper, crumpled tissue paper, fabric, sandpaper, corrugated card, card labels, sequins, doilies, string, etc.)
- printing paper (mixed-media paper, cartridge paper or another heavier paper)
- cutting mat
- scissors or craft knife
- printing ink
- roller (brayer)
- inking tray or slab
- spoon or baren or clean roller
- pencil
- paper clips (optional)
- PVA glue
- glue brush or applicator
- disposable gloves
- rags
- warm water
- washing-up liquid
- oil (baby or vegetable) (optional)
- baby wipes and/or a damp cloth

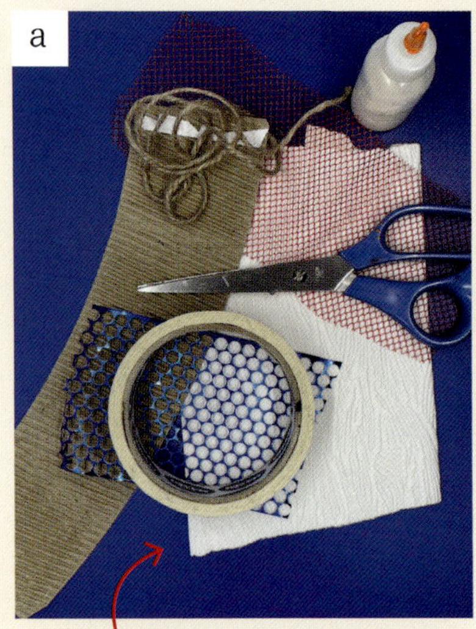

A selection of
textured materials

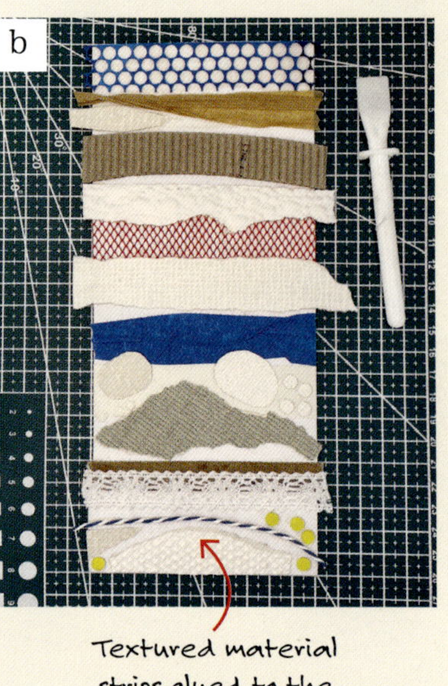

Textured material
strips glued to the
card plate

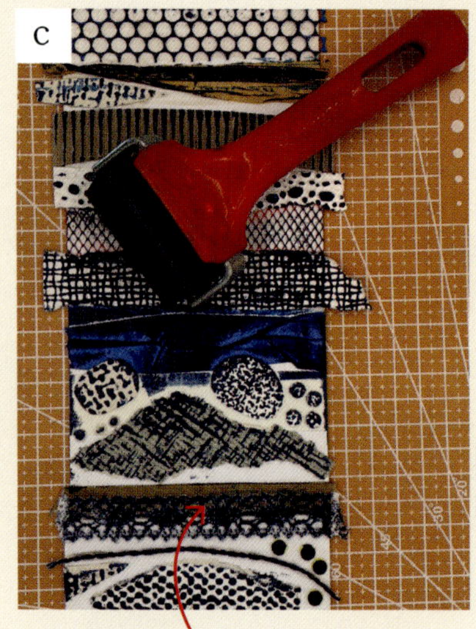

Printing ink rolled over the
surface of the plate once
the glue has dried

1. Take the piece of card you will use as your plate.

2. Cut strips or shapes from your textured materials. You can also incorporate found textured objects, as long as they are flat and not sharp (sharp or hard raised pieces can cut into your paper when you print). (a)

3. Collage your pieces on to the plate using PVA glue. This is an activity in which you can experiment and find out how materials produce different textures when printed, so don't try to create a picture. Ensure that the materials lie flat on the plate and are securely sealed around the edges. If you are using netting or lace, it is best to apply the PVA to the base card and press the material into it. You may need to apply pressure until the glue dries, or clamp it with paper clips. (b)

4. Once your plate is finished, it needs to be allowed to dry completely. As this is a test plate, there is no need to seal it all over with glue or varnish before applying the ink.

5. Squeeze a blob of printing ink on to your inking tray or slab. Work the ink with your roller until you have a thin, even covering of ink on the surface of the roller.

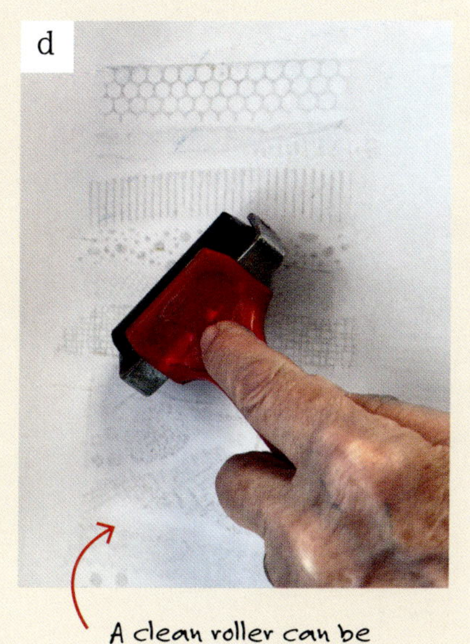

d

A clean roller can be used to apply pressure over the paper

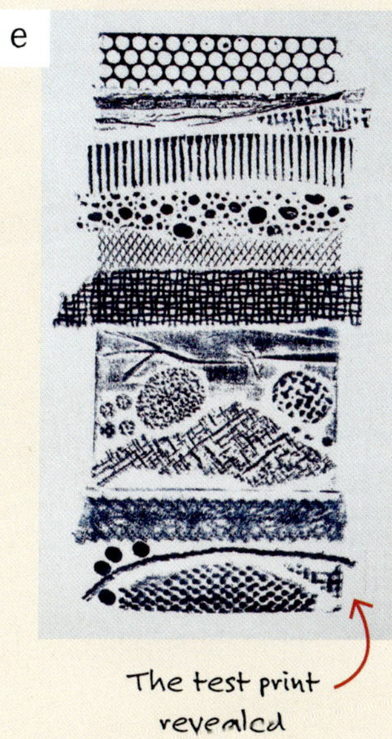

e

The test print revealed

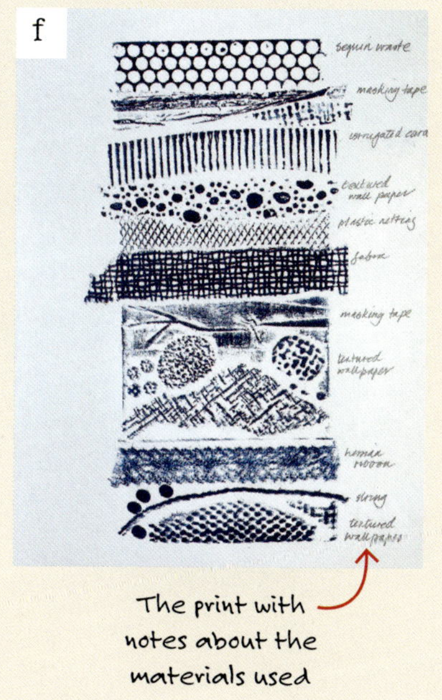

f

The print with notes about the materials used

6. Roll a layer of ink over your test plate, making sure that you cover all the collaged pieces evenly. Spread the ink sparingly – too much ink will result in a messy print. (c)

7. Place a piece of paper over the inked surface and use a spoon or baren to press down over the paper. Burnish the surface right up to the edges, rubbing in circular movements. You can also use a clean roller to roll over the surface with firm pressure. (d)

8. Peel the paper to reveal the print. (e)

9. Add this test print to your sketchbook with notes about the materials you used. You could include comments about which materials worked and which were not so successful. (f)

Cleaning up

■ You do not need to clean your collagraph plate – just let it dry!

■ Clean up your inking tray or slab by wiping the excess ink away and then washing your tray or slab in warm water and a little washing-up liquid. You can use oil and a rag to clean off most of the ink before washing. Wear disposable gloves to keep your hands ink free.

STILL-LIFE COLLAGRAPH PRINT

Once you have tried out this method of printing, you are ready to create a more interesting print. Try putting together a still-life image, using different textures to create the tones and details.

YOU WILL NEED

- mountboard or packaging card (cereal box or similar) (approximately 16 × 20 cm)
- textured materials (cut shapes from thin card, textured wallpaper, crumpled tissue paper, fabric, sandpaper, corrugated card, card labels, sequins, doilies, string, etc.)
- printing paper (A4 mixed-media paper or cartridge paper)
- tracing paper
- spare paper or sketchbook
- cutting mat
- scissors or craft knife
- printing ink
- roller (brayer)
- inking tray or slab
- spoon or baren or clean roller
- pencil
- PVA glue (for collage)
- PVA glue or shellac varnish/button polish (for sealing your plate)
- glue brush or applicator
- disposable gloves
- rags
- warm water
- washing-up liquid
- baby oil (optional)
- baby wipes

1. Draw your still-life image on paper or in your sketchbook and transfer it on to a piece of sturdy card. (a)

2. Build your printing plate in the same way as the test plate, collaging materials and making sure they are well stuck down. I always trace the drawn image and use the tracing to mark out pieces of textured material. If you do this, make sure you transfer the traced shape to the back of the textured material so it fits your drawing correctly. (b)

3. Leave the glue to dry, then paint a layer of diluted PVA glue (or shellac varnish/button polish) over the entire surface. This will help to secure all the collaged pieces and, when dry, will make your plate more durable. Leave it to dry fully. (c)

5. Ink up the plate by rolling an even layer of ink over the surface with your roller. (d)

6. Place a sheet of printing paper over the inked plate and use a spoon or baren to burnish the surface, or roll over the surface with a clean roller, applying firm pressure.

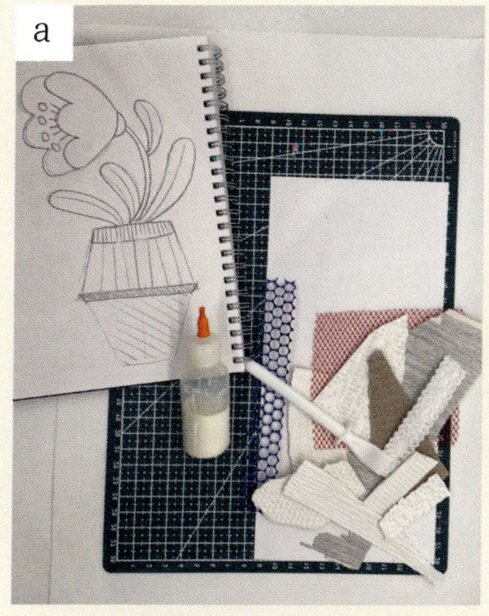

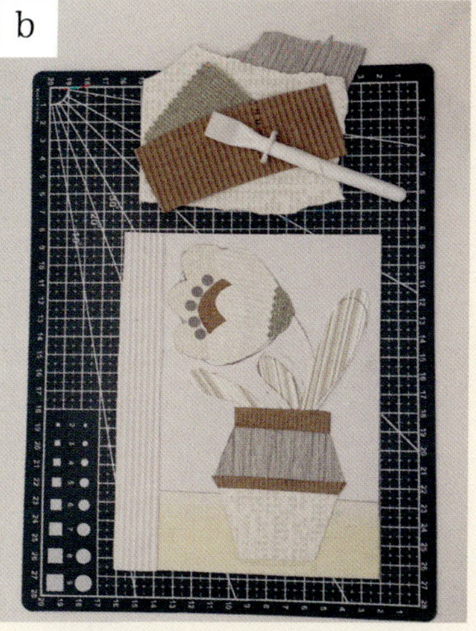

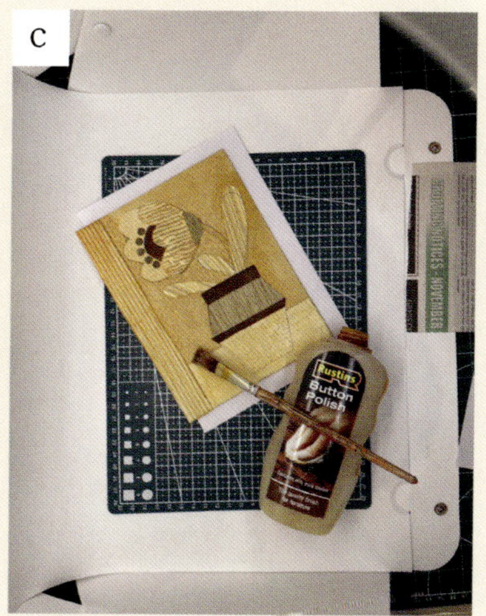

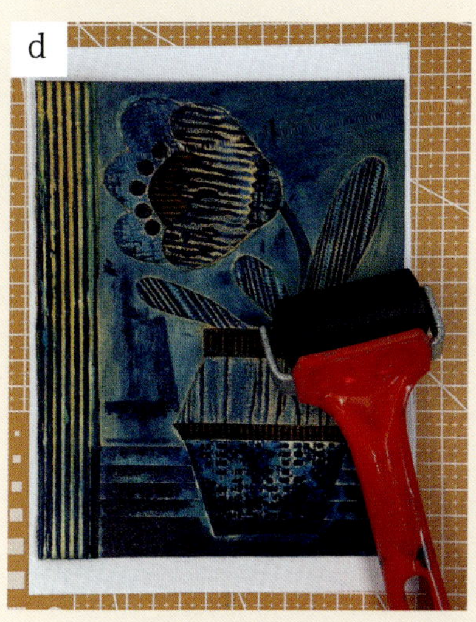

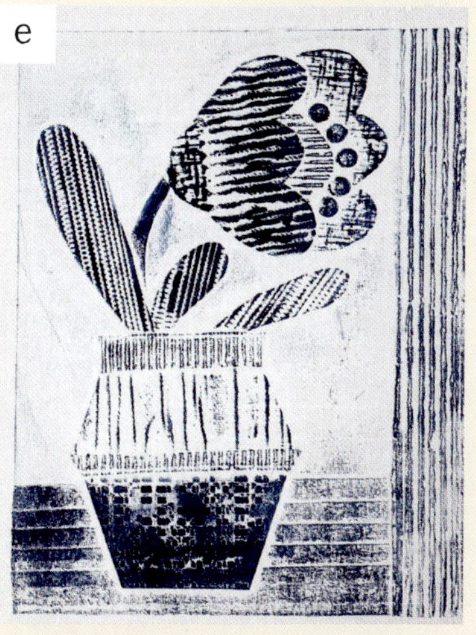

Try printing your plate again but add different colours of ink to selected areas. (Clean the roller between colours by rolling it on to scrap newspaper and wiping with a baby wipe.) Every print from your plate will be slightly different as it is not easy to ink consistently unless you are using a single colour.

7. Peel the paper away carefully to reveal your print. (e)

8. Place somewhere flat to dry.

CLEANING UP

- You do not need to clean your collagraph plate after use – just let it dry!

- Clean up leftover ink with baby wipes or baby oil and a rag. Then wash in warm soapy water, rinse and leave to dry. Wear disposable gloves to keep your fingers ink free.

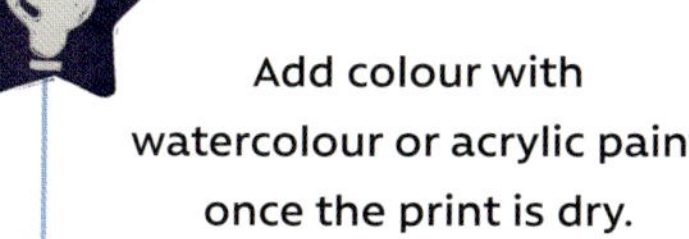

Add colour with watercolour or acrylic paint once the print is dry.

Suzie MacKenzie — printmaker

'I enjoy the playful simplicity of relief collagraph prints and often like to work in this way for print exchanges and artist's books. Unlike an intaglio print, a relief collagraph is characterised by the white 'haloes' that show around the raised area of the printmaking block. While this method doesn't allow the range of tonal values possible with an intaglio print, with careful inking and printing it can show very fine textural detail which can work as areas of tone. And although intaglio collagraphs require high-pressure printing using an expensive press, relief collagraphs can be printed without a press using hand pressure alone. An added benefit of this method is that the textures are less likely to compress when printing by hand, so it is possible to take more prints from the block before it degrades.

'I make my relief collagraph blocks using two different methods, or a combination of both. Both begin with a piece of mountboard as the base. The first method creates layers by cutting into the board with a scalpel and peeling off the surface. This reveals a rough texture; the deeper the cut and the more of the top layers peeled, the lighter this area is likely to print – or it can be cut out and removed entirely for a completely white area. Tools such as dressmakers' tracing wheels and fluted pasta-cutting wheels can be used to create interesting marks on the block. The second method adds texture by gluing materials onto the block, building up layers on the board; textured papers and tapes work well for this. For your first attempts, it is best to start on a small scale – printing by hand can be quite hard work!'

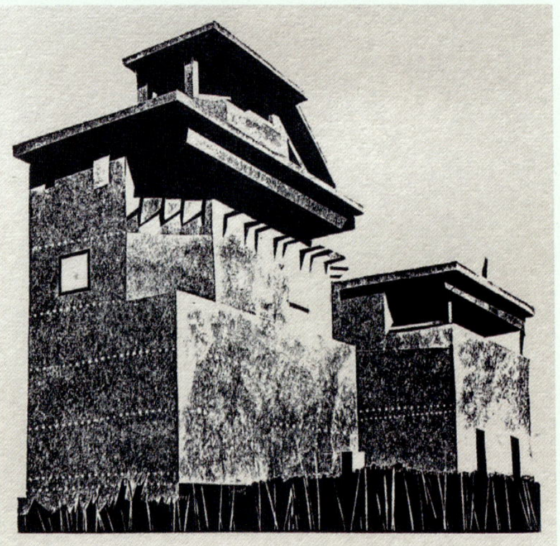

Above: **This simple architectural image was made with shapes cut and peeled from the surface of a piece of mountboard. A dressmakers' tracing wheel was used to create the dotted lines. The background area was removed so that it appears completely white in the printed image. Nothing was added to this block.**

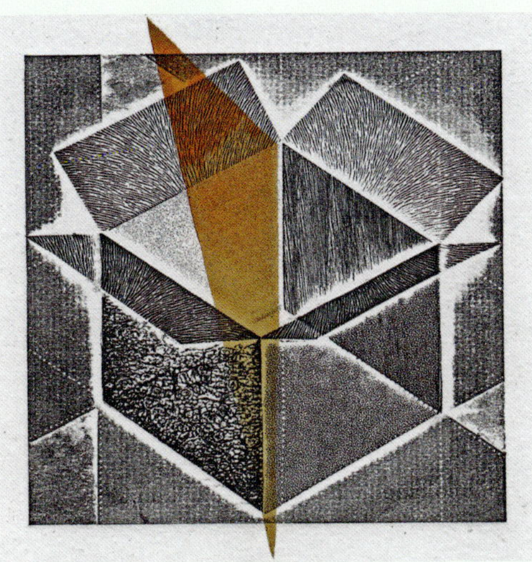

Left: This image was made by adding layers of textured papers to the block. It is a good demonstration of the fine textural detail that is possible with this technique. The white 'haloes' characteristic of a relief-printed collagraph also show well. Materials used for making the block were brown kraft paper, wallpapers, blackboard sticky-back plastic, sandpaper and wood veneer. The coloured area was added post-printing, using acrylic ink and a stencil.

Right: This print uses a combination of both techniques — the bird shapes were revealed by cutting away and peeling off layers of the cardboard base surrounding them, and then textures were added as in the image above, including one created using an inexpensive crafter's embossing machine. This print was made using two colours simultaneously — a soft wallpaper seam roller (widely available from DIY and online stores) was used to apply turquoise ink all over the block, then a medium print roller passed over it to add black to the upper surfaces. Because the seam-roller is so soft, it can reach down into areas of the block that the print roller isn't able to, and these will remain turquoise. As in the image above, other colours were added post-print, using acrylic ink and stencils.

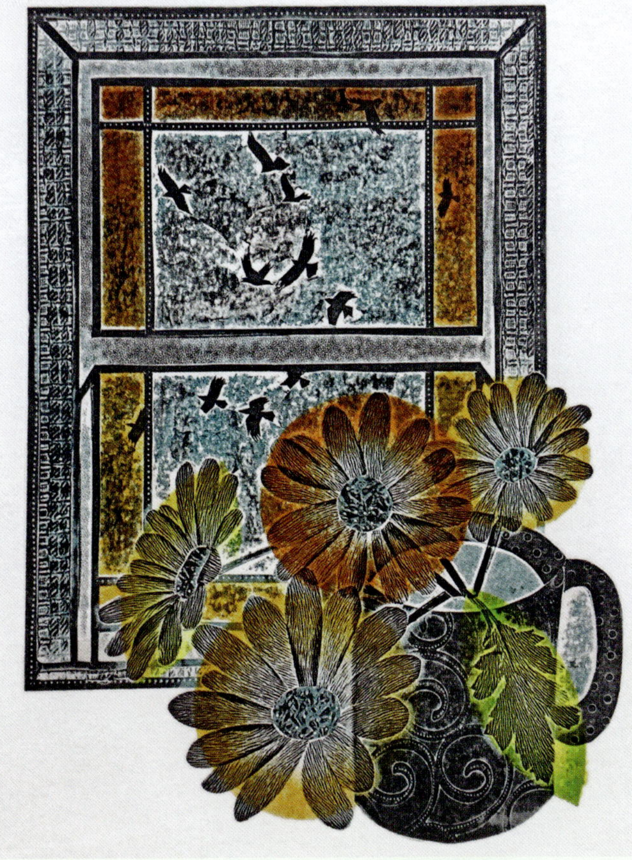

8

PRINTING WITH PACKAGING

Many types of packaging come into our homes and can be used for printmaking.

Small card packages, when opened out, have interesting shapes and fold lines and can be used for collagraph printing. The card is easily cut into different shapes and some packets have intriguing apertures.

The waxy surface inside juice, milk and soup cartons is a cheap and effective printmaking material. The folds and creases add texture to monoprints or drypoint etchings. You can use a scalpel or sharp pointed implement to score or scratch a design, or cut and peel away areas to expose the absorbent material under the surface. You can print these without a press, but the pressure of an etching press produces a more defined print.

A printing plate made from Tetra Pak®, corrugated card from a coffee cup sleeve, labels and a cereal box.

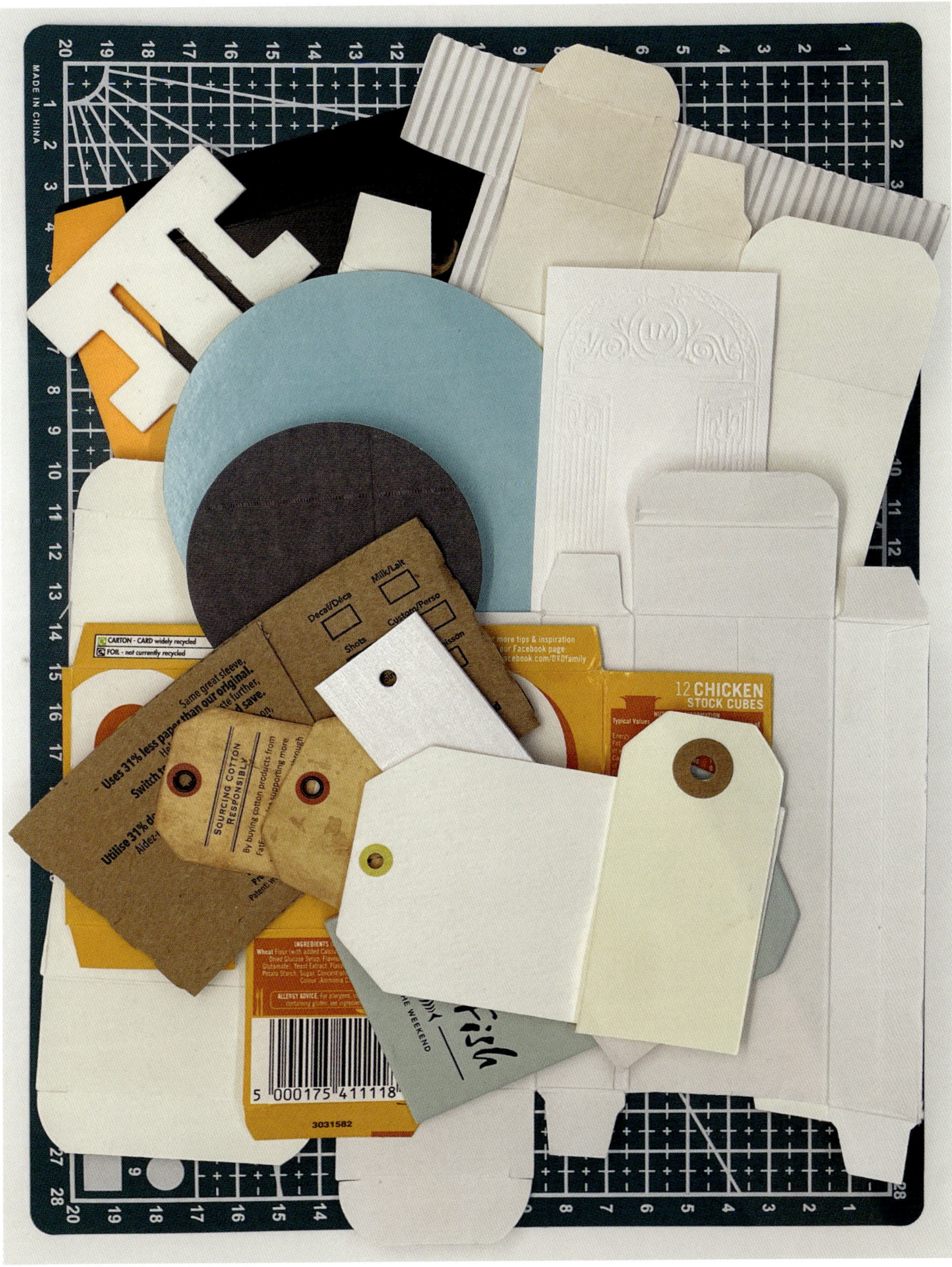

Above: A collection of flattened packaging, labels and card offcuts ready for creating collagraph plates.

Monoprinting with packaging

YOU WILL NEED
- carton packaging such as Tetra Pak® (clean and dry)
- printing paper (copy paper, sketchbook paper, cartridge paper or any smooth paper)
- scrap paper
- scissors or craft knife
- ink pads
- spoon or baren
- damp cloth or baby wipes

1. Cut out several pieces of packaging, varying the sizes of your shapes (squares, rectangles, circles, etc.). (a)

2. Fold each shape up in multiple ways to create creases in the surface. (b)

3. Take an ink pad and dab it over the shiny, waxy surface of a piece of crumpled carton packaging to get a fairly even cover of ink. (c)

4. Place the inked piece ink side down on to a clean piece of paper. Place a piece of scrap paper over it. Rub firmly using a spoon.

5. Lift the paper and carton piece and admire your unique print. (d)

6. Ink up the other pieces of packaging (use the same colour or different colours of ink) and repeat the printing process on the same piece of paper. (e)

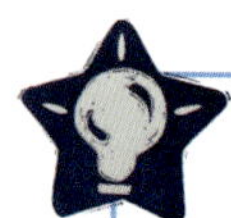

Instead of cutting shapes, use a whole unfolded carton. Fold and crease it in different directions, apply ink from an ink pad and print as a unique background to use with other print techniques.

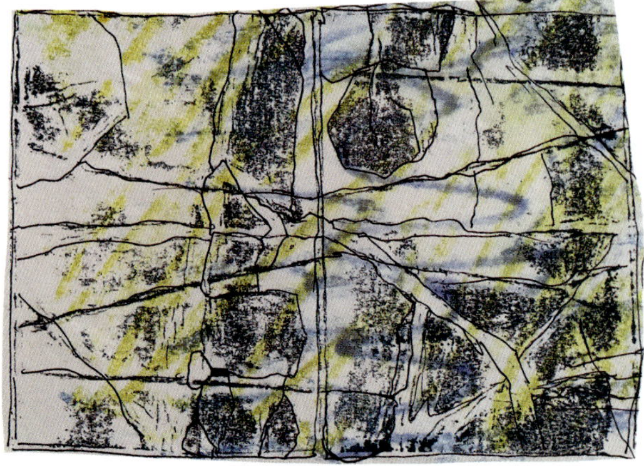

Above: **Crumpled print using carton packaging with fineliner for added detail.**

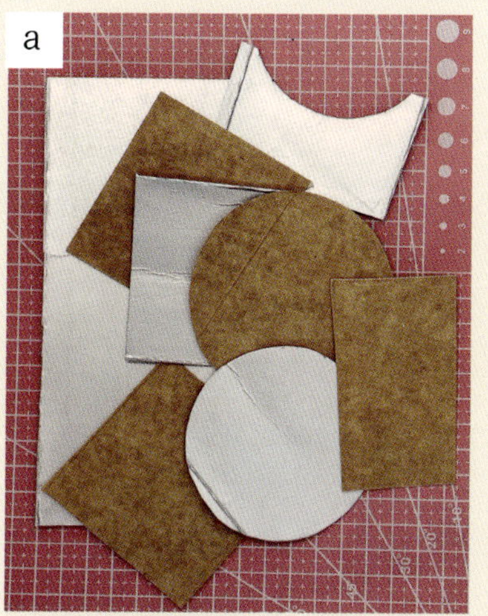

a

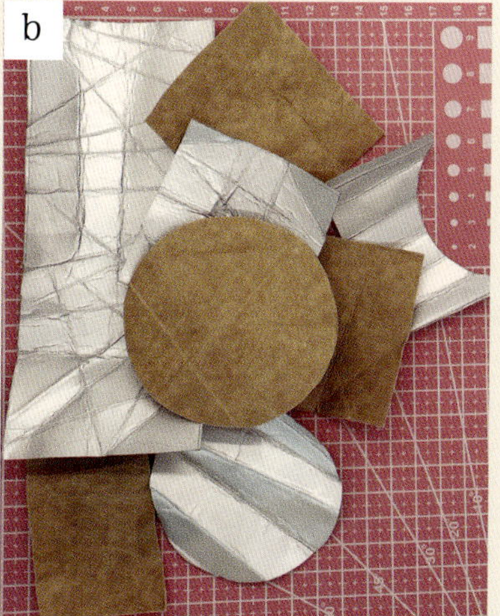

b

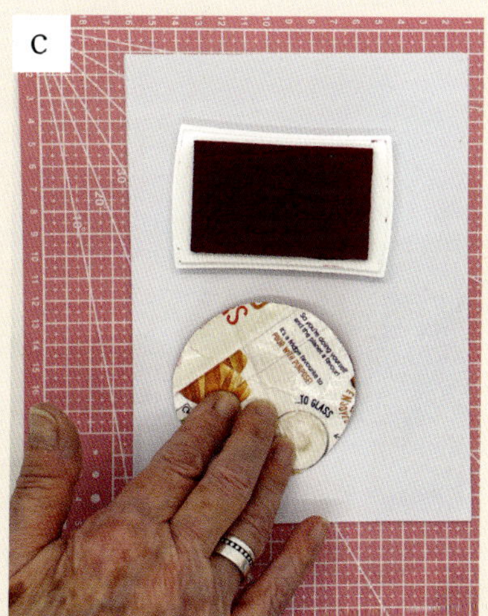

c

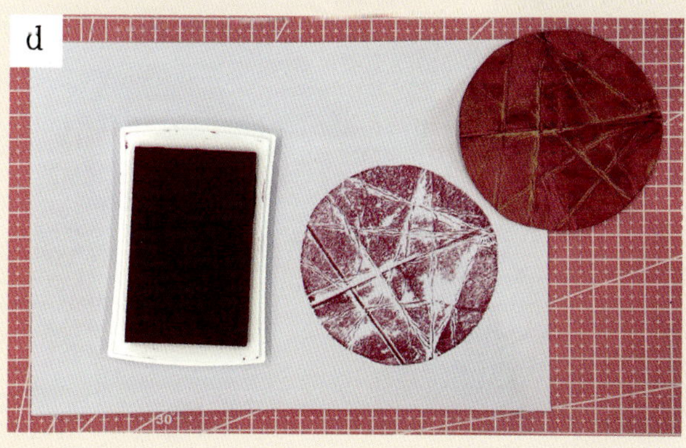

d

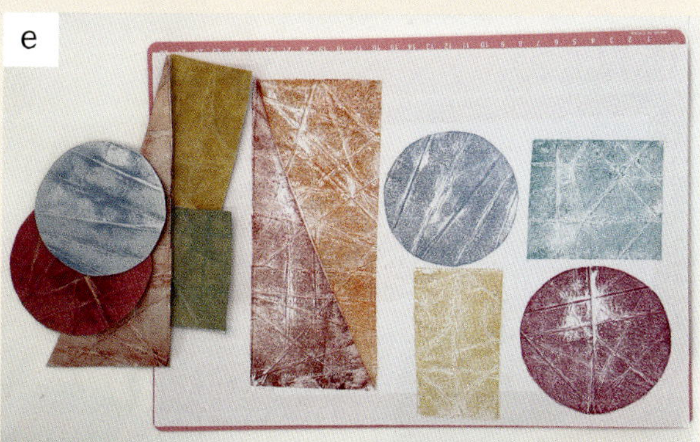

e

Look for images in the creased print patterns, such as mountains, water, buildings, or even vases of flowers. Add to the prints by using a fineliner pen to outline and define areas or add colour with crayons or watercolour.

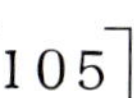

CLEANING UP

■ Use a damp cloth or a baby wipe to clean ink from your carton pieces.

Drypoint etching with packaging

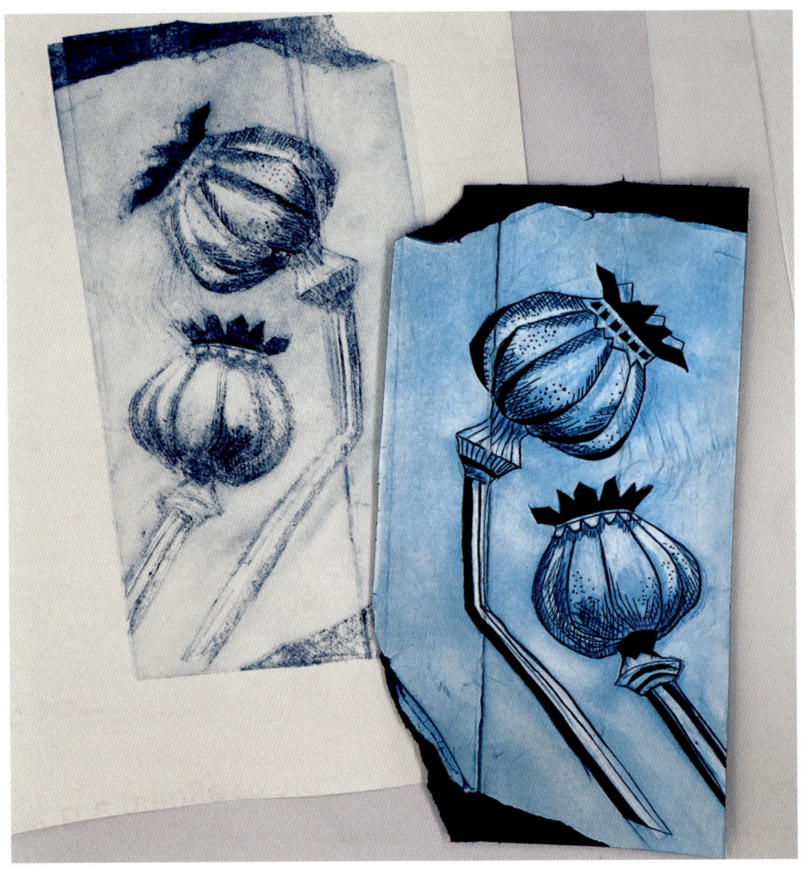

Left: **Drypoint etching plate and print using carton packaging.**

Drypoint etching is a simple form of printing that you can do at home with or without a press. Normally it is done by scratching an image into the surface of an acrylic sheet. The etched lines have a slightly rough edge or burr to which the ink clings. The finished etching plate is then inked up by spreading printing ink on to the plate and working into the scratched lines. The plate is then wiped and the ink that stays in the incised marks prints on to the paper.

The waxy surface of the packaging inside milk, juice or soup cartons is a cheap and effective way of creating a printing plate and serves as an introduction to this printing technique. Use a sharp etching tool, a nail or even the point of a compass to incise the lines of your image. You can cut into the surface with a craft knife and peel areas away, revealing the absorbent layer below the smooth top layer. This soaks up the ink and produces much darker areas in the print.

The print is made on dampened paper, allowing the paper to pick up the ink that has collected in the marks cut into the surface of the plate. You need a heavier paper with a smooth surface to print on as it will be soaked and then blotted dry; thinner paper would be too fragile when wet. Somerset® Satin 200 is a good paper to use.

Drypoint etching is usually printed using an etching press which allows the roller to exert really strong pressure on the plate and pushes the damp paper into the etched lines where the ink has collected. Without a press, you will need to use your trusty spoon and plenty of elbow grease to burnish the plate and transfer the image to the paper. You will not achieve a crisp print, but it can be very pleasing and benefits from being worked into once dry to give more definition or to add colour.

YOU WILL NEED

- carton packaging such as Tetra Pak® (clean and dry)
- printing paper (mixed-media heavy paper with a smooth surface – Fabriano® or Somerset® Satin)
- copy paper or greaseproof paper
- newspaper or tissue paper
- tracing paper
- scrap paper
- small rectangular pieces of card or mountboard
- cutting mat
- etching tool or sharp nail or thick sharp needle or the point of a compass
- craft knife
- printing ink (black or a mix of phthalo blue/black; use Caligo Safe Wash – this does not work with water-based printing inks)
- inking tray or slab
- spoon or baren or clean roller
- pencil
- cotton buds
- disposable gloves (optional)
- rags or scrim
- blotting paper or two clean tea-towels
- damp cloths or baby wipes
- washing-up bowl
- warm soapy water

1. Prepare your mixed-media or heavy paper for printing – soak it in cold water for about five minutes, drain it and place between two sheets of blotting paper or a couple of tea-towels to blot the water but leave the paper damp.

2. Look at your packaging and see if the shape, including folds, flaps and creases, suggests the start of an image to you. You might see a building, a mountain range, a fence or wall with a bird perched on it, or an abstract or geometric design. The creases and folds can add interest to a finished print. If you don't think you want these

Notice how areas have been scored with a craft knife and the surface shapes peeled away to create darker areas once it is inked and printed.

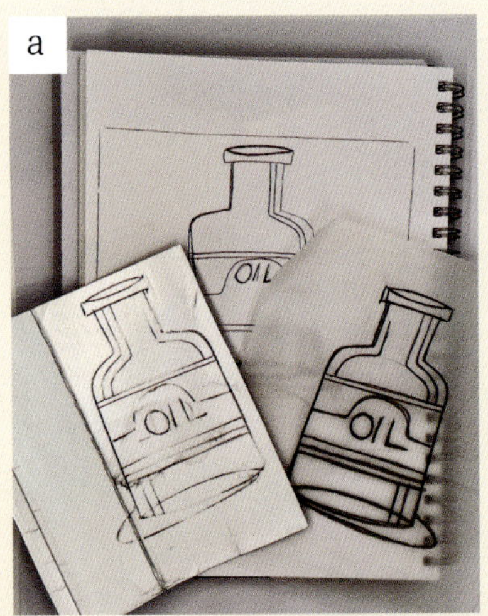

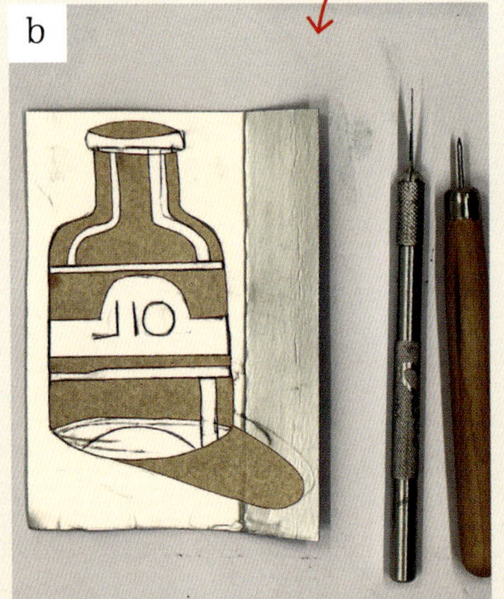

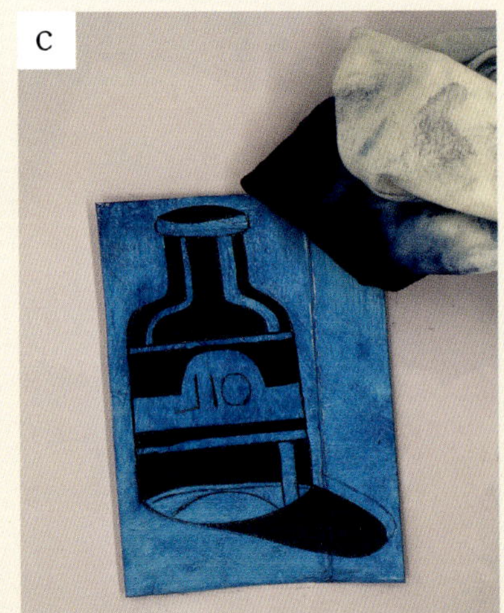

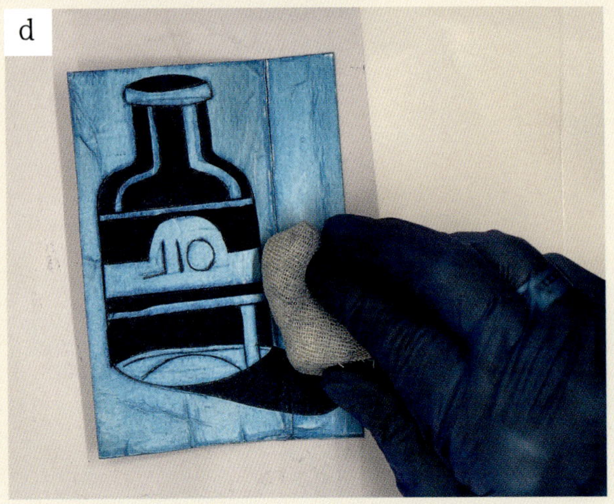

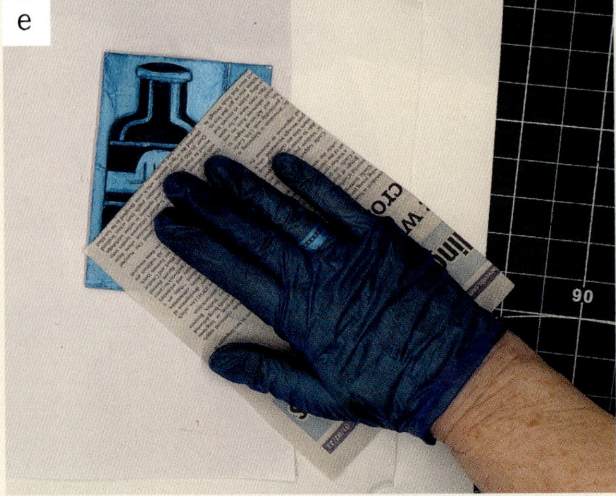

additional marks, cut a piece of carton packaging that is smooth and uncreased. The packaging can be trimmed into a specific shape to match your image once you get creating.

3. Draw the picture on a piece of tracing paper – you could trace from an image in your sketchbook, a picture from a magazine or a photo. (a)

4. Flip the tracing paper over (if you have any lettering or numbers in your image, this is important as they need to be transferred to the packaging in reverse) and place it over the waxy side of the packaging. Use a pencil to draw firmly over the lines so that the image transfers to the surface of the plate. It may show as an indentation but should be clear enough to follow.

5. Use your etching tool or sharp implement to score into the lines of the drawing, piercing the wax surface to expose the core of the packaging. Once you have scored around the outline, you can add additional marks, scratching the surface in lines (cross-hatching). Any area of the plate that you want to print in a darker tone can be scored with a craft knife and the surface carefully peeled away. (b)

6. You may wish to wear disposable gloves for inking up your plate. Squeeze some printing ink on to your inking tray or slab and make the rag/scrim into a pad which you dip into the ink and then dab over the drawn lines of your plate. Use small rectangular pieces of card or mountboard (offcuts are fine) to spread the ink thinly over the surface of the plate, working the ink into the scored lines and peeled areas with the edge of the card. (c)

7. Take another piece of rag/scrim to gently remove the surface ink, taking care not to lift it from the incised lines. Most of the ink should now have been removed from the plate, revealing your scratched and peeled image. Take care not to remove too much ink from the etched marks or your print will be very faint. (d)

8. Take a piece of newspaper or tissue paper and place it flat on to the piece of carton. With your fingers flat on the paper, use circular movements to polish the surface. As you do this, a film of ink will be left on the waxy surface of the plate; this will give a pale background colour to the print. If there are areas that you want as highlights or to print with no colour, use a cotton bud to lift the ink completely from these parts of the plate. Wipe the edges of the plate carefully with a dry rag or piece of paper. (e)

9. Place your printing plate, ink side up, on a clean piece of scrap paper and position your slightly damp paper over it. Put a piece of copy paper or greaseproof paper over the top to protect the damp paper and, with your spoon or baren, rub over the surface using circular movements. Focus on the areas where the image is and press down firmly. You want to press the dampened paper into the etched lines. You will need to apply quite a bit of pressure, but take care not to move the paper as you burnish or you will get a smudged print. (f)

10. Lift the paper carefully to see if your image has transferred to the paper – you may need to rub harder in some areas. If you have wiped too much of the ink away, or your scratches are not deep enough to hold the ink, go over the etching again with your sharp tool and then repeat the inking and wiping process as before. It is worth persevering with this process until you have worked out how much ink to leave on the plate and how much to wipe away. (g)

If you want to be a bit more adventurous, try using a piece of sandpaper to rough up a part of the surface of the packaging, use a thick needle to make a series of pierced dots or use a dressmaker's wheel to create dotted lines.

You will achieve more definition by using an etching press for both collagraph and drypoint etching. Taking a class in printmaking or joining a print studio will provide the opportunity to expand on these techniques.

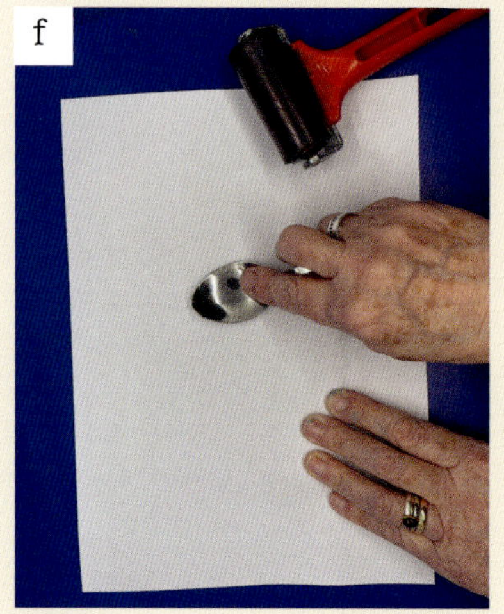

f

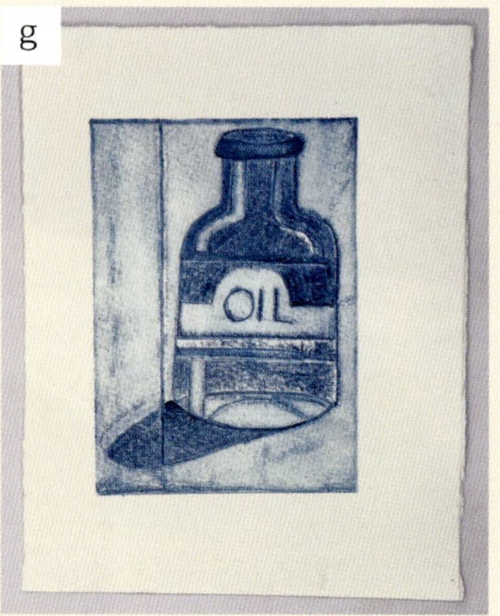

g

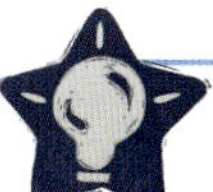

Carton packaging such as Tetra Pak® is easy to cut with scissors — cutting around the shape on your plate to print without a background can be very effective. Here you can see that the bottle has been cut to be printed without any background.

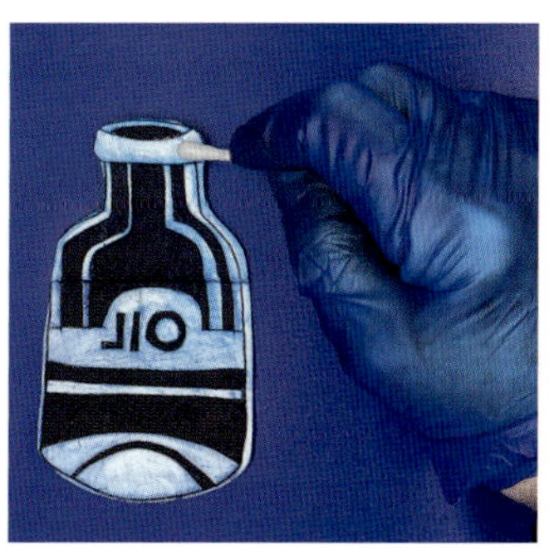

CLEANING UP

■ Clean excess ink from your plate with a damp cloth or baby wipe and leave to dry on a flat surface. Carton packaging such as Tetra Pak® is not particularly sturdy, but you should be able to print from the plate several times before it falls apart.

■ Roll excess ink from the roller on to scrap paper and wash the roller in warm soapy water, making sure you clean the round edges and the space between the handle and rolling surface. Rinse and leave to dry.

■ Clean ink from the inking tray or slab with scrap paper or a damp rag, and wash with warm soapy water. Rinse and leave to dry.

Relief printing with packaging

Collect some pieces of cardboard packaging and open them out carefully. The shapes with their flaps and folds can be interesting on their own or as a composite picture with others. Some have a shiny surface on one side and are matt on the other. Some surfaces will hold on to the printing ink more than others, so a mixture of both can be useful. Put out a variety of these and move them around, looking for images — maybe you see buildings, robots, creatures or just a collection of abstract shapes. Place a few together and have a play. Once you have completed this print activity, you will see packaging differently!

YOU WILL NEED

- mountboard or packaging card (cereal box or similar)
- variety of packaging (opened out), clothing labels (made from card)
- printing paper (copy paper, sketchbook paper, cartridge paper or any smooth paper)
- scrap paper
- cutting mat
- scissors or craft knife
- inking tray or slab
- printing ink
- roller (brayer)
- clean roller
- hole punch (optional)
- PVA glue
- glue brush or applicator
- damp rags
- washing-up bowl
- warm soapy water

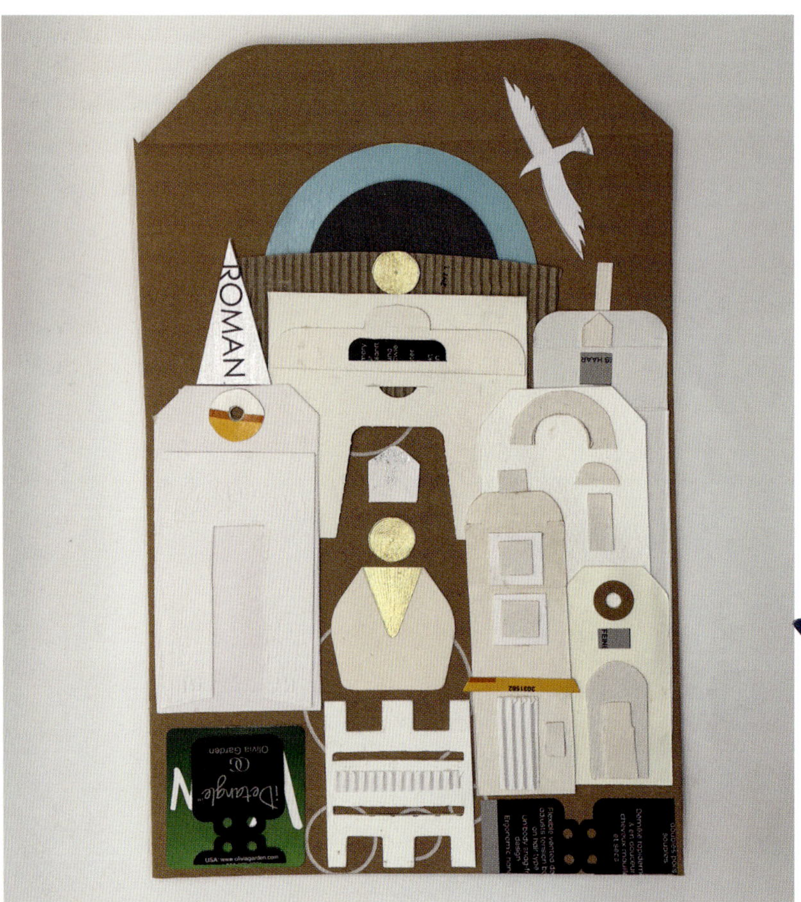

Left: **A printing plate made from packaging and labels collaged on to a cardboard base.**

> Use different colours of ink on areas of the plate or, once the plate is dry, add colour to the print with watercolour or draw definition with a fineliner pen.

1. Take a piece of sturdy card as your base plate and begin to assemble your packaging picture on it. You can overlap pieces, add additional shapes, cut areas away, punch holes or cut them with a craft knife. (a)

2. Once you have decided on your design, stick the pieces firmly to the base card with PVA glue. You will probably change your design several times before finally fixing it all together. Leave overnight or until the glue is dry.

3. Once your printing plate has completely dried, you can print from it. Squeeze some blobs of ink on to your inking tray or slab. Then, roll out some printing ink over the surface of your plate. It will cover the raised areas and may also mark out the periphery and edges of the shapes on the printing plate. Don't use too much paint as it will result in a smudged print. (b)

4. Place a piece of paper over the plate and use your fingers to press it down on to the printing plate, paying attention to the edges as well as the centre. Use a clean roller to roll over the paper. (c)

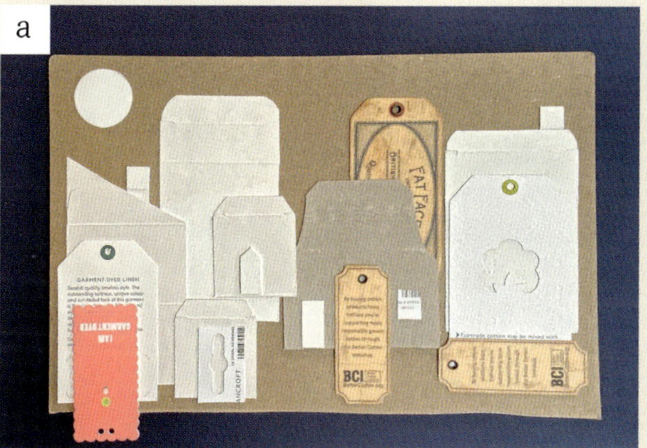

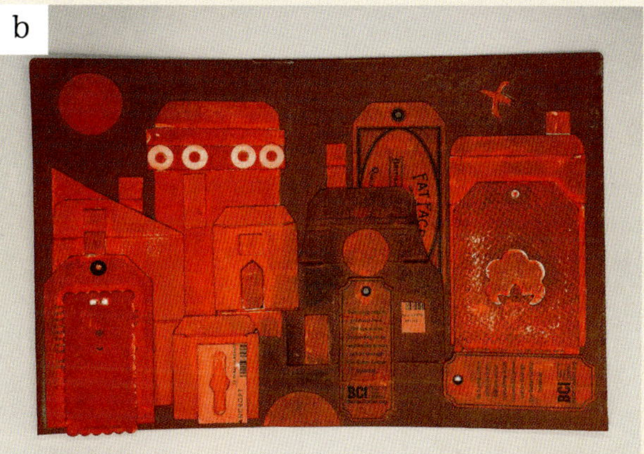

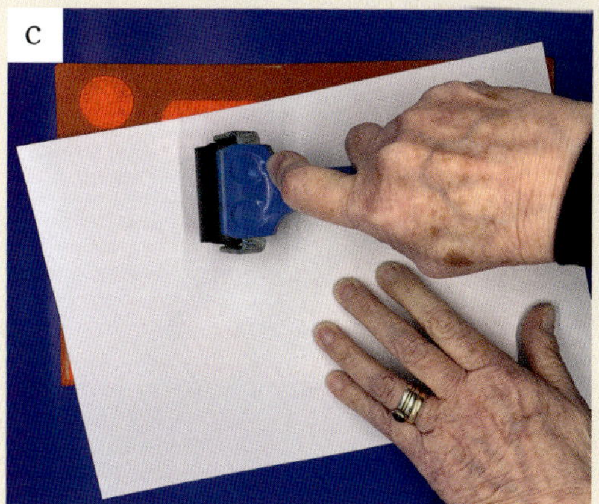

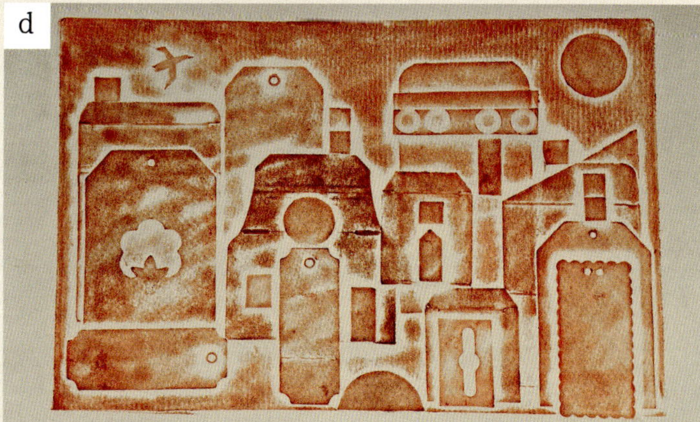

Make small plates and prints which are ideal for cards or for putting in a small frame.

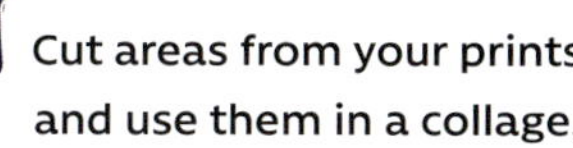

Cut areas from your prints and use them in a collage.

5. Lift the paper to reveal your print. You can use your printing plate several times, but it will eventually fall apart. (d)

CLEANING UP

■ There's no need to clean the plate – just leave the ink to dry over a few days. It will then be reusable if you wish to print from it again.

■ Roll excess ink from the roller on to scrap paper and wash the roller in warm soapy water, making sure you clean the round edges and the space between the handle and rolling surface. Rinse and leave to dry.

■ Clean ink from the inking tray or slab with scrap paper or a damp rag, and wash with warm soapy water. Rinse and leave to dry.

9

ECO PRINTING

Eco printing is a way to use leaves and flowers, with their wonderful variety of shapes and textures, to create unique prints on paper and fabric. These can then be used for a range of end products such as book covers, framed prints or cards.

Eco printing is unpredictable, experimental and very addictive! It can also be a bit smelly and stains your fingers so wear disposable gloves and an apron, and either take your experiments outdoors or turn on the extractor fan. I have used a camping gas stove outdoors to great effect, but you need to choose a sheltered area and avoid windy days (a gust of wind can spread the flame and quickly become a fire hazard).

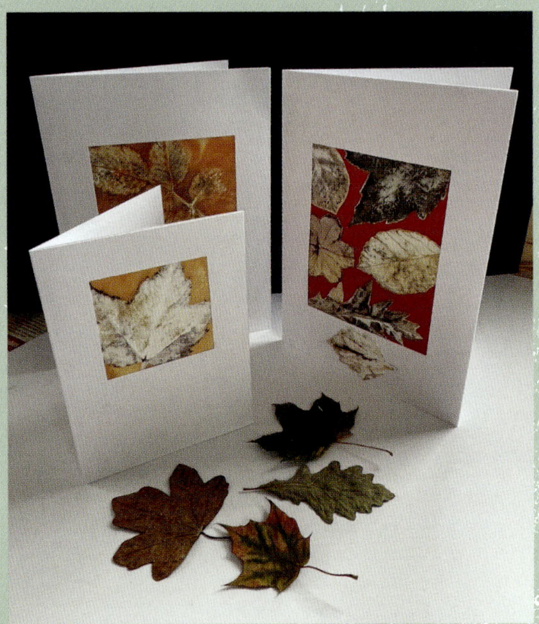

Above: Cards made using eco printing.

Right: Leaves printed on paper using onion skins and 'iron water' for colour.

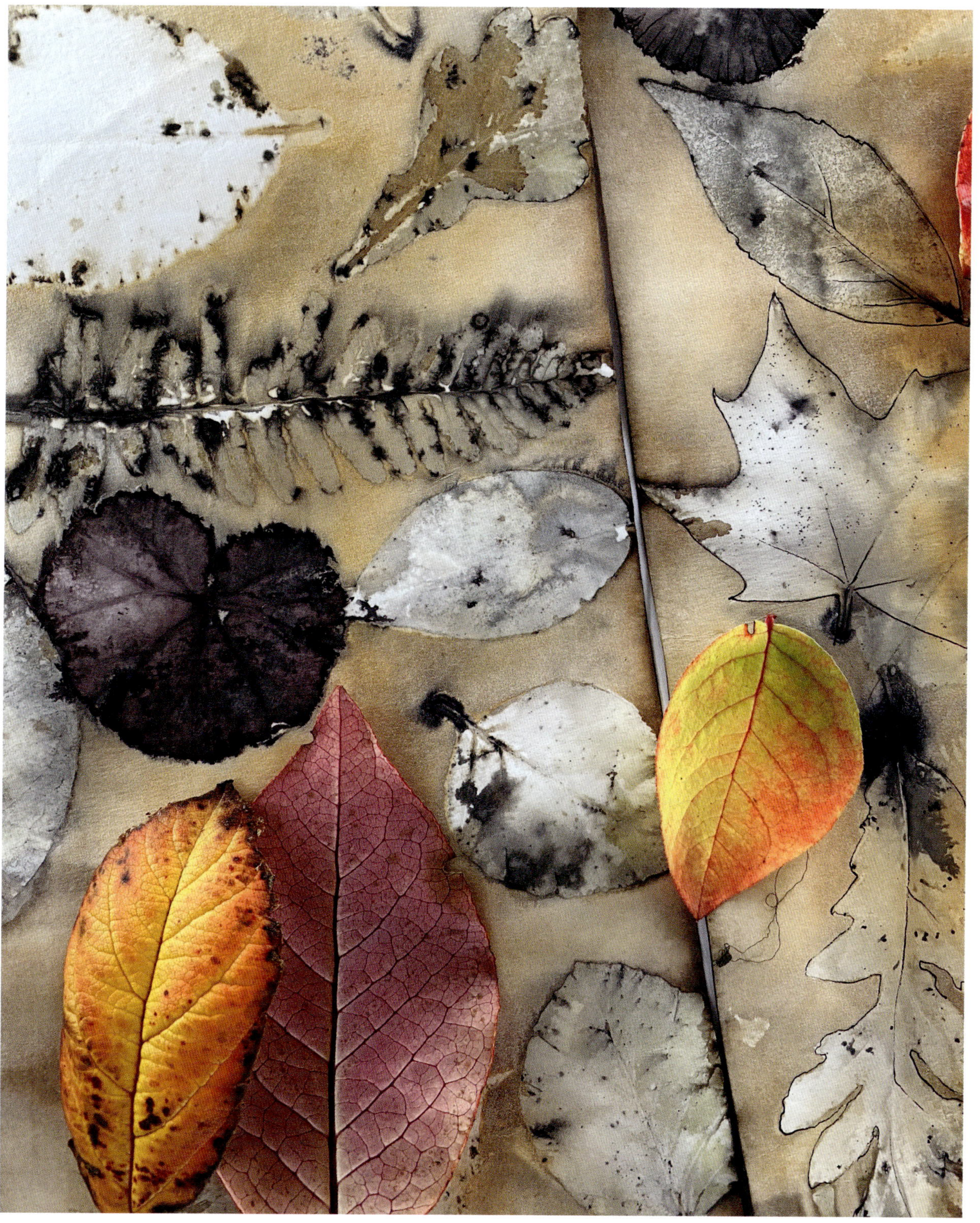

Cooking up botanical prints

Leaves that produce good prints contain a lot of tannin; these include rose, geranium, cotinus, St John's wort, aquilegia, artichoke and strawberry leaves; leaves from eucalyptus, ginkgo, oak, sycamore, maple, apple, pear and cherry trees; and bracken and ferns.

For this activity, you will need 'iron water'. Prepare this a couple of weeks in advance by collecting some rusty nails and putting them in a jar with equal quantities of water and vinegar. Leave for at least two weeks outside to develop. Before using it for eco printing, strain it through a cloth or coffee filter to remove any rusty debris. You can make a simpler version of 'iron water' by mixing a teaspoon of ferrous sulphate crystals (see list of suppliers on p.172) with a cup of water; keep in a jar.

> **Try using different leaves and flowers to place on the fabric.**

YOU WILL NEED

- wooden dowels (that fit flat in your saucepan)
- strips of torn cotton sheeting (20 × 60 cm, one strip for each length of wooden dowel)
- onion skins (brown and/or red onions)
- leaves
- four strips of cartridge or watercolour paper (approximately 20 × 60 cm – the width should match your cotton strip or be slightly narrower; you can also use a larger number of shorter strips)
- several layers of newspaper
- plastic sheet for your work surface
- mordant – 'iron water' (see above)
- string or strong rubber bands
- disposable gloves
- large saucepan (not used for cooking food)
- stove
- old wooden spoon
- tongs
- shallow container
- rack (optional)
- washing-up bowl
- warm soapy water

1. Cover your work surface for protection – I use an old plastic tablecloth and several layers of newspaper. Put on disposable gloves to prevent staining your fingers.

2. Half fill your saucepan with water and add your onion skins. The more skins you add, the darker the colour will be – red onion skins add a pink tinge, whereas brown skins give a golden hue. Put the pan on the stove and bring to a boil. Simmer for approximately 30 minutes, then remove the onion skins and discard them. (a)

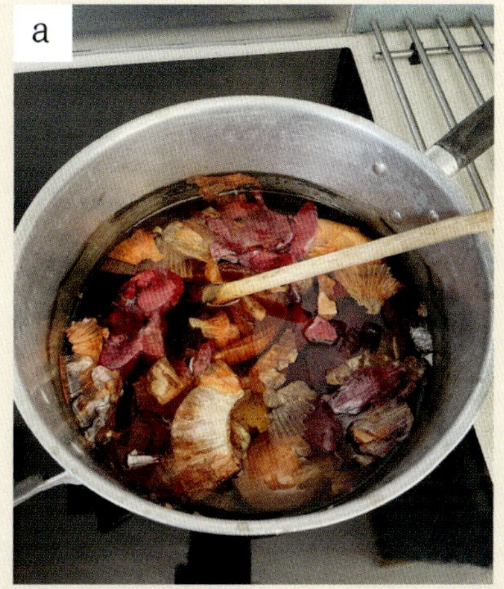

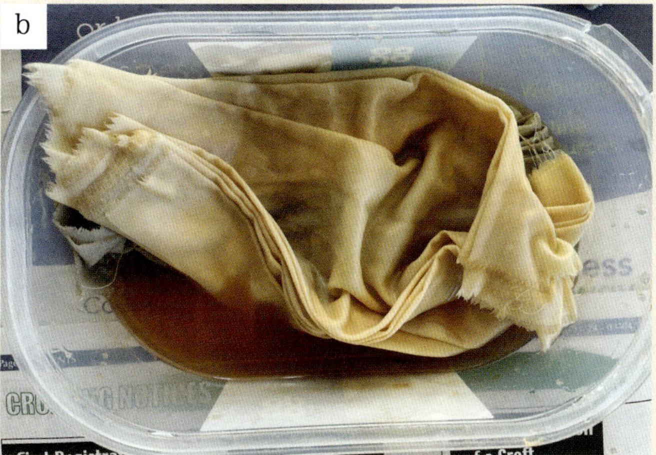

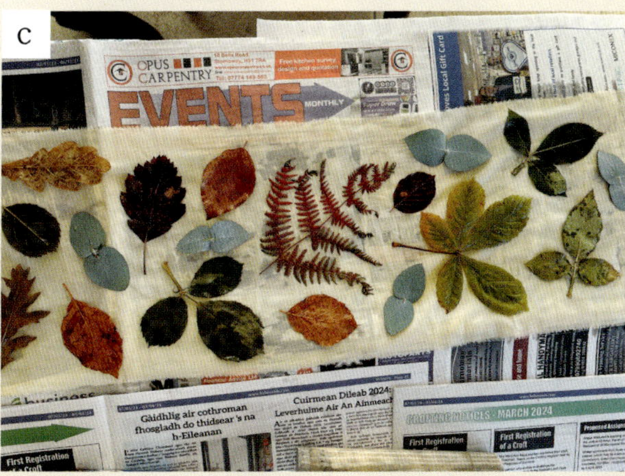

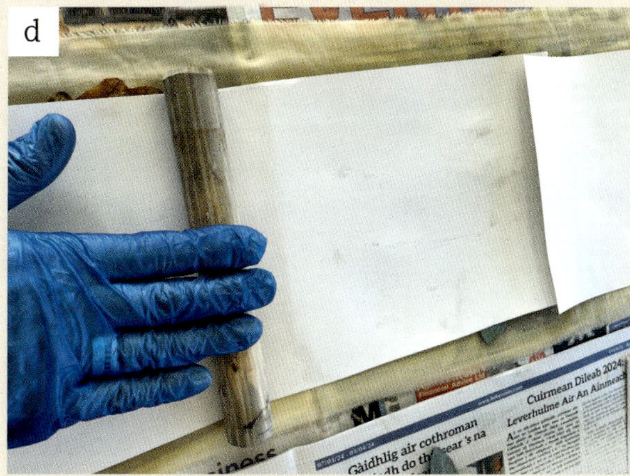

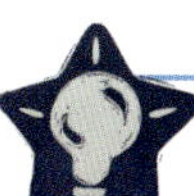

Experiment with coloured spices and natural dyes in the pan instead of the onion skins — these could be teabags, turmeric, cochineal or rose madder.

3. Strain some of your 'iron water' into a shallow container and soak a strip of fabric in this — then squeeze out any excess liquid. (b)

4. Spread your strip of soaked fabric on the work surface on plenty of newspaper. Place leaves on the fabric in a pattern. They can be close together or overlapping. (c)

5. Cover the fabric and leaves with a strip of cartridge or watercolour paper. You may need to use two strips of paper if you don't have large sheets to cut the strips from. Roll the fabric-foliage-paper sandwich flat with a dowel to get good contact between the fabric, leaves and paper. (d)

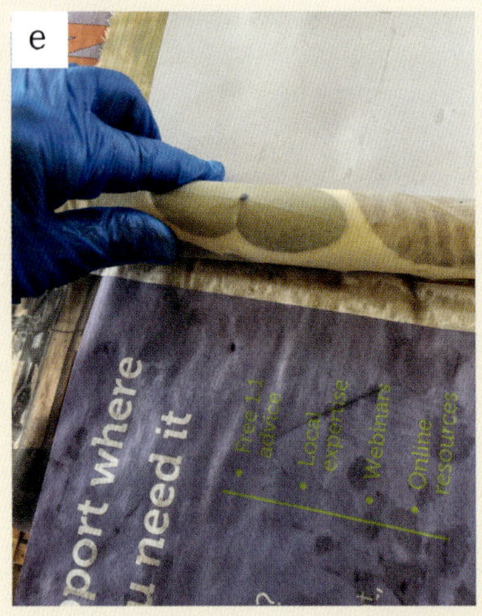

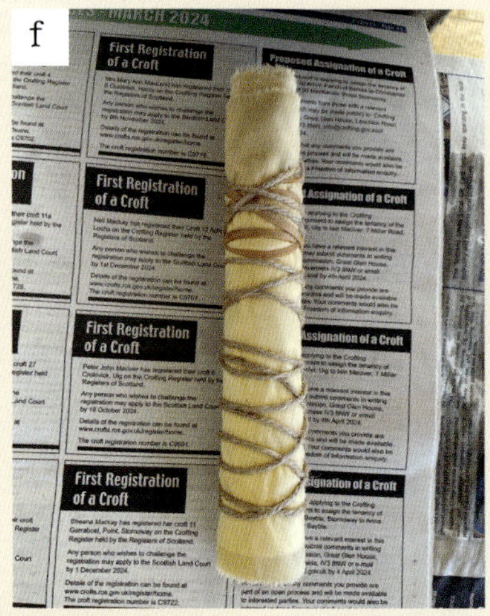

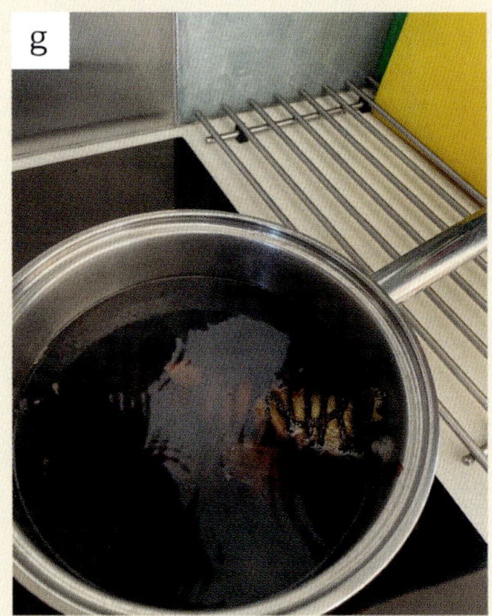

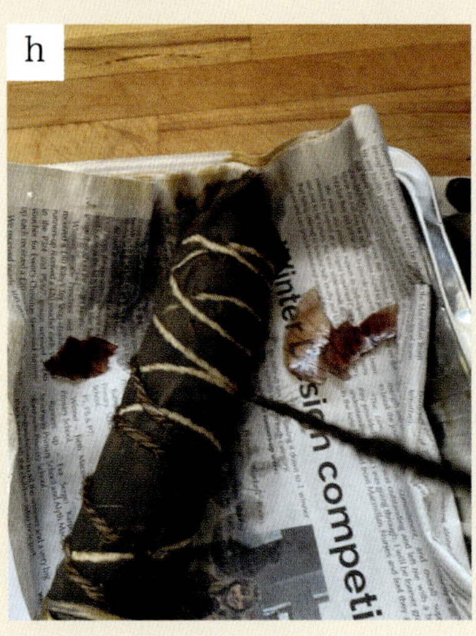

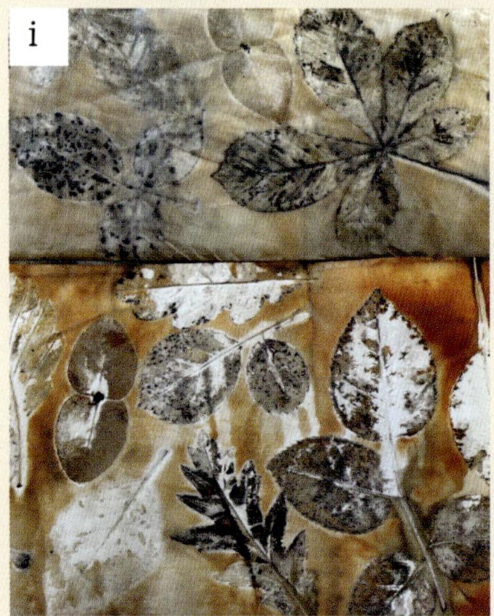

6. Place a dowel at one end of the strip of fabric and paper. Roll the strips tightly around the dowel, keeping the fabric and paper flat to the dowel with the leaves sandwiched in between. (e)

7. Secure the bundle firmly with a binding of string, wrapping it round tightly from one end of the bundle to the other. You can also use strong rubber bands to do this. (f)

8. Place the bundle in the pan and simmer for approximately 20 minutes. Make sure that it is completely submerged in the liquid. (g)

The fabric can be stitched into or appliquéed on to a garment or cushion, or you could cut squares and make a quilted piece.

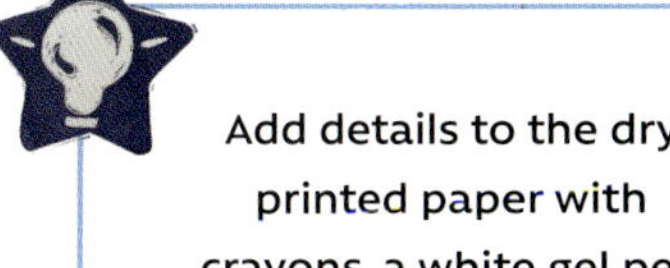

Add details to the dry printed paper with crayons, a white gel pen or fineliner pens.

9. Remove the bundle with tongs and place on a thick layer of newspaper. (I put it in an old baking tray to make sure it doesn't roll away, but this is optional.) When it is cool enough to handle, release the string (ensure you are wearing gloves) and carefully unwrap the bundle. Remove the leaves and discard. (h)

10. You should have some interesting images of leaves on both the paper and the fabric as well as the stripy marks from the string binding. (i)

11. Rinse the fabric strip in clean water and hang outside to dry. Rinse the paper strip under the tap to remove excess iron solution. Handle the wet paper carefully as it can tear easily at this stage. Blot the wet paper with kitchen paper to speed up drying and lay flat on a rack or on sheets of newspaper to dry out completely. Once dry, it can be ironed with a cool iron to remove any creases. Once you have learned the process using one bundle, you can 'cook' several bundles at the same time, depending on the size of your pan.

CLEANING UP

- Dispose of your cooking liquid in the garden or down an outside drain rather than down the sink — it is not highly toxic but could stain the sink.

- Wash out your pan and spoon, and store them to be used for eco printing only.

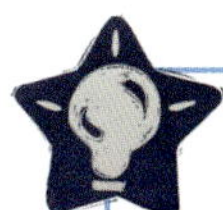

Use the printed paper to make cards, book covers or bookmarks, or to add to journals. Or choose a good leaf print and pop it into a frame. These all make lovely gifts.

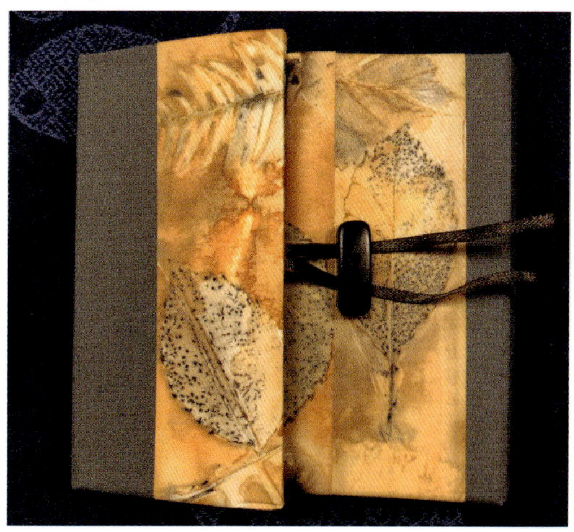

10

SUN PRINTING –
CYANOTYPES AND
ANTHOTYPES

Cyanotypes and anthotypes are forms of photographic printing invented in the mid nineteenth century. Both are ways of printing an image on to paper using sunlight or ultraviolet light. You do not need a camera for this, but you will need a sunny day or a UV lamp, and some patience. Both printing processes are fun to do, and the results are beautiful.

Cyanotype printing uses photosensitive chemicals to coat paper on which flowers and leaves and other objects are placed. The areas of paper that are exposed to light from the sun or a UV lamp turn a dark blue, whereas the areas covered by the leaves are a lighter blue or white.

Anthotype printing is another way of creating alternative photographic images by using plant dyes which contain natural photosensitive pigments. With this method, the solution used is yellow. When exposed to sunlight, the area around the leaves becomes lighter, leaving a darker image from the leaves. Once the paper is rinsed, the image becomes a deeper reddish brown colour. The image fades faster than cyanotype prints but you can photocopy the images soon after printing them and use these for cards or to work into with pens and/or crayons.

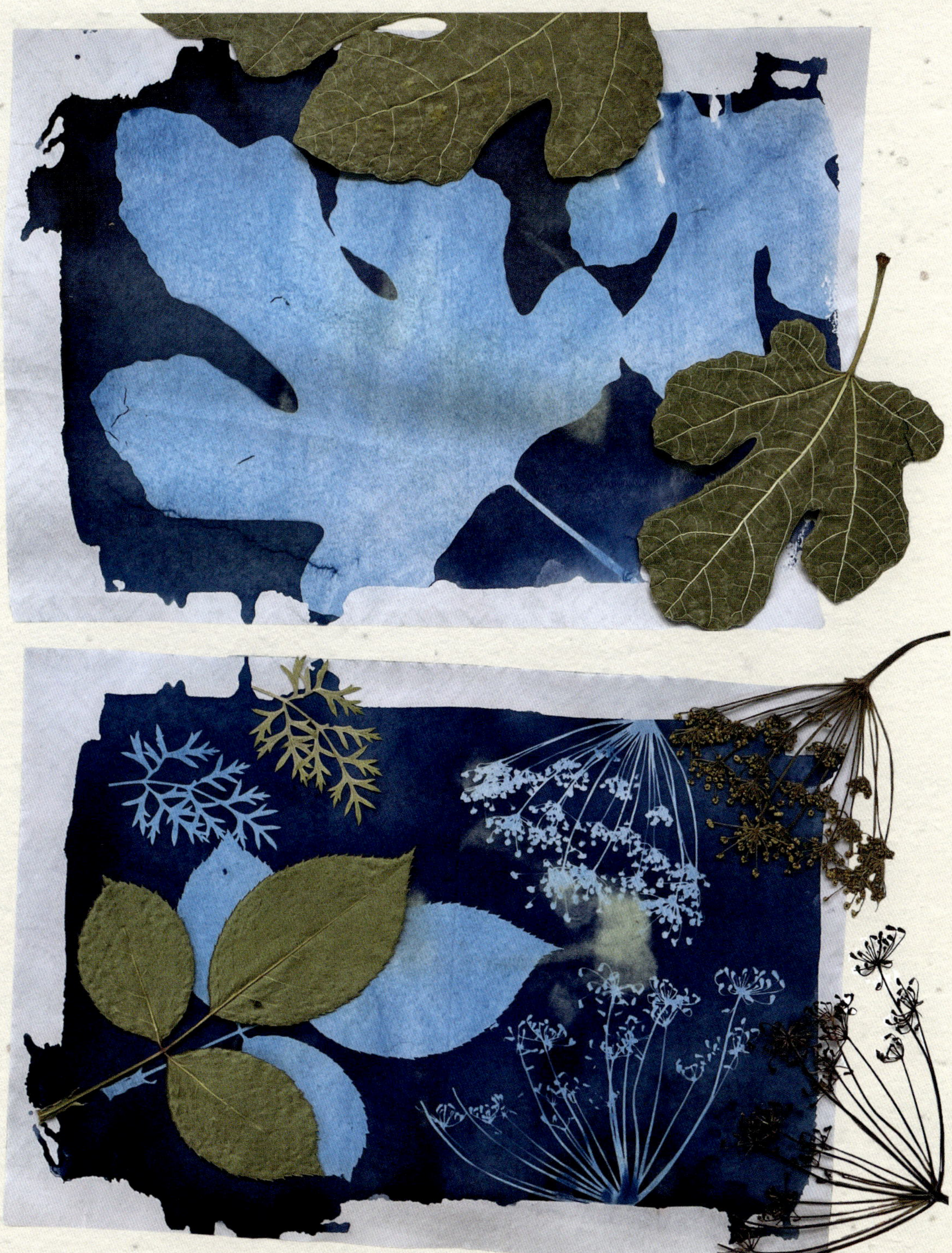

Two cyanotype prints and the leaves used. This shows the
typical blue colouring resulting from exposure to sunlight.

Cyanotype prints

You can buy cyanotype kits which contain the chemicals you need to create the photosensitive mix for coating the paper. These come ready mixed as solutions A and B. Ordinary copy paper can be used, but a more robust paper, such as watercolour paper, is preferable, as it will be submerged in water. An alternative to using cyanotype solutions that you apply to paper is to buy ready-coated cyanotype paper (see p.172).

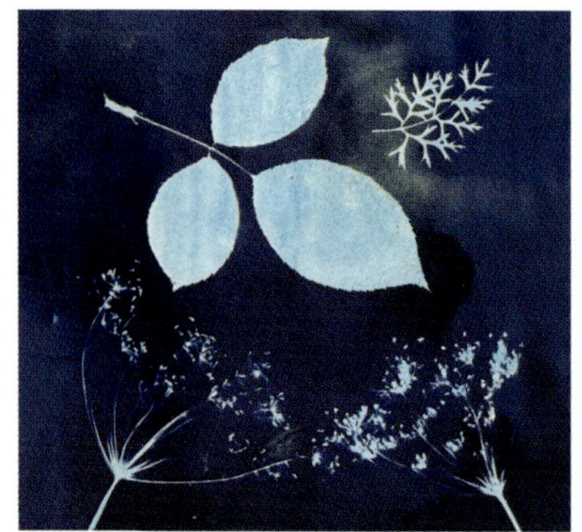

YOU WILL NEED

- leaves, grasses or feathers
- printing paper (watercolour paper or other robust paper)
- newspaper or plastic sheet
- cyanotype chemicals – Part A and Part B
- glass click frame (or sheet of glass/clear acrylic, strong card and binder clips)
- spoon
- paintbrush or sponge applicator
- glass or plastic container
- UV lamp (optional)
- cardboard box with a lid (big enough for your paper)
- disposable gloves
- apron
- masking tape (optional)
- washing-up bowl
- warm soapy water

USING CYANOTYPE CHEMICALS

■ The chemicals used are potassium ferricyanide and ferric ammonium citrate. Both these chemicals are relatively safe to work with, but wear disposable gloves and an apron and protect your work area with newspaper or a plastic sheet.

■ Avoid ingesting the chemicals or letting them get in contact with your skin.

■ It is best to work in a dimly lit area to mix the chemicals and coat the paper so that they do not start reacting to light too soon.

■ You can dispose of small amounts of the chemical solution in the sink.

■ Wash the container you work with thoroughly after using or use a plastic pot and dispose of it.

1. Mix equal amounts of cyanotype solutions A and B in a glass or plastic container with a spoon – 100 ml of each solution will provide enough mix for quite a few pieces of A4 paper. Place your paper on several sheets of newspaper and coat the paper with the solution using a paintbrush or sponge applicator. If you want a white frame around the coated area, use masking tape around the edges of your paper while painting the solution on and then remove this when your paper is dry. (a)

2. Leave the coated paper to dry in a cardboard box with a lid or in a dark room or cupboard. If it is exposed to light, it will begin reacting too soon. Any spare coated paper can be stored in an envelope, away from the light.

3. Cut your dried coated paper to the size of your click frame or strong card. Place it on the card or the backing board of the click frame. Place leaves, grasses or feathers on the surface. Place a piece of glass or a clear acrylic over the paper and leaves and use the click frame clips or binder clips to hold the 'sandwich' together. This will keep the leaves flat against the paper and prevent sunlight seeping under them. (b)

4. Place in full sunlight, glass side up. You could also use a UV lamp to expose the print. (A simple light box can be made from a cardboard box with a UV lamp suspended from a batten over the top.) When the coated paper has changed from a green/blue colour to a darker grey/brown, it has finished exposing. Depending on the time of year and the strength of the sunlight, this can take from 15 minutes to an hour. (c)

Use the chemical solution on fabric and process it in the same way – the resulting prints can then be used for textile work.

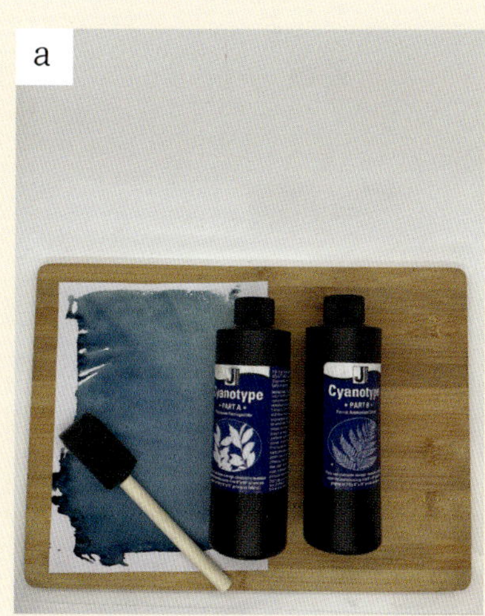

a

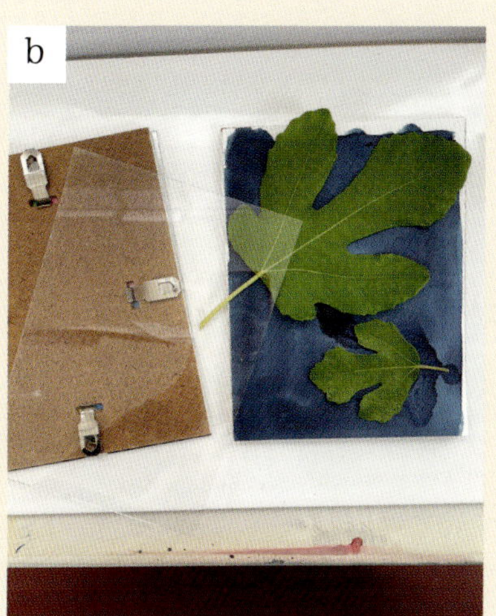

b

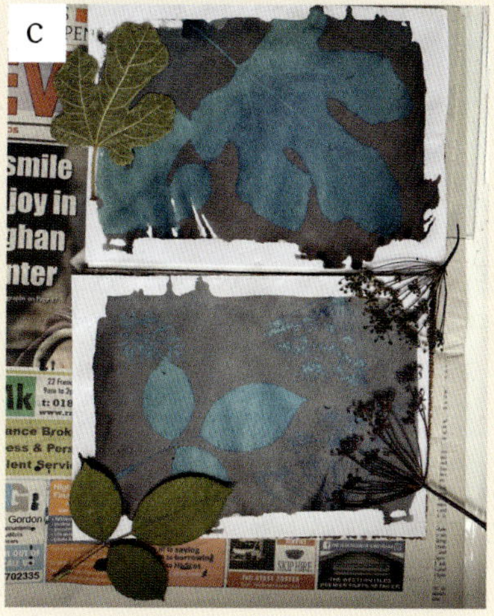

c

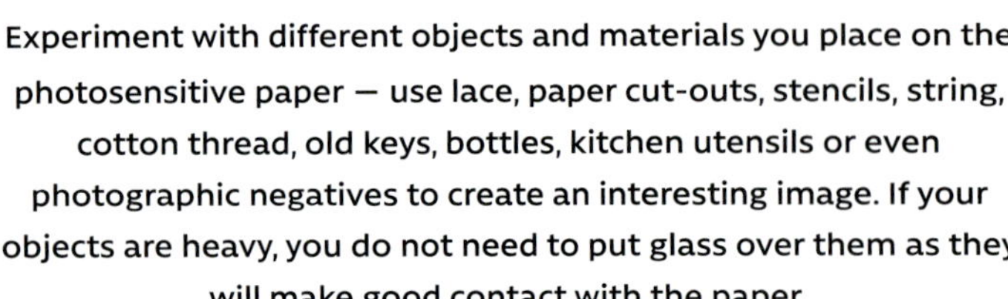
d

5. Undo the clips, take the paper out of the 'sandwich' and remove the leaves. Rinse the paper under cold running water until the image is blue and white.

6. Leave to dry. (d)

CLEANING UP

■ Cyanotype is one of the safest of chemical photographic processes but, although the solution is not poisonous, it can be an irritant, so avoid getting splashes on your skin. Dispose of the solution down the sink, diluting it with plenty of running water.

■ Wash any spoons, brushes, sponge applicators or containers in warm soapy water.

Use up your mixed solution by coating several pieces of paper, drying them and storing them in a card envelope in a dark drawer or cupboard — that way you have a reserve of papers ready for the next time you want to do cyanotype printing.

Experiment with different objects and materials you place on the photosensitive paper — use lace, paper cut-outs, stencils, string, cotton thread, old keys, bottles, kitchen utensils or even photographic negatives to create an interesting image. If your objects are heavy, you do not need to put glass over them as they will make good contact with the paper.

Anthotype prints

YOU WILL NEED

- leaves and grasses
- printing paper (watercolour paper or other robust paper)
- newspaper
- plastic sheet (optional)
- 2 tsp bicarbonate of soda
- 1 tsp ground turmeric
- 4 tsp cheap vodka or isopropyl alcohol (from a pharmacy)
- 120 ml warm water
- glass click frame (or sheet of glass/clear acrylic, strong card and binder clips)
- spoon
- acrylic wax (optional)
- large paintbrush or sponge applicator
- UV lamp (optional)
- funnel or sieve
- small glass container
- two cups or glass containers
- shallow container (optional)
- cardboard box with a lid (big enough for your paper)
- disposable gloves
- apron
- kitchen paper or coffee filter paper
- washing-up bowl
- warm soapy water

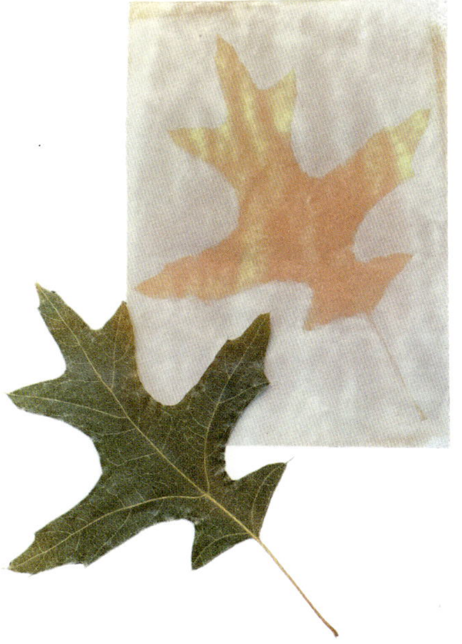

1. Prepare for this activity by putting on disposable gloves and an apron, and covering your work surface with newspaper and/or plastic sheeting. Turmeric stains everything it touches with a strong yellow colour!

2. In a small glass container, mix the turmeric and vodka/isopropyl alcohol. It will make a bright yellow/orange paste. If it is too thick, add a tiny bit more alcohol and then pour the solution into another container through a coffee filter paper or two layers of kitchen paper placed in a funnel or sieve to filter out any undissolved solids. Squeeze to release the liquid and dispose of the filter and contents so it cannot stain anything. Being organic, it can go into your compost bin. (a)

3. Place your paper on to some layers of newspaper. Use a paintbrush or sponge applicator to apply the turmeric dye to the paper in an even layer. Alternatively, you can strain the liquid into a shallow dish and dip your paper into the dye to soak it up.

4. After coating your paper, place it in a cardboard box with a lid or in a dark room or cupboard to prevent it reacting to light too soon.

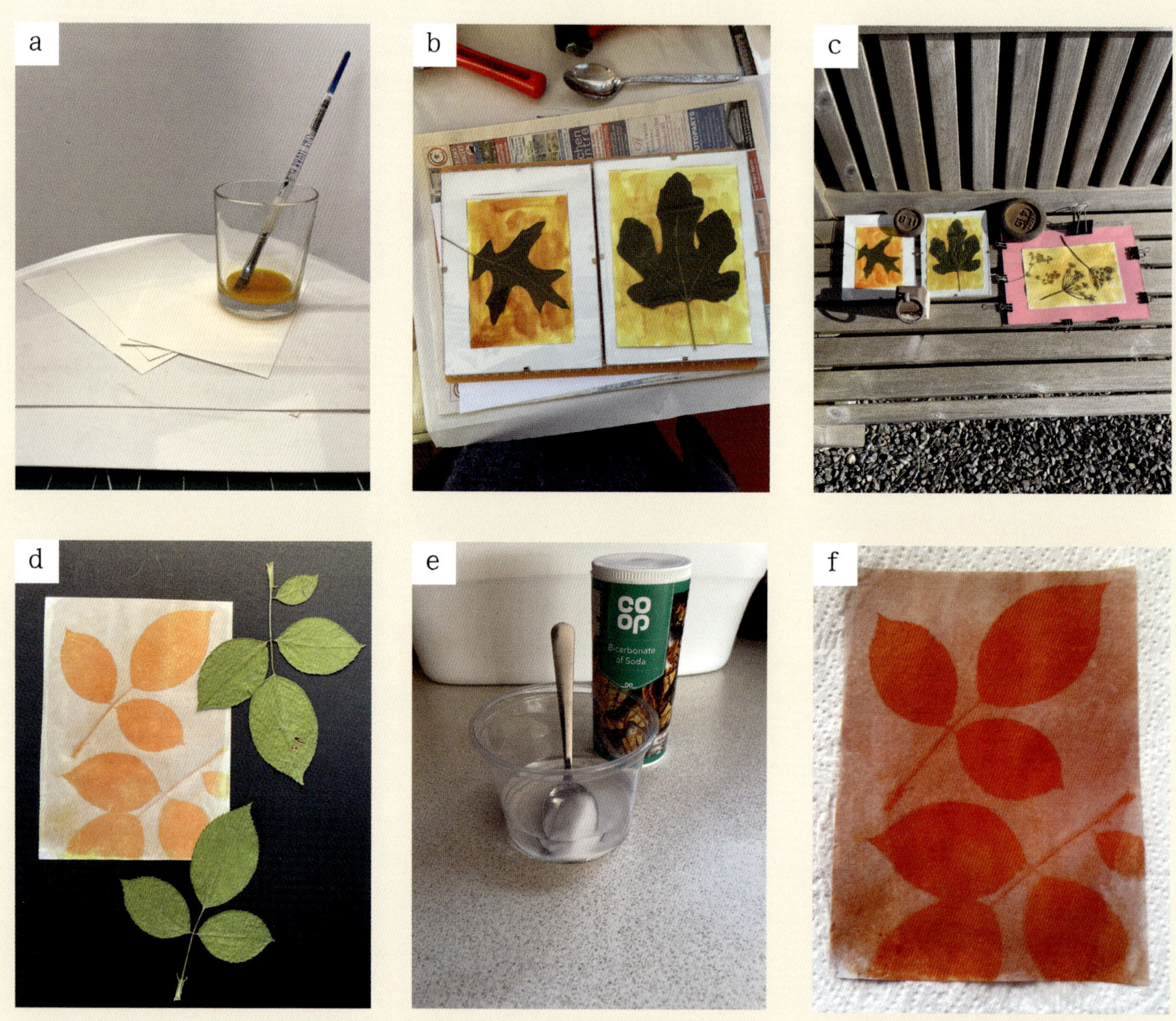

5. When the paper is completely dry, lay it flat on a piece of card and place some leaves on the paper, spacing them out and arranging them in a pattern. Place a piece of glass or clear acrylic over the leaves and fix the 'sandwich' firmly together with binder clips or, if using a click frame, with the clips provided. This is to ensure a good contact between the leaves and the coated paper without allowing the sunlight to seep under the leaves. (b)

6. Move the 'sandwich' to a flat surface in full sun. Expose the paper and leaves to direct sunlight, undisturbed, for three to four hours or longer, depending on the strength of the sun. (A sunny day in summer is best as the sunlight is much stronger than earlier in the year.) (c)

7. The UV light from the sun will fade the exposed part of the paper whilst the areas covered by leaves will remain a bright yellow colour. (d)

8. In a cup or container, mix the bicarbonate of soda with the warm water and stir with a spoon until dissolved. (e)

9. Put your print into the washing-up bowl. Slowly pour the bicarbonate mixture over the printed image and swish it around. You should see the image changing from yellow to a darker brown.

10. Once It stops changing colour, rinse the picture with water to remove the bicarbonate mixture.

11. Place the print on several layers of newspaper in a dark place to dry. You will have a reddish brown image of the leaf/leaves against a pale yellow background. Over time, your anthotype print will fade, but you can keep it in a journal or scrapbook or coat it with acrylic wax (see p.172) to help preserve it. (f)

Experiment with other dyes made from beetroot, spinach, flower petals or blackcurrants. Mash the plant or berries to form a paste, mix with a small amount of alcohol and strain through a coffee filter or muslin. Use the resulting liquid to coat your piece of paper. This can result in some really interesting prints and it's worth having a go.

CLEANING UP

- Any unused turmeric solution can be disposed of down the sink, diluted with cold running water. Take care not to let the solution splash on to clothing or work surfaces as it stains!

- Other utensils (containers, spoons, funnel, sieve, etc.) can be washed in warm soapy water.

11

MIXING IT UP – HYBRID PRINTS AND PRINT COLLAGES

Hybrid prints

Hybrid printmaking involves combining more than one printmaking technique to create a single image. Where two or more techniques are used together, they produce elements of richness and texture, creating a very special and unique print.

Linocut printing is very graphic, etching gives lines and soft tones, and gel-plate prints can have a random textural or patterned quality. Print a linoprint over a monoprint and you immediately add a different dimension. This is an approach to printmaking that is worth trying out; here are some ideas for different combinations.

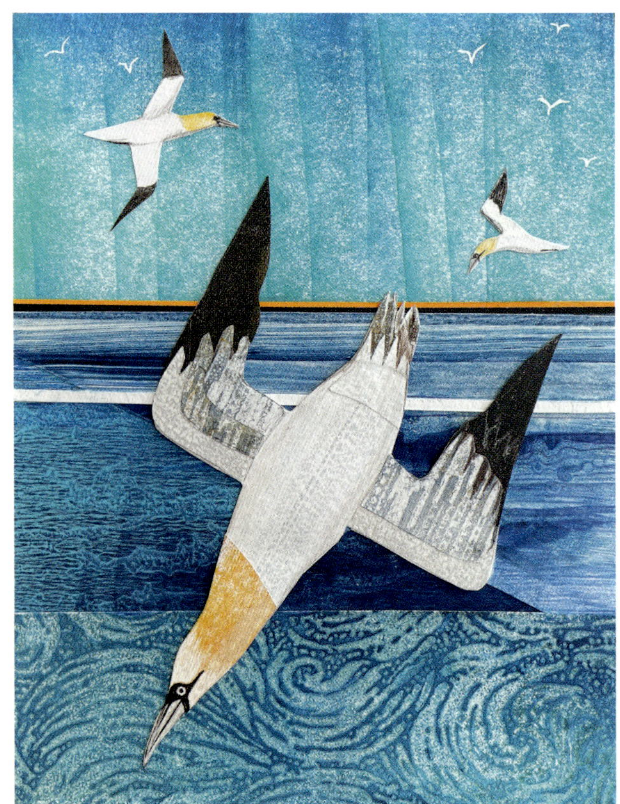

Right: A collaged image made using gel-plate prints.

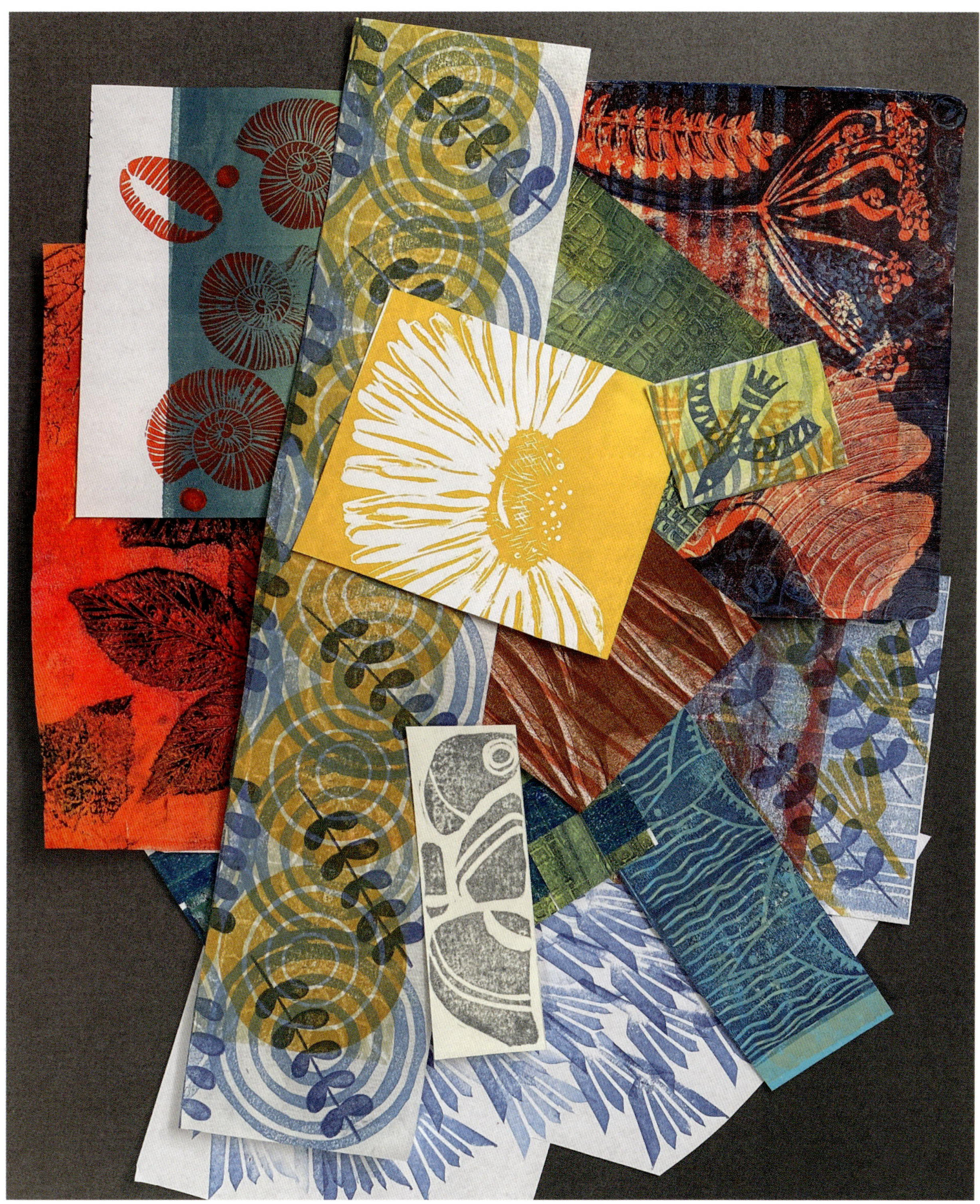

Above: **A selection of printed papers which can be used for printing over with a different print technique.**

COMBINING STAMPING WITH MONOPRINT

Use your carved Speedy Carve™ stamps or carved erasers over a textured gel plate monoprint background. This technique can be very effective as it allows the colour and texture of the monoprint to show through the cut areas of the relief print. This is ideal for making cards as each one will be slightly different and the image is quickly made.

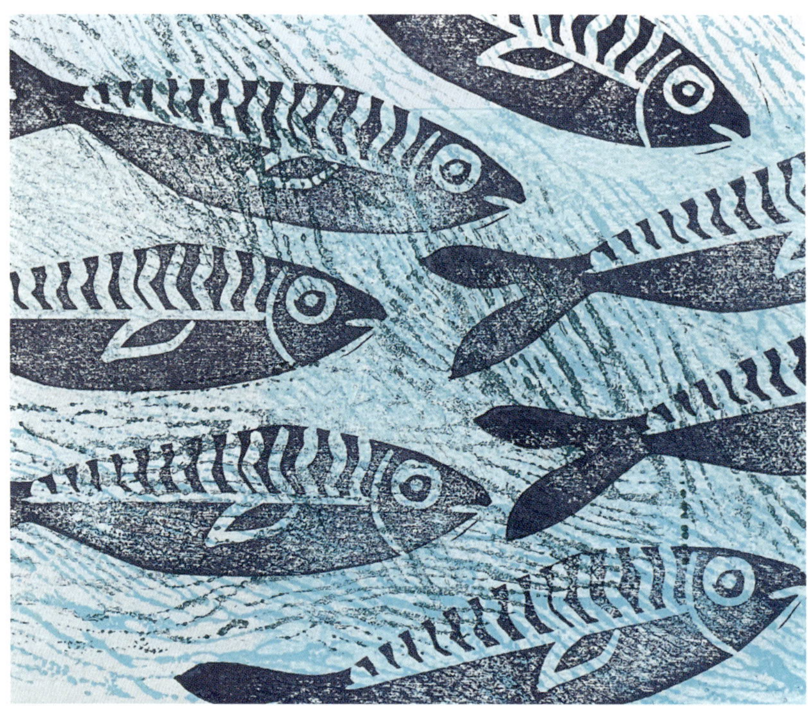

Right: Relief printed fish on a gel-printed sea.

COMBINING LINOPRINT AND MONOPRINT

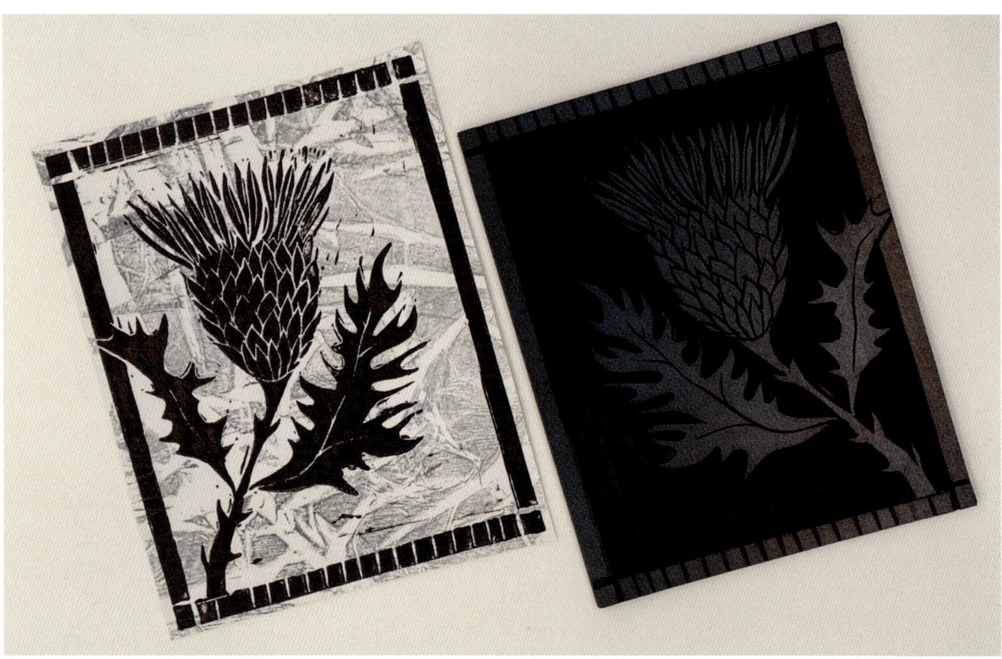

Above: A card made from a linoprint thistle printed on a monoprint background, together with the lino plate.

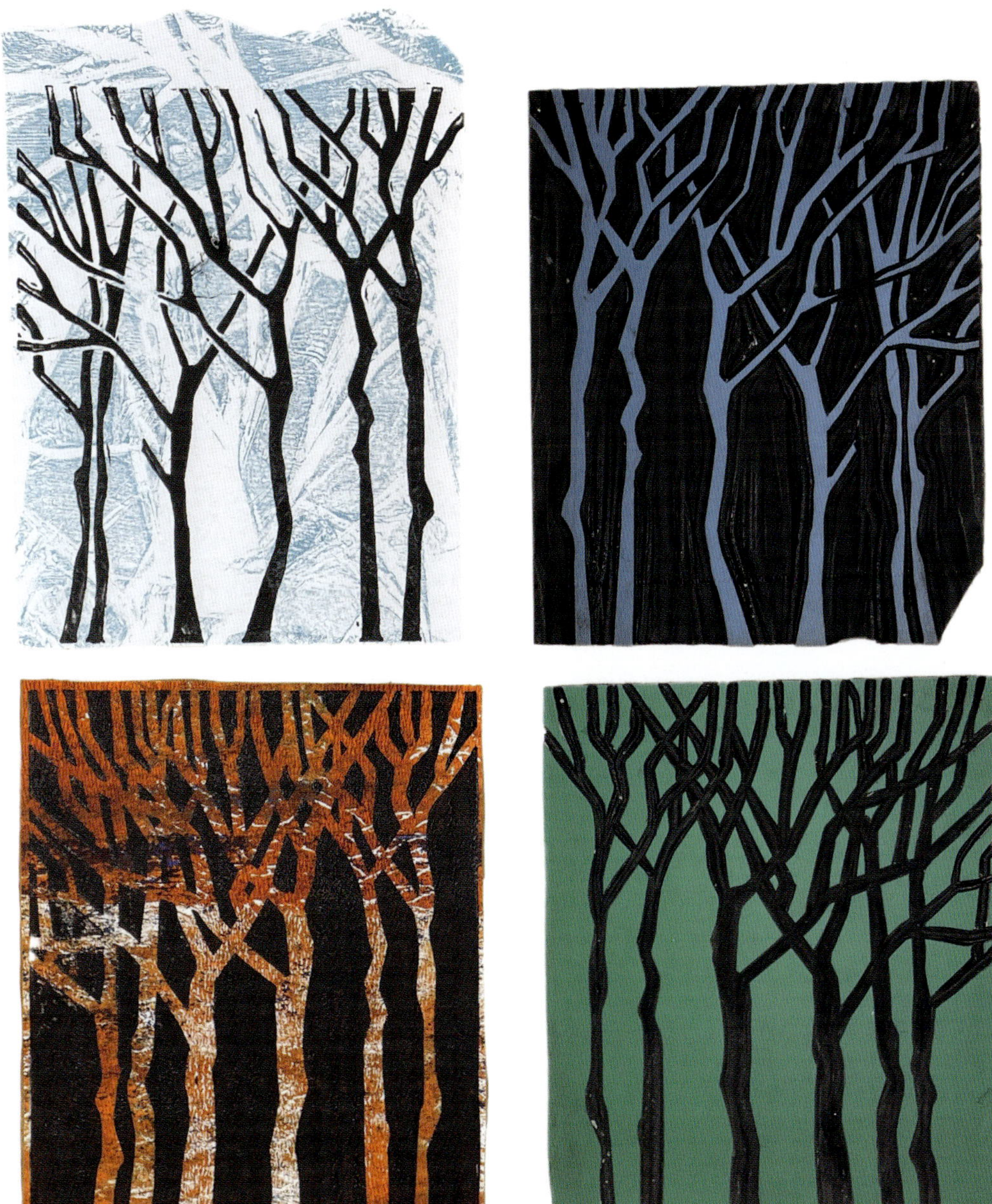

Two ways of printing with lino over monoprinted backgrounds.

Top: **'Black-line' linoprint over a gel printed background and the carved lino plate.**

Bottom: **'White-line' linoprint over a textured gel print background and the carved lino plate.**

A monoprinted background can add a contrasting layer to your linoprint, making it stand out boldly or adding colour and texture to a linoprint. You can match the background to the subject of your linoprint – for example, a feather-printed monoprint would work well with a linoprint of birds, as would a foliage background.

WARP AND WEFT

YOU WILL NEED
- paper or thin card
- two printed papers (same size)
- cutting mat
- scissors or craft knife
- double-sided tape
- glue stick

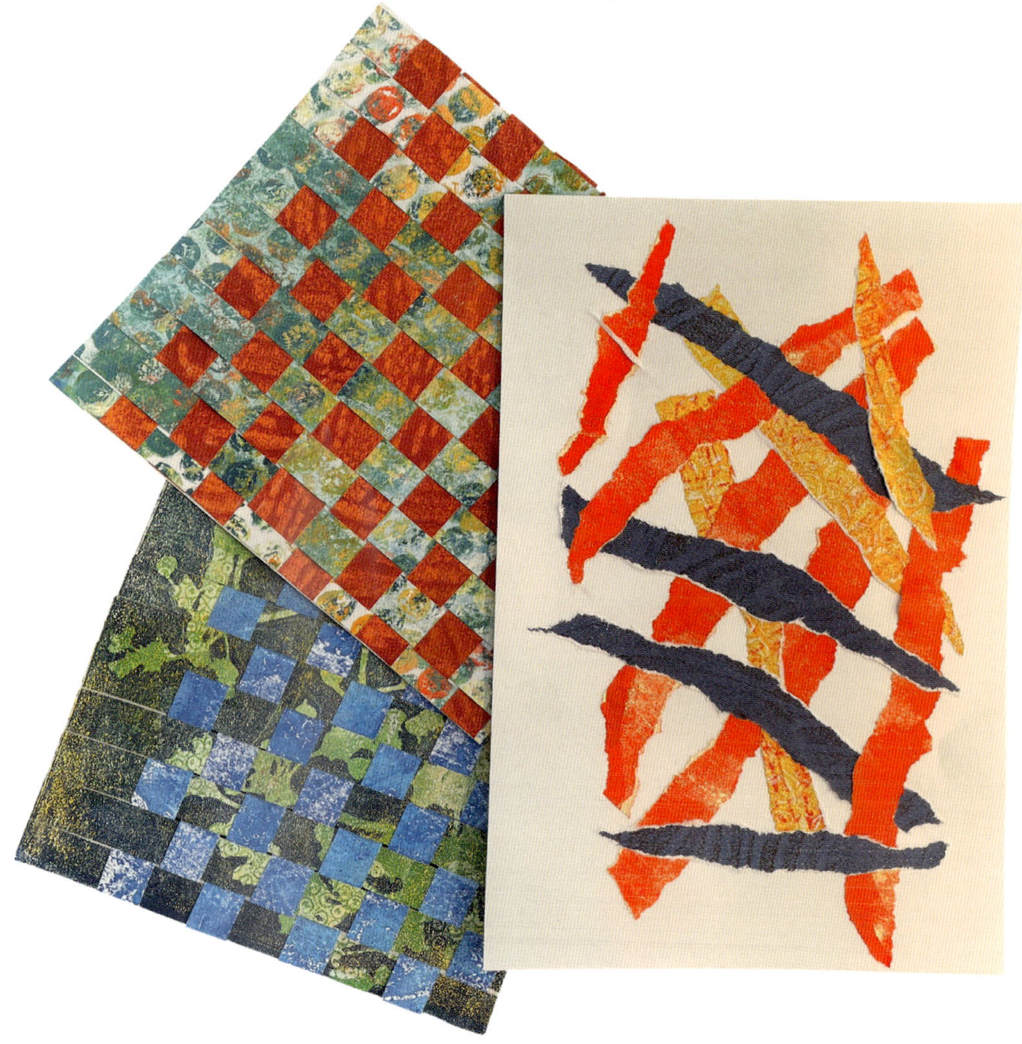

Above: Weave strips cut from two different printed papers to give you an interesting patchwork piece to use as a background or to make a card.

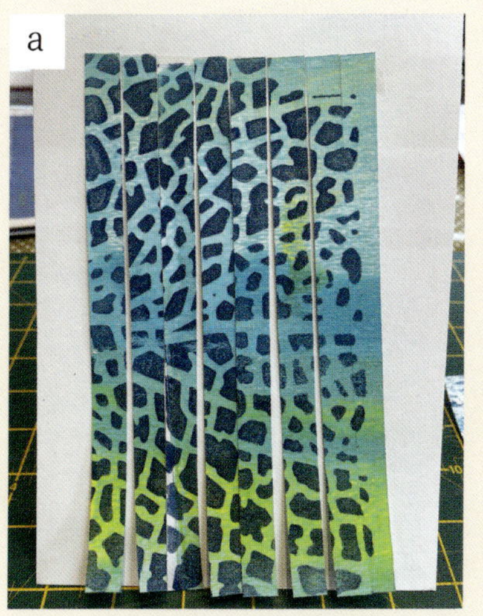

a

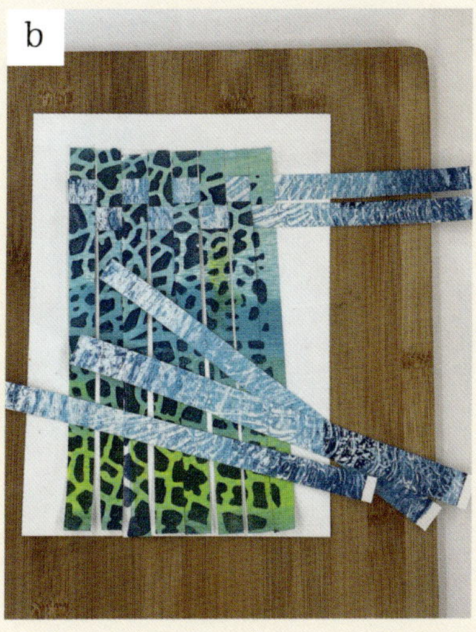

b

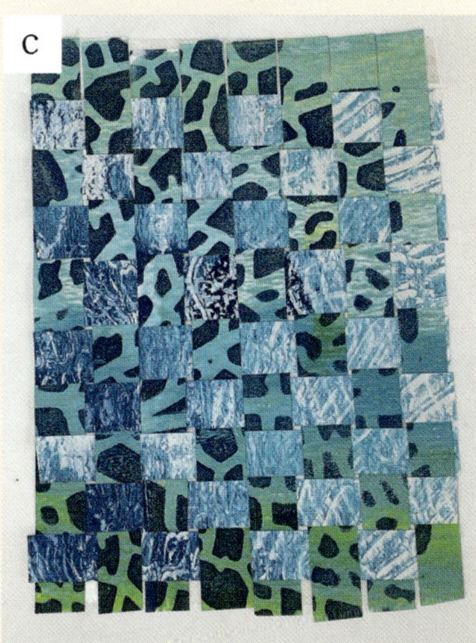

c

1. Cut each printed paper into vertical strips approximately 1 cm in width.

2. Attach a piece of double-sided tape to a piece of paper or thin card. Secure one set of strips, side by side, at the top, leaving the lower part of the strips free. (a)

3. Weave the second set of printed paper strips horizontally through the vertical strips, working them over one strip and under the next. (b)

4. Once the weaving is complete, trim any excess around the edges and use a dab of glue to secure the end of each strip to the base paper. (c)

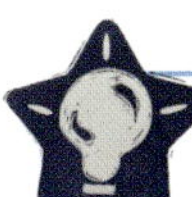

This can be used on its own as a picture or a card, or you can use it as a background and print or stamp an image over it. Stamping or linoprinting can work well as long as the printing ink is darker to contrast with the woven background.

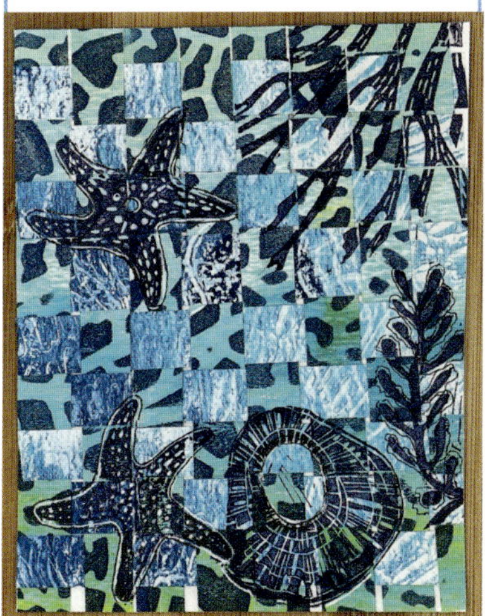

You can use this technique more loosely to create an abstract woven design.

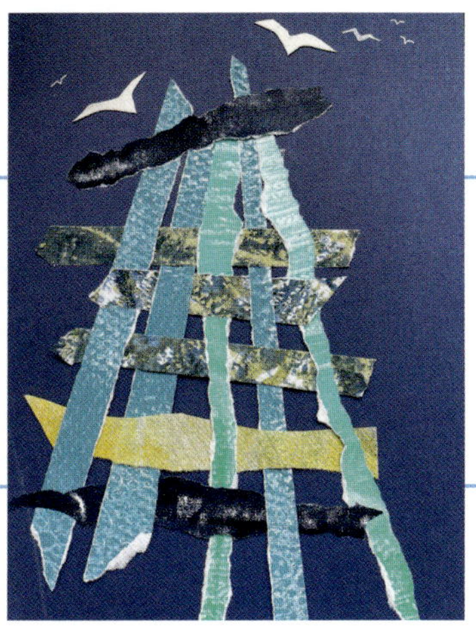

PRINTING OVER READY-MADE BACKGROUNDS

You can use all manner of ready-made backgrounds to add interest to your prints — pages from old books, maps, gift wrap, the patterned inside of envelopes, or old sheet music. If you are reluctant to tear out pages from a book or cut up a map or music score, photocopy a page and use that.

I have made Christmas cards by printing a mistletoe linoprint over a photocopied page from a natural history book or a poem about mistletoe, and I have printed cars and bicycles over sections of maps.

Similarly, you can print on to fabric that already has a design on it using your carved stamps or linoprints (see p.90). If you have created a particularly satisfying gel-plate print, make some colour photocopies to use for printing over. This works well for cards as their life is short-lived (the photocopy colours fade over time).

Below: **Bicycle linoprint over a section of a map.**

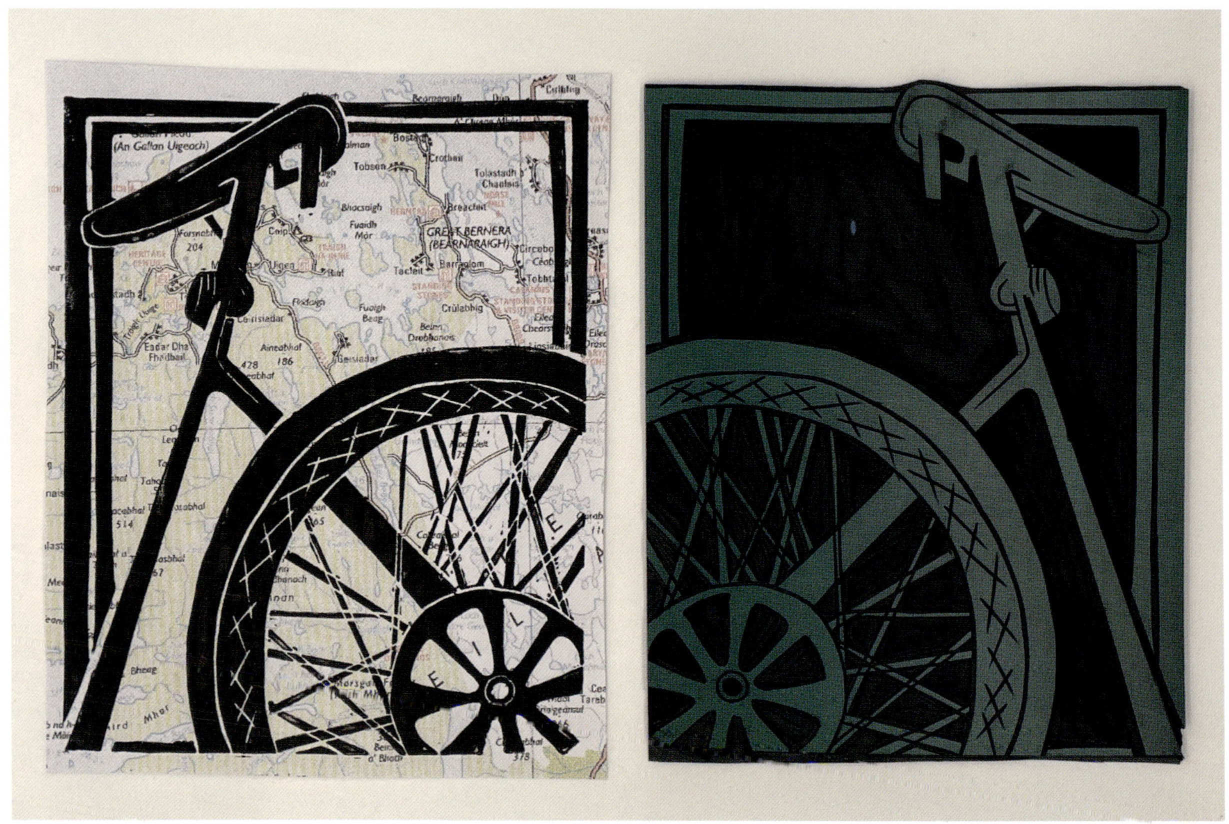

Print collage

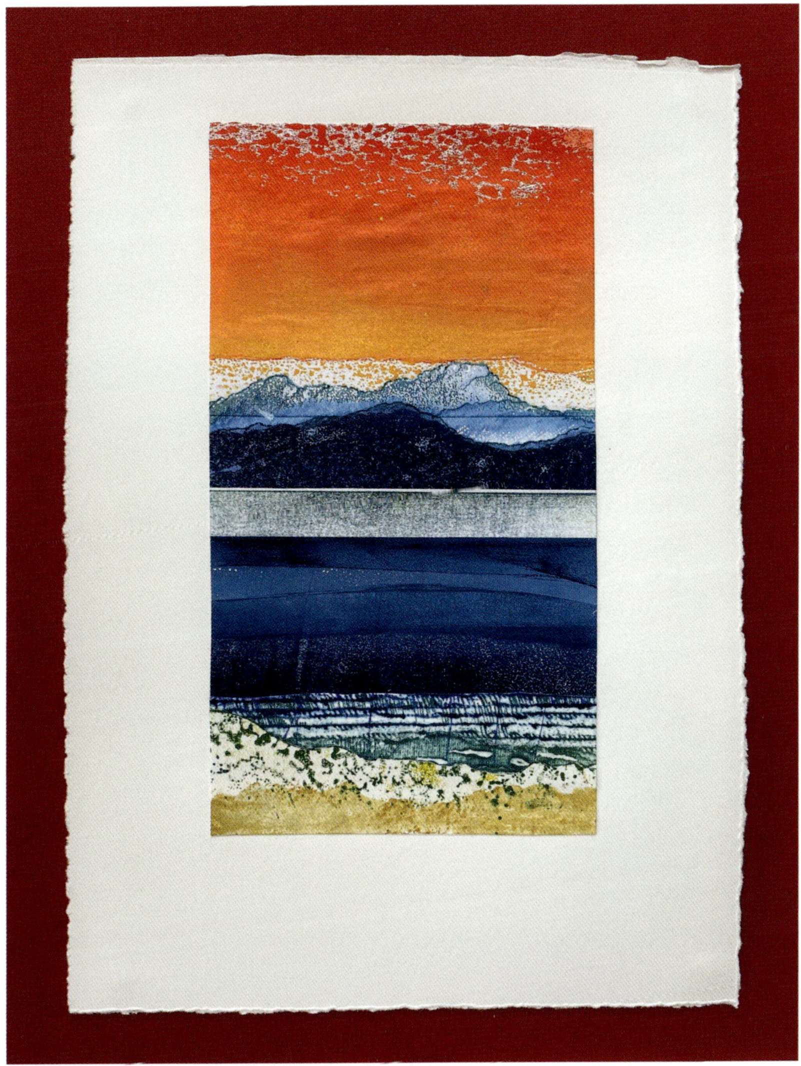

Right: **A landscape created by layering printed papers to represent sky, mountains, sea and foreground.**

I rarely throw prints away. Even failed lino or monoprints can be great for collage, and your stash of printed papers offers you a wonderful opportunity to create pictures. They can be simple abstract images with torn shapes grouped together, or you can piece together a detailed image combining texture, pattern and colour in a unique way.

You can add newspaper scraps or other printed pieces to your own printed papers and, once you have experimented, you will see the potential of this and even make some printed papers intentionally to use as elements in your collages (sky, water, hills, flowers, etc.).

I organise my printed papers into folders according to colour, which makes finding suitable pieces easier.

Once you have collaged your picture, you can use a black fineliner pen or a white gel-roll pen to outline or highlight areas of your picture.

YOU WILL NEED
- card or paper
- printed papers
- tracing paper
- white/contrasting card or mount (optional)
- frame (optional)
- scissors
- pencil
- glue (glue stick, PVA glue or Mod Podge®)
- glue brush or applicator (optional)
- Mod Podge® or acrylic wax (optional)

1. Choose a piece of paper or thin card as a base.

2. Draw the image that you want to make — keep it simple. A layered seascape or landscape is a good place to begin. You can add birds, clouds, a sun to the sky and grasses or rocks to the foreground. (a)

3. Sort some printed papers in the colours that you want to use and cut or tear them to shape. Torn pieces often have a rough white edge which can be very effective as part of the design. (b)

4. You could trace the drawn picture and cut out the individual shapes to use as templates when cutting your collage pieces.

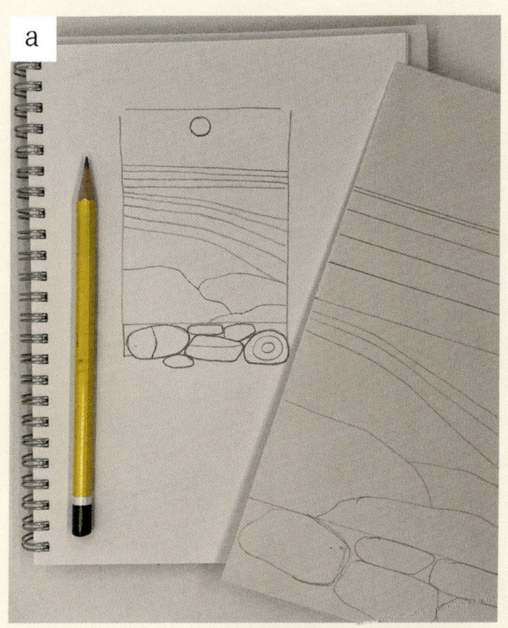

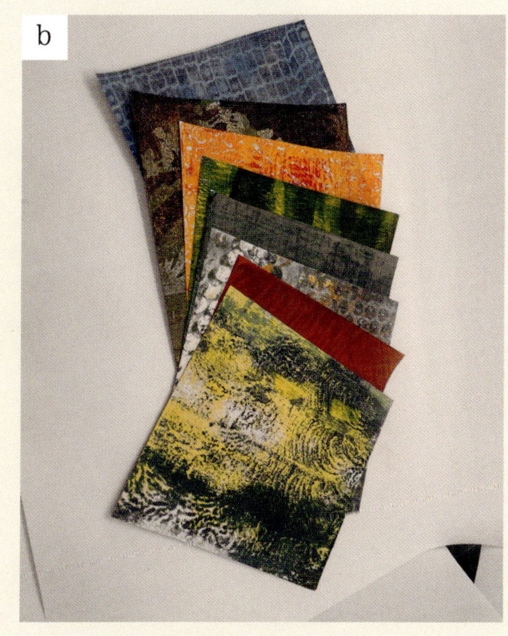

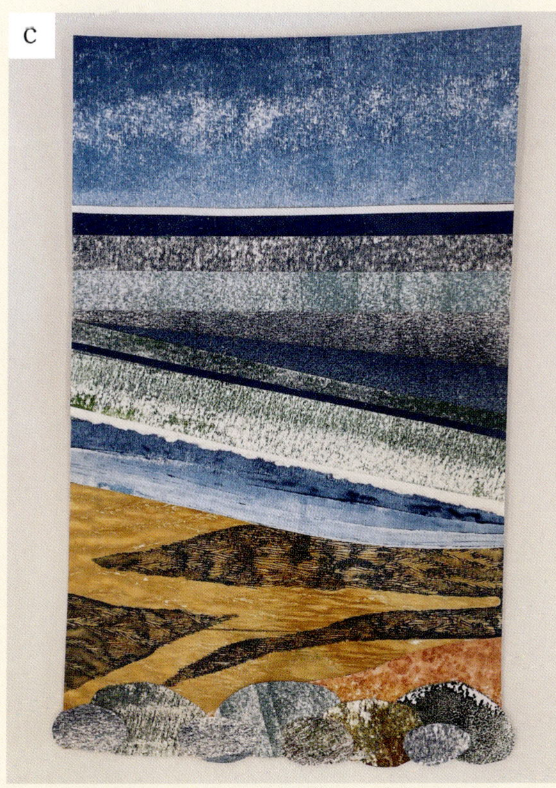

5. Assemble your pieces so you can see how the collage comes together. Make any adjustments to achieve the best effect, and then begin sticking the shapes together. I like to get the sky in place first and then, depending on whether the pieces are torn or cut, you might want to continue working down, layering the different textures and patterns as you stick them down. If you are using the white torn edge of a patterned paper as part of the design, you will need to ensure this is visible. (c)

6. Once completed, you can seal the picture with a layer of Mod Podge® or acrylic wax.

7. You may decide to trim the edges to neaten the picture or leave them to give an abstract element.

8. Stick the collage to a white or contrasting colour of paper or mountboard or give it a simple card mount (see p.166).

9. It is now ready to pop into a frame.

Monoprinted papers used to create a variety of collaged work.

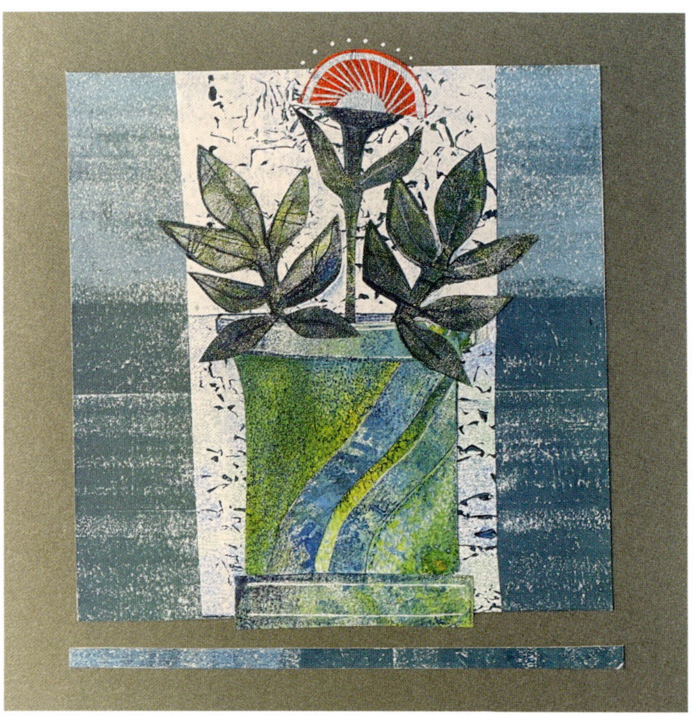

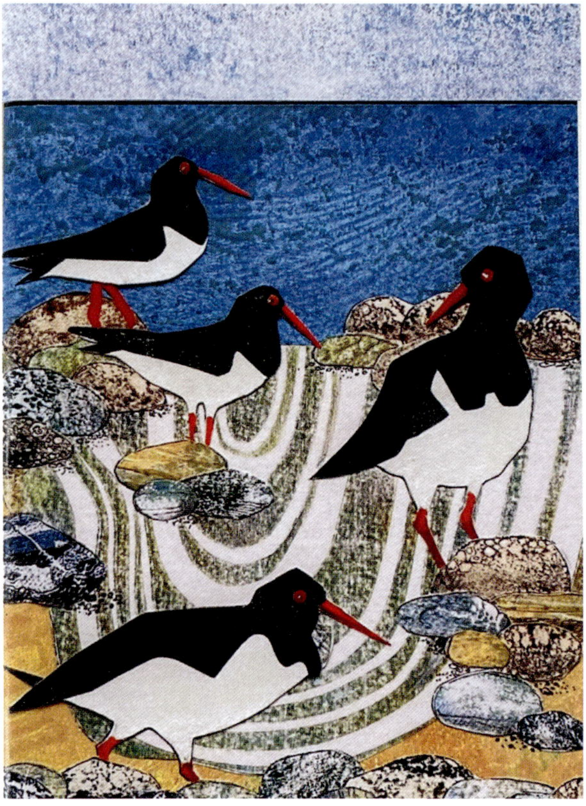

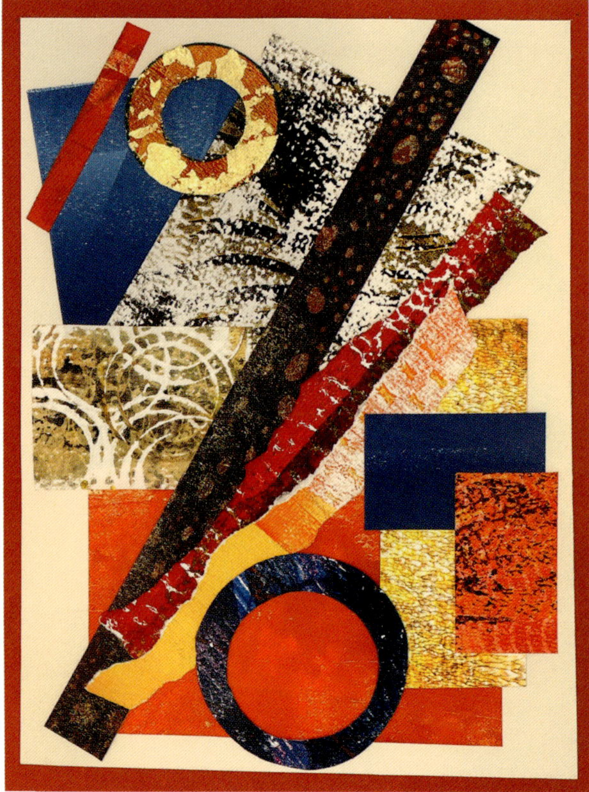

Clare Youngs — collage artist

'I have always loved the art of collage. When I was seven years old, my school entered my collage of a hedgehog into an art competition, and it won a prize. Even though I went on to study graphic design at art college, printmaking and illustration have always played an important part in my creative journey.

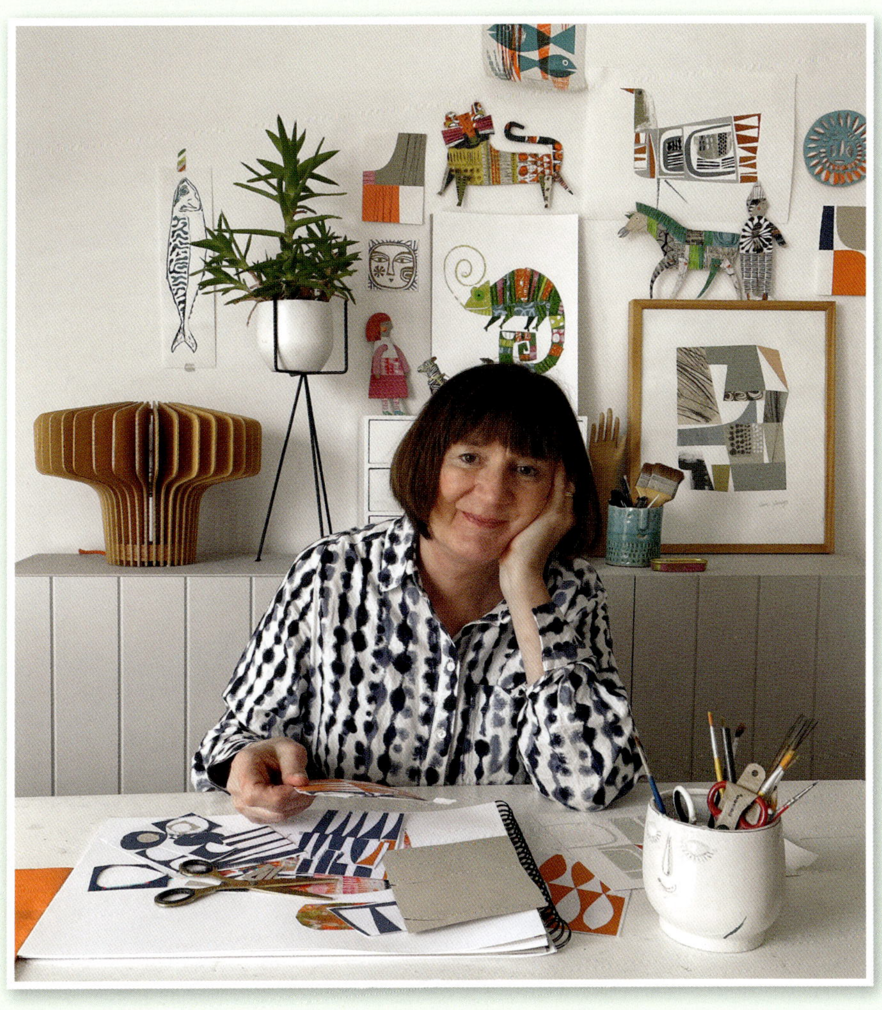

'A few years ago, I decided to join in with an Instagram challenge. You commit to doing a creative piece every day for 100 days and share the results. I decided to create a collaged, cardboard, articulated animal every day. I soon realised that to get the results I wanted, I would have to make my own papers to cut up and use on the artworks. I used mark-making and printing techniques to create a wonderful variety of textures and patterns to cut up and use in my creations. I discovered the method of gel printing in the last couple of years and I love it. It is a good way to experiment with making a range of textures and layering different colours and shapes. It is quick to build up a great selection of papers to use, and great fun.

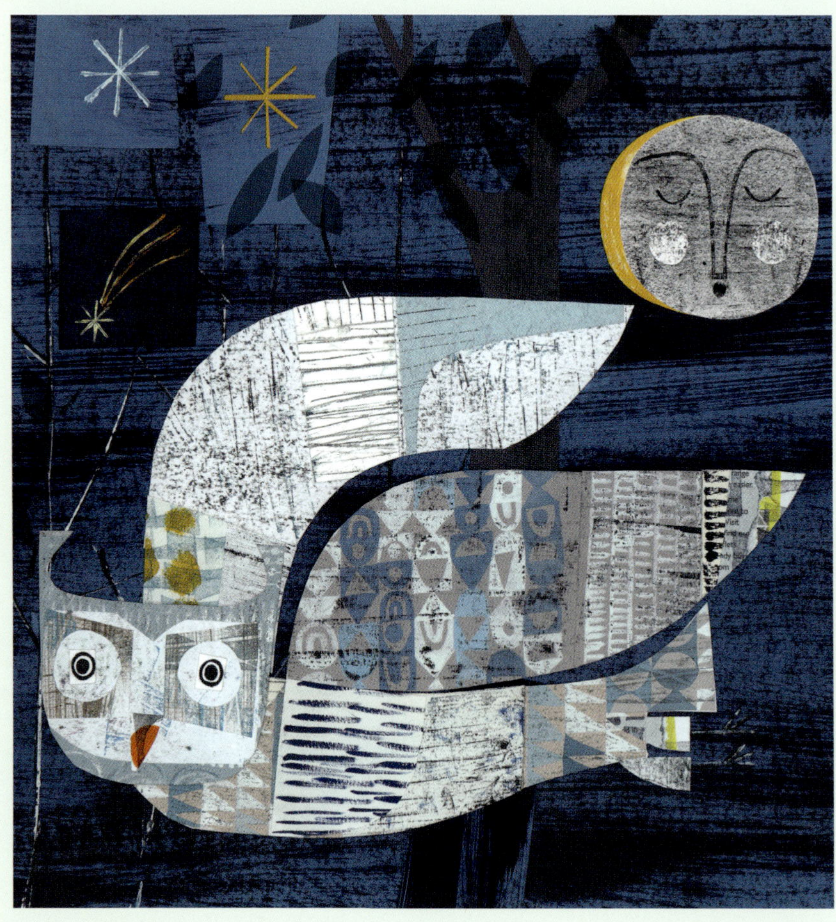

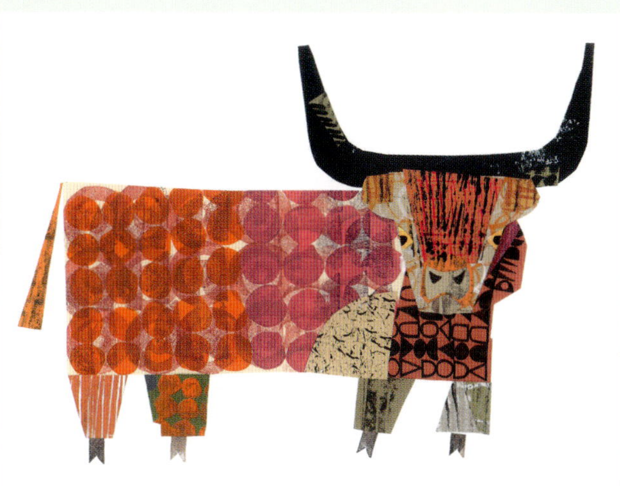

'Areas of repeat pattern appear frequently in my work. I love cutting up erasers into different shapes and then using an ink pad to print the patterns. I use all sorts of things to make a printed texture. One of my favourites couldn't be simpler. I use a cut-up piece of card pressed into an ink pad to create lines. I print lots of lines, often printing them in different directions over the top of each other, to create a lovely, scratchy texture. I also use linoprinting techniques. I like to paint some pattern work and then overprint with a piece of lino that I have cut into. I use sticks, sponges and things from the garden to print with, really anything that makes a mark. I like to build up layers so that the end result of the animal I am working on is richly textured.

'Producing all these paper samples is a part of my working process that is hugely enjoyable, and it is a way of making each collaged piece individual and unique.'

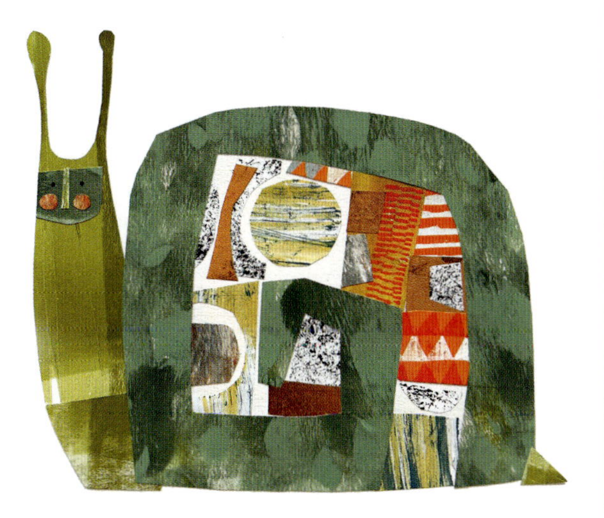

12

CREATIVE PROJECTS USING YOUR PRINTS AND PRINTED PAPERS

Cards

You can use your printed papers and print techniques in a variety of ways to make cards.

- Packs of blank cards are inexpensive and come with matching envelopes. You can make your own cards by folding a sheet of plain card but I find this makes a flimsy card which then needs an envelope, so I buy cards in packs. (a)

- Use a glue stick, PVA glue or Mod Podge® to attach a piece of printed paper to the front of your card; it is entirely up to you how you go about it.

- Your card can have an abstract image of overlaid shapes, a picture, a flower, a butterfly – let your imagination fly. (b)

- Aperture cards are great as they provide a small mount for your artwork and the small aperture version can highlight a miniature work of art. (c)

- Another method is to wrap a long strip of printed paper around the front and back of the card, which can be very effective. (d)

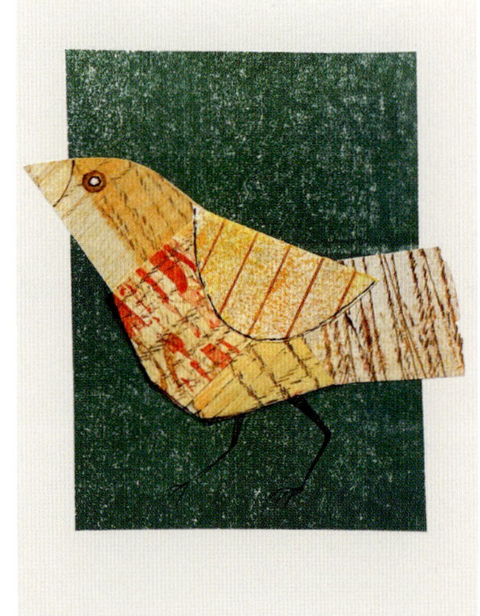

Above: **A card with a 3D folded bird (see p.159).**

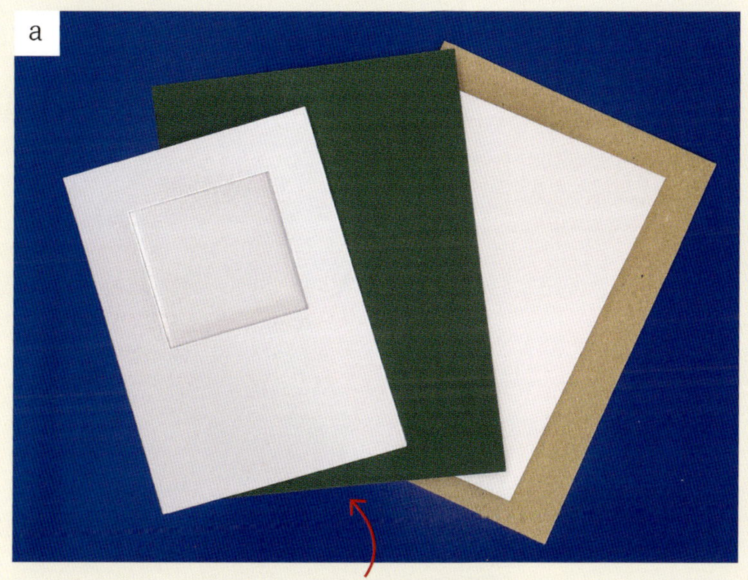

Blank cards come in a variety
of shapes, colours and sizes

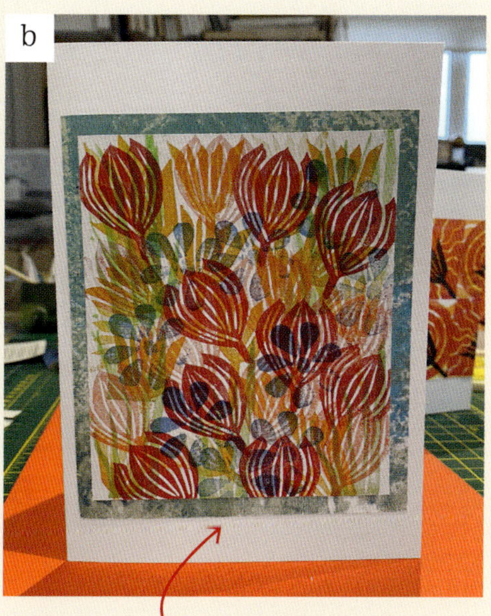

Stamped images overlaid to create
a multi-layered card image

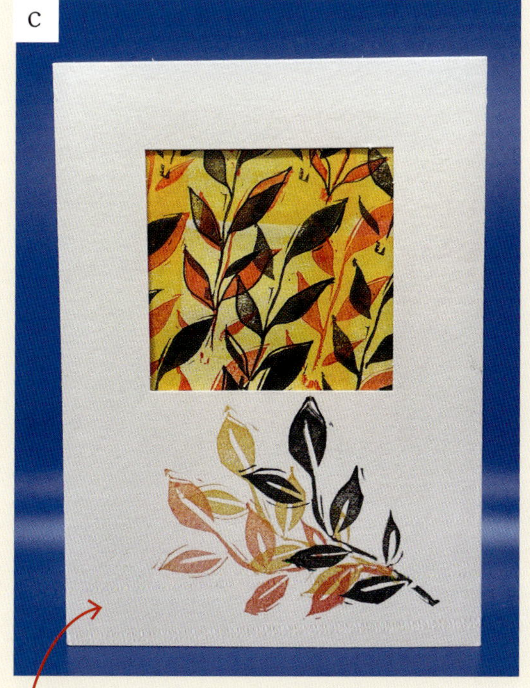

An aperture card acts as a mount for an image
– this one also has a stamped image printed
directly on the card below the aperture

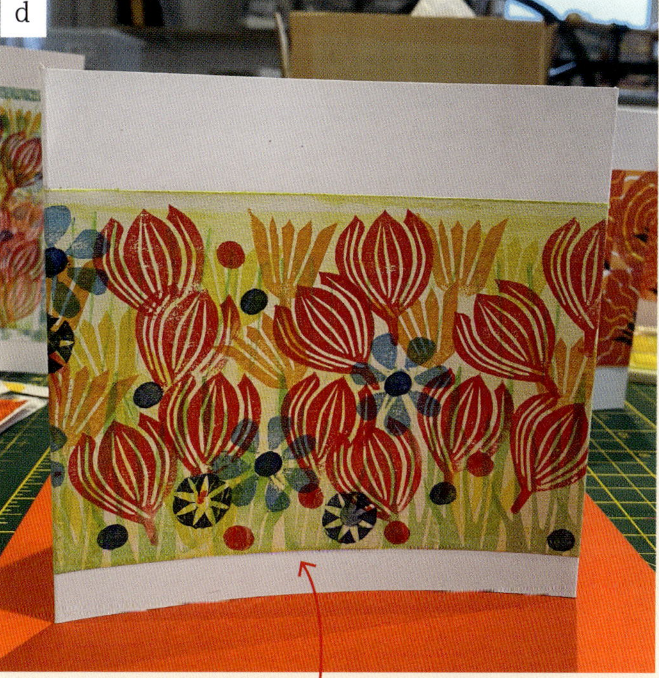

A long strip of printed paper is wrapped
around the front and back of the card

■ I like to mount a printed image on to a contrasting background before gluing to a card as it shows the image off to good effect. (e)

■ Use your carved stamp to print directly on to your card. (f)

■ I design and carve linoprints specifically for printing on cards and often have 20 or more cards drying on my rack. It makes Christmas and gift cards very personal and, once you have your lino plate, you can print in multiples. (g)

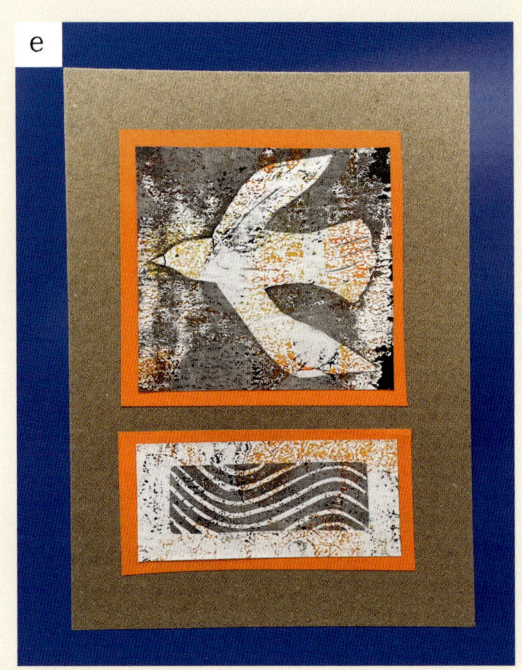

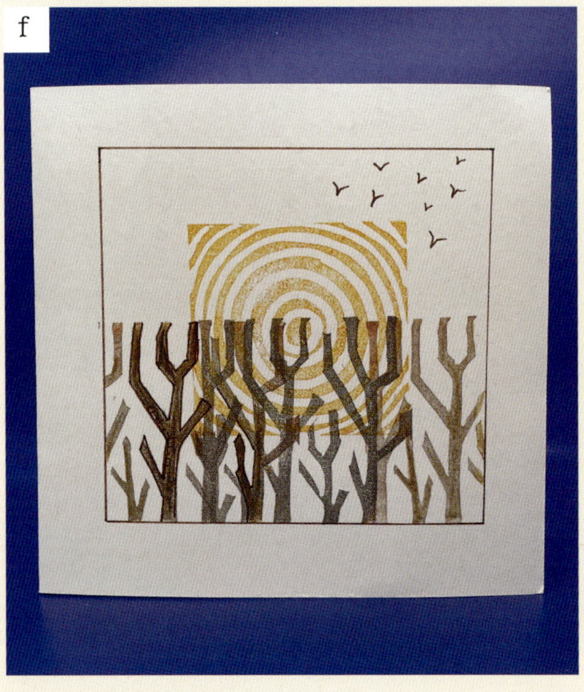

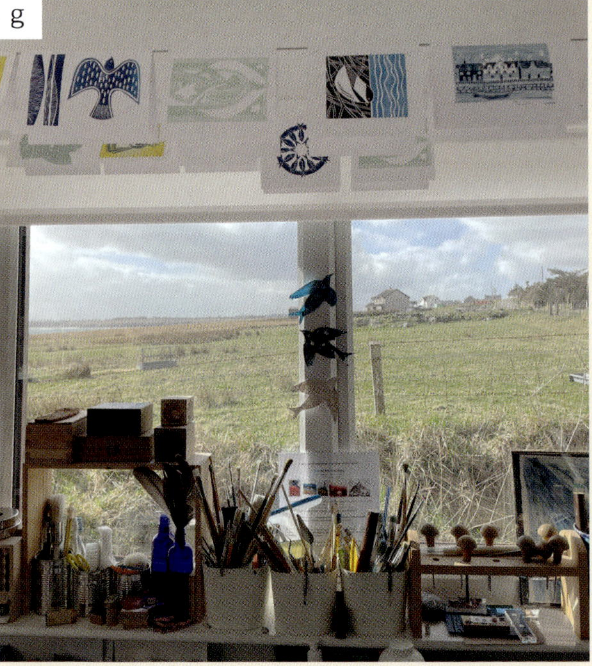

Gift tags

■ Gift tags can also be purchased in bulk and come in a variety of sizes and shapes. You can, however, make your own from rectangles of card with a hole punched to take a piece of string or ribbon. Use your stamping blocks to print directly on to the gift tags. If you buy tags, the surface needs to be a matt finish for printing on; printing ink does not print well on a shiny surface and tends to smudge.

■ You can cut shapes from printed papers and collage them on to gift tags. Craft punches for shapes such as hearts, birds or stars can be used to great effect.

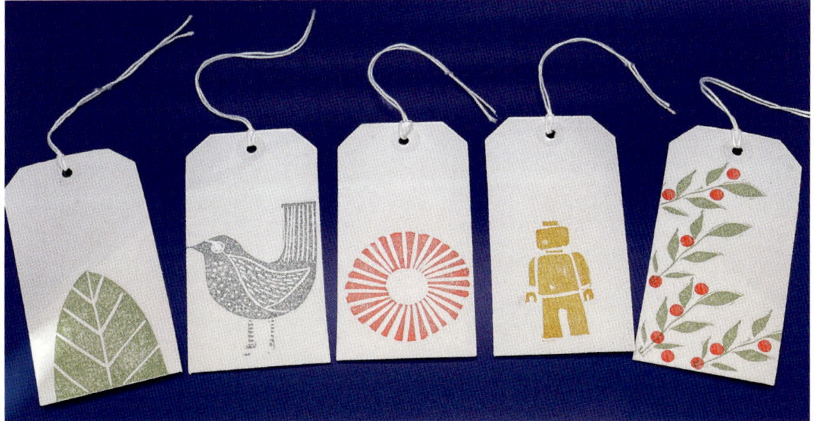

Bookmarks

These make a welcome gift and look great when made with printed papers. You can also put your contact details on the back and use them as business cards.

YOU WILL NEED

- thin card
- printed papers
- printed words cut from magazines (optional)
- cutting mat
- scissors or craft knife
- pencil
- ribbon
- ruler
- hole punch
- glue (glue stick, PVA glue or Mod Podge®)
- glue brush or applicator (optional)
- laminator (optional)
- damp cloth

1. Measure and cut strips of card (each 15 x 80 mm) – if the card is very thin you can glue two pieces together.

2. Collage printed paper on one side, leaving the back plain or decorating both sides, which stiffens the bookmark and looks great. You can go for a whole piece of printed paper to cover the bookmark or make a patchwork of strips. Collage them to the card with glue.

3. I have an envelope with 'book' words and phrases that I have cut from magazines – these can be combined with your printed papers to good effect.

4. To make the bookmarks more durable, you can laminate them and then trim around them. (I have a useful little gadget that cuts rounded corners.)

5. Punch a hole at the top edge and thread some ribbon through.

CLEANING UP

- Save larger offcuts of printed paper or words in envelopes for future use.

- Clear away any small scraps.

- Make sure lids are firmly replaced on glue sticks.

- Clean glue from your cutting mat or work surface with a damp cloth.

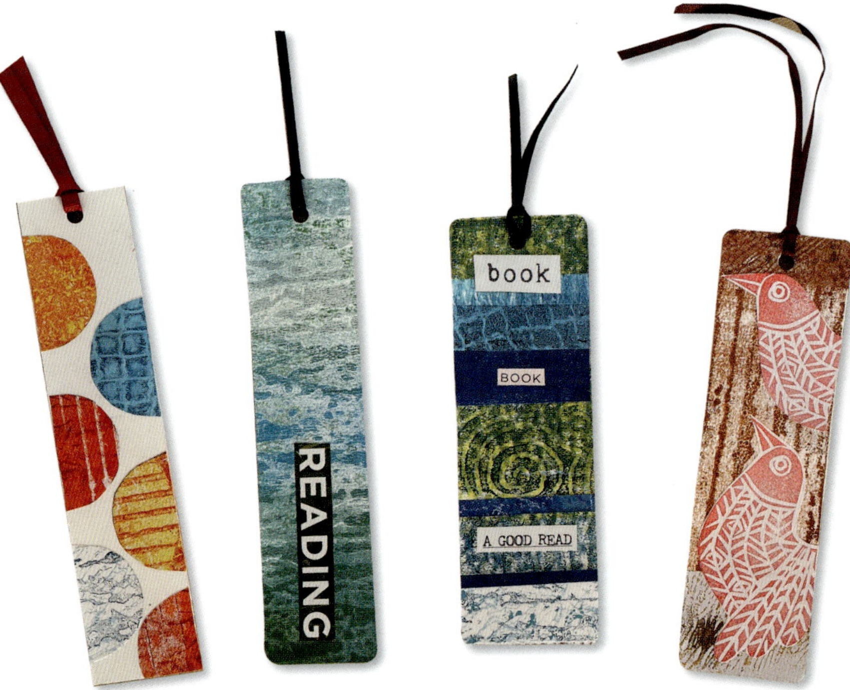

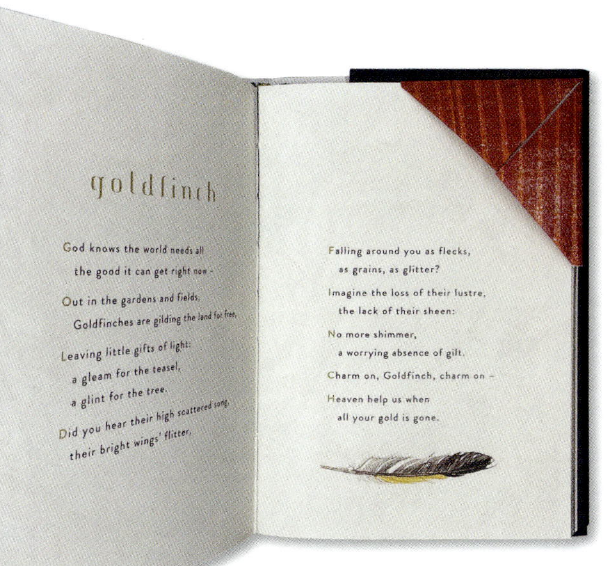

Corner bookmarks

With some careful folding, you can make an origami bookmark which is unusual and looks a bit special.

YOU WILL NEED
- square piece of printed paper (15 × 15 cm) (ideally cartridge paper)
- bone folder or ruler

1. Place the paper in front of you in a diamond position with the printed side down and bring the lower corner up to meet the top corner. Use a bone folder or ruler to flatten the crease. (a)

2. Take one of the lower corners of the triangle and fold it to align with the top corner – crease the fold. (b)

3. Repeat with the other corner so that you have a small diamond shape. (c)

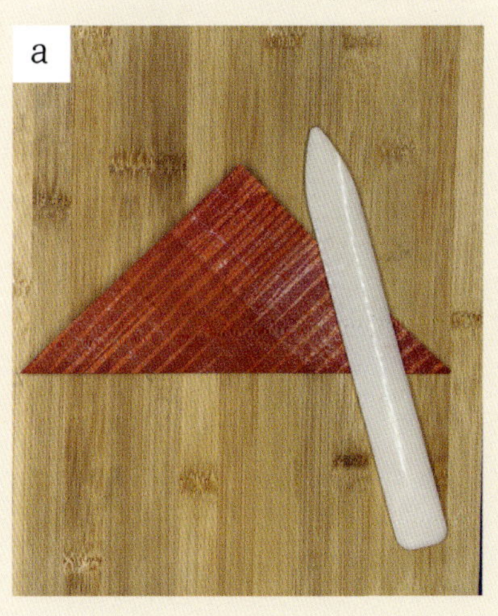

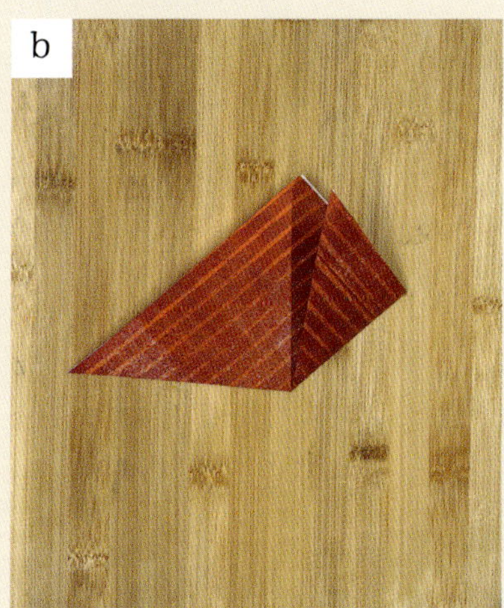

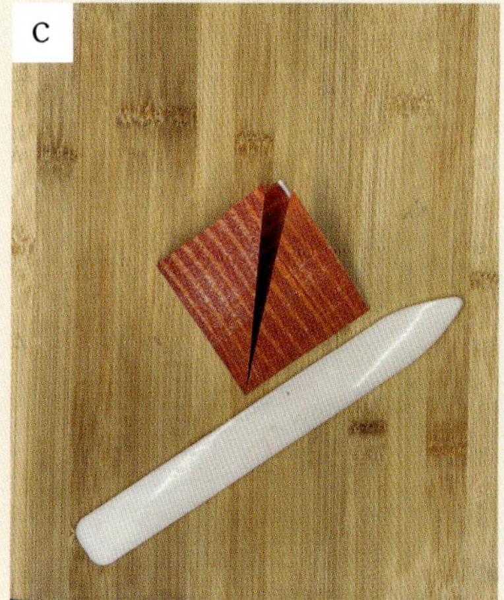

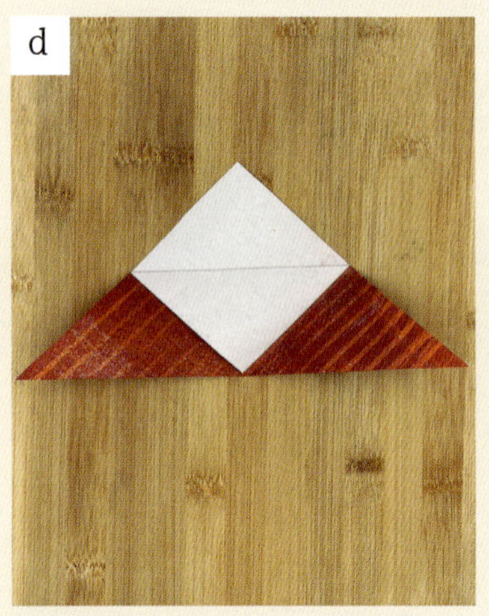

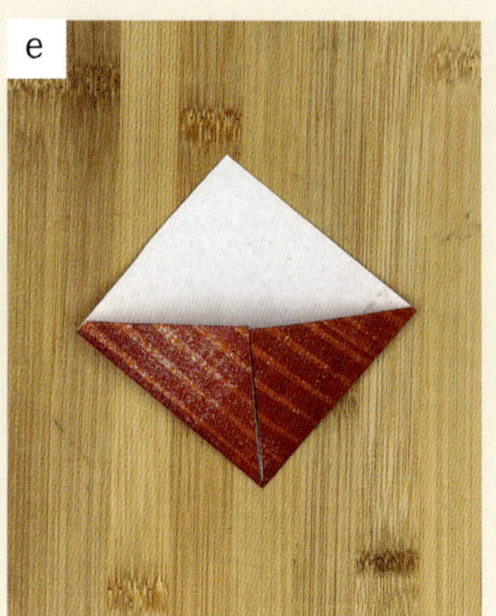

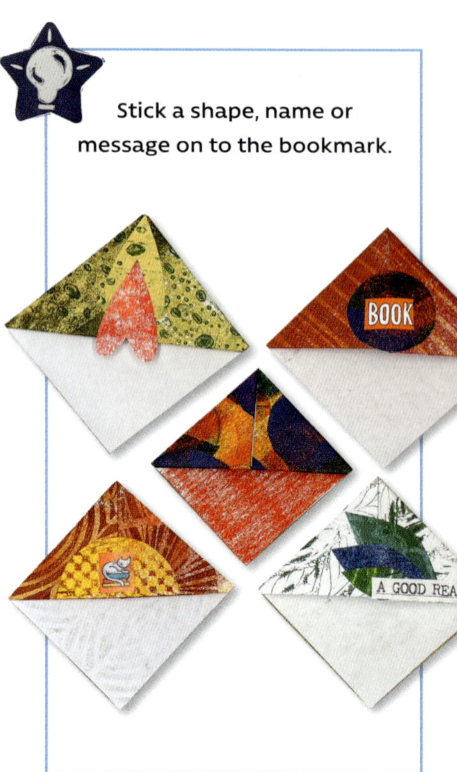

4. Open out the two lower corners and take the front flap from the top point and fold it down to the bottom edge. (d)

5. Fold one of the lower corners back up and tuck it neatly into the horizontal fold. Repeat with the other corner to make your basic corner bookmark. (e)

Envelopes

There are many ways of making your own envelopes but I am going to show you a very simple method which makes a small 10 × 8 cm envelope. Use a larger square of paper to make a bigger version.

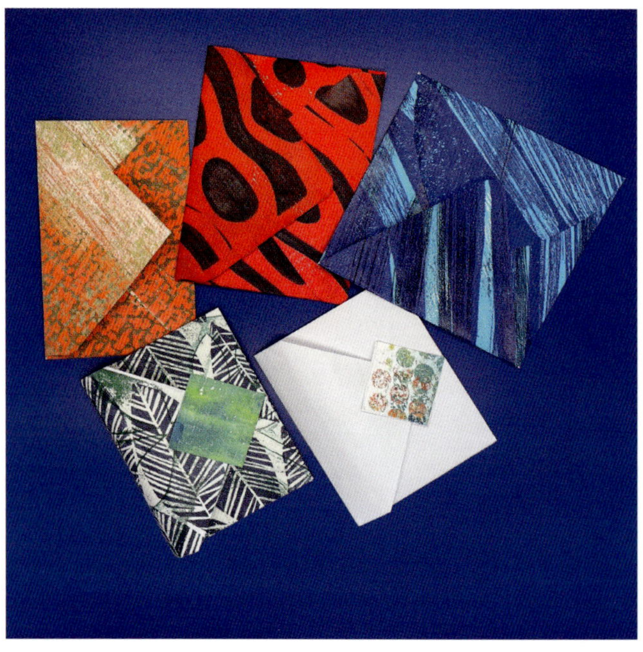

YOU WILL NEED
- square piece of printed paper (21 × 21 cm)
- bone folder or ruler
- glue stick

1. Place the paper on the work surface with the printed side down. Fold it in half diagonally to make a triangle with the printed side on the outside and press the fold with the bone folder or ruler. (a)

2. Fold the corner of the top layer down to the bottom fold and crease the new fold. (b)

3. Fold the right corner one third over to the left. Repeat with the left corner to the end and crease the fold. (c) (d)

4. Fold the left corner back on itself to meet the left edge. (e)

5. Fold the point of the flap up to the top and then open out this folded section and squash it into a diamond shape. (f)

6. Fold the top down to the bottom edge and tuck it into the diamond 'pocket'. (g)

7. Use a dab of glue under each flap of the diamond shape to secure it.

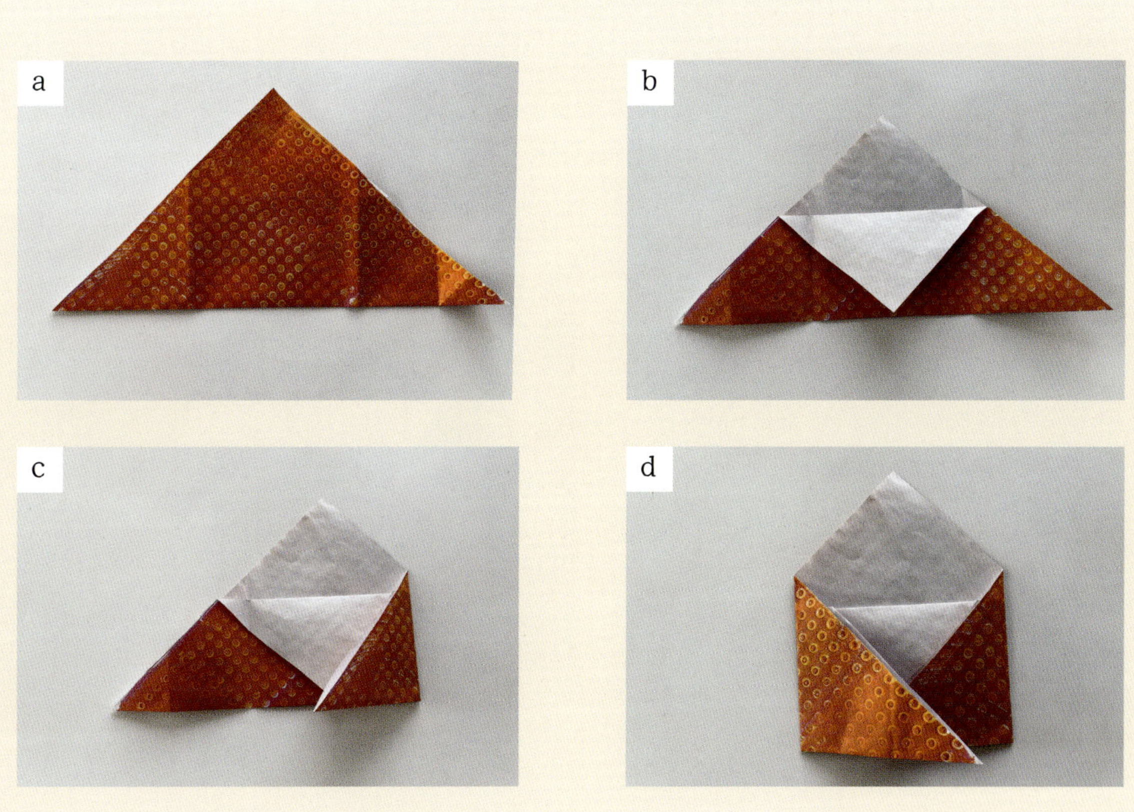

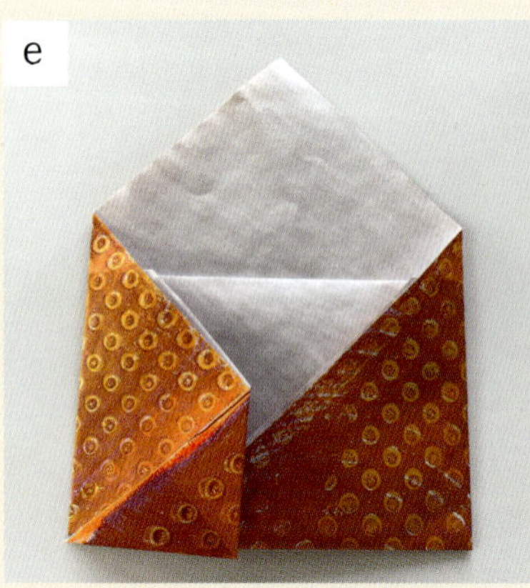

e

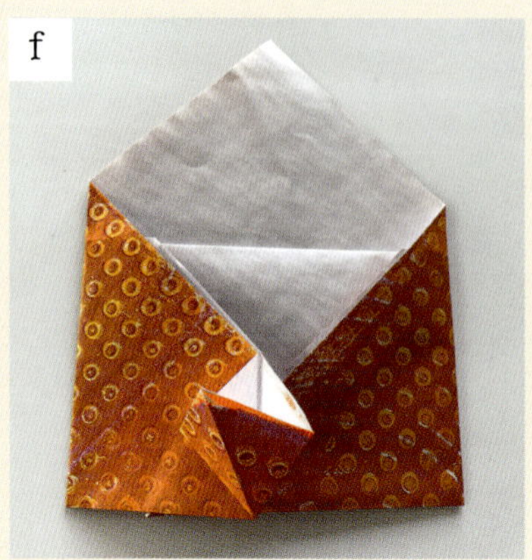

f

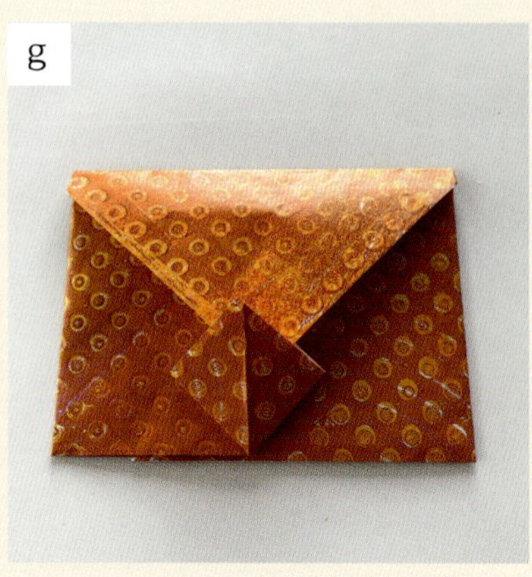

g

Pop a gift inside or stick a plain adhesive label on the front and use it to post a card or letter (glue the flap down if you post it to keep the contents safe).

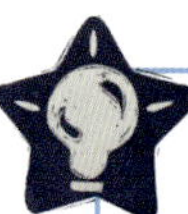

Add a contrasting piece of printed paper over the diamond.

Mini folders

These little folders are quick to make and look great with a covering of hand-printed paper.

YOU WILL NEED
- strip of printed paper
- three C6 envelopes (114 × 162 mm)
- cutting mat
- scissors or craft knife
- ribbon or string
- hole punch
- glue stick

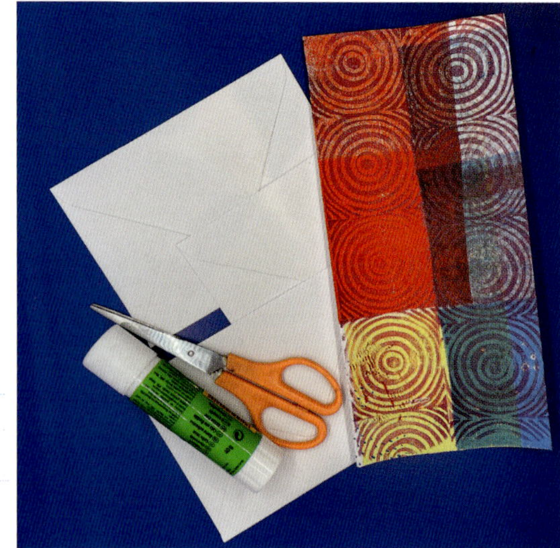

1. Cut a piece pf printed paper that measures 114 × 250 mm.

2. Take your three envelopes and glue down the flaps. (a)

3. Fold each envelope in half by bringing the short ends together and cut a sliver off the two ends opposite the centre fold. (b)

4. The folded envelope now has an opening at each end. Open it out and use the glue stick to glue a line across the inside centre fold. From the centre of this line of glue, glue another line out to the cut edge, creating a T-shape. Press the folded envelope together so the centre sticks together and you have two pockets. (c)

5. Glue the other folded envelopes together in the same way. Put the folded envelopes together with the cut edges all at the top, and then glue the T-shape on the outer face of each folded envelope and join it to the next one, making sure the cut edges remain at the top. You should now have a folder with six pockets. (d)

6. Take your printed paper strip and glue it to the outside surface of the folder.

7. Trim any excess. Alternatively, you could fold and stick any excess printed paper over the edge so the pattern shows inside the flap (this makes it stronger for the next step).

8. When the glue is dry, punch a hole centrally in the flap and attach a piece of ribbon or string long enough to wrap around and hold the folder together.

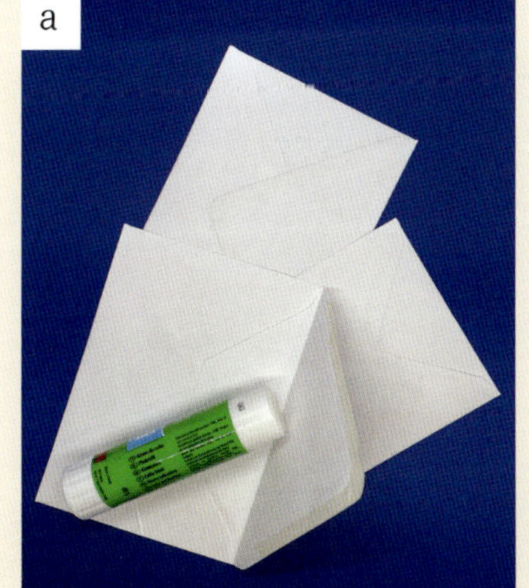

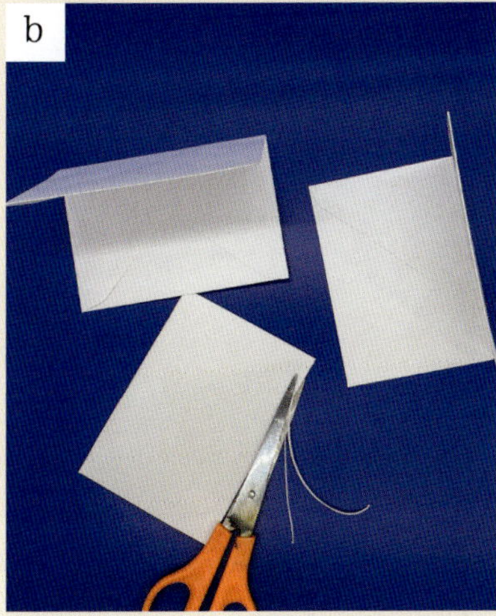

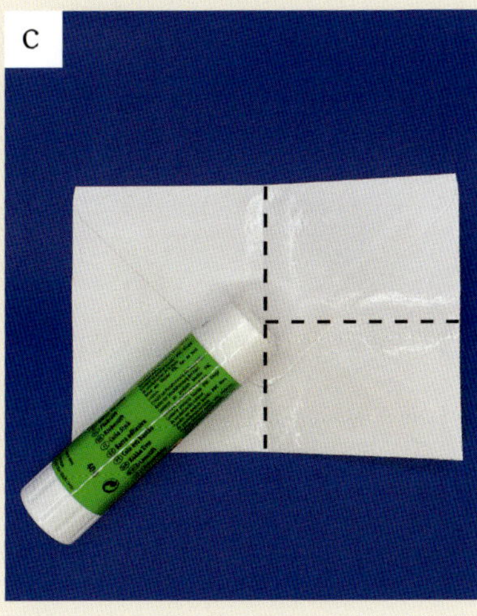

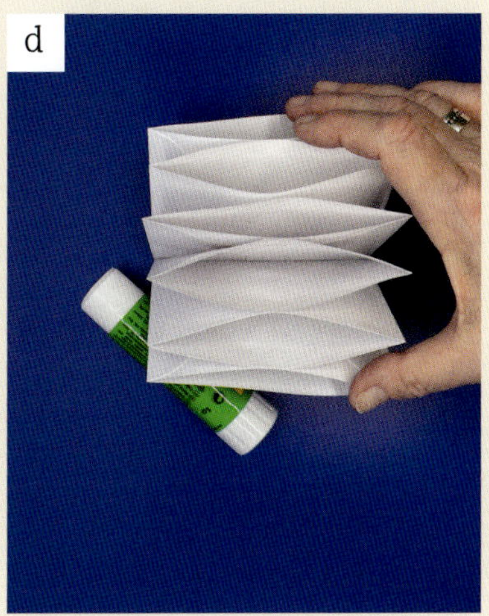

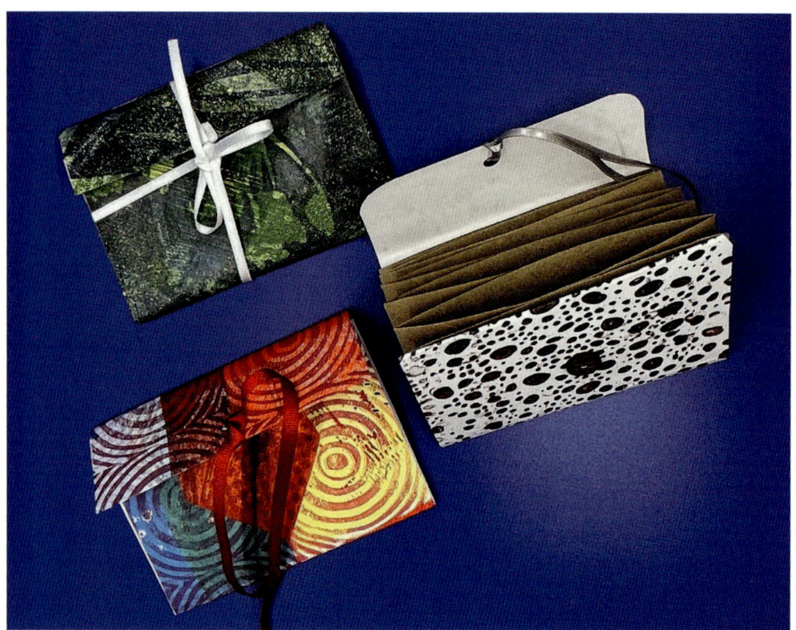

Left: Examples of mini folders.

This makes a useful small folder for stamps, business cards, small cards or scraps from magazines and newspapers (for example, words that you cut out), and it would make a lovely gift.

Handmade books

Your printed papers can be used to make some beautiful handcrafted books which are ideal to use as sketchbooks, journalling or for displaying your prints. I will show you some simple ways of creating books but, if it interests you, there are a great number of books available which will show you more complex bookbinding techniques.

ZINE BOOK

A zine book is a small, folded leaflet made from a single piece of paper. It is not difficult to make and can be created with plain paper to which you can add your prints; or you could make it from a printed piece of paper and then embellish it with more printed scraps, words and drawn or printed images.

YOU WILL NEED
- sheet of A4 paper (plain or printed cartridge paper)
- scissors
- bone folder or ruler for creasing the folds
- glue stick

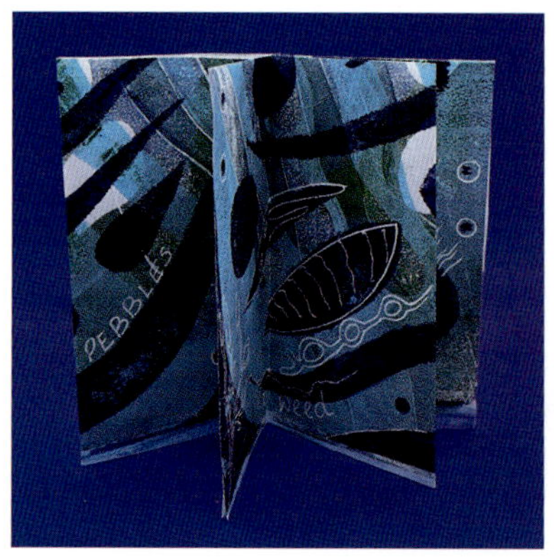

1. Fold the piece of paper in half lengthways and crease the fold firmly. (a)

2. Open it out again, fold it widthways and crease the fold. (b)

3. Unfold the paper and fold the short side to the centre crease. (c)

4. Repeat with the other short side. (d)

5. Unfold the paper so it is flat – you should see eight sections. (e)

6. Fold the paper in half, bringing the two short sides together. Take your scissors and carefully cut along the central horizontal fold from the central fold to the central vertical fold. Take care to stop cutting once you reach the centre. (f)

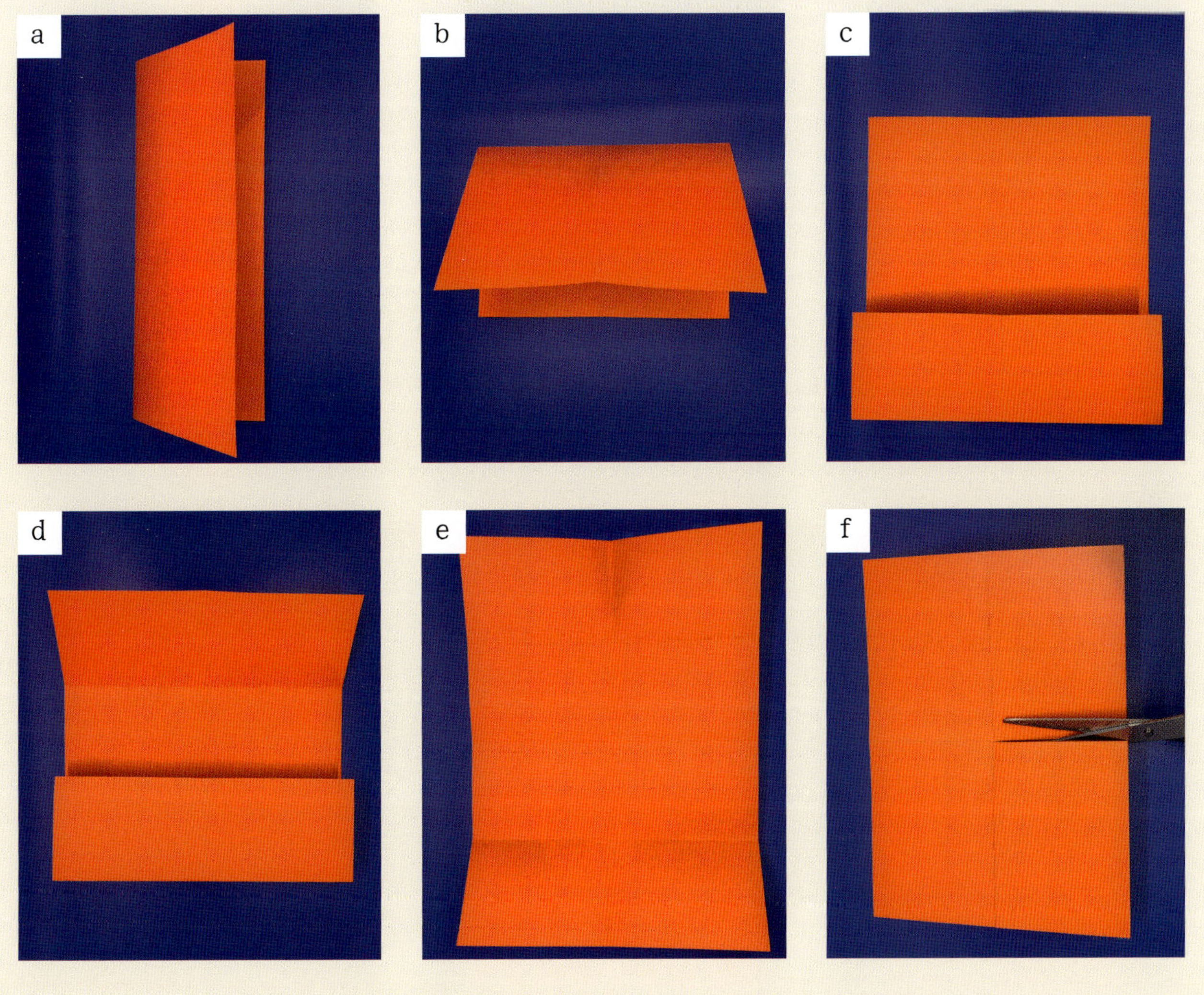

7. Open the folded paper and fold it in half lengthways, bringing the two long sides together. Hold the two ends and push them towards each other, opening up the centre into a diamond shape and then pushing the centre folds together to form a cross. (g) (h)

8. You can now fold the arms of the cross together to form the booklet. A dab of glue will hold the folded pages together. (i)

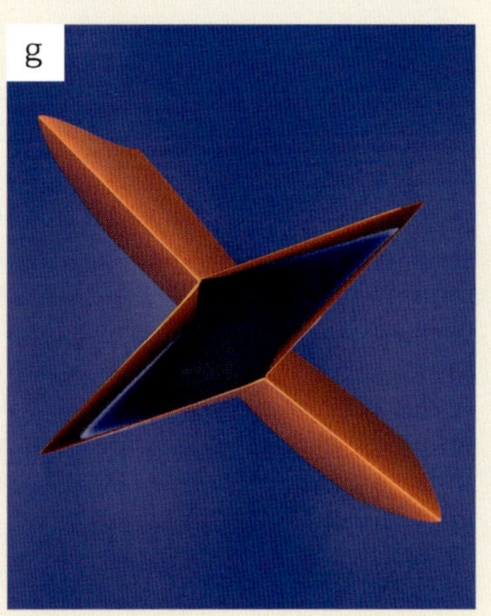

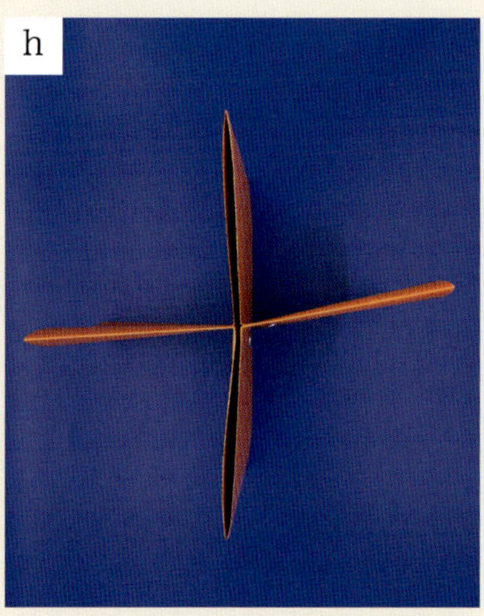

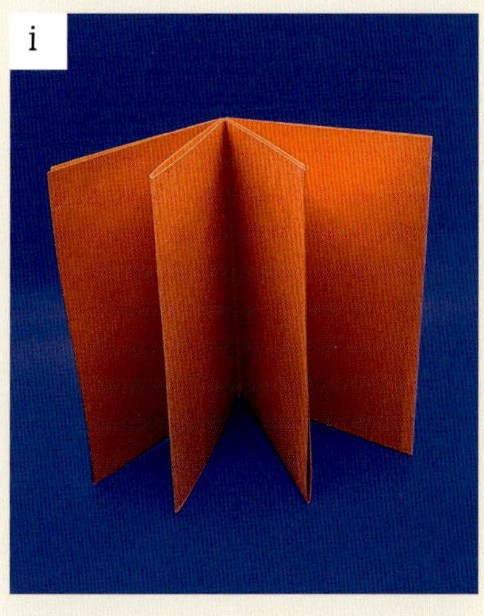

Add drawings, words or collage prints, or create small pockets.

Make a larger version in the same way with a sheet of A3 paper.

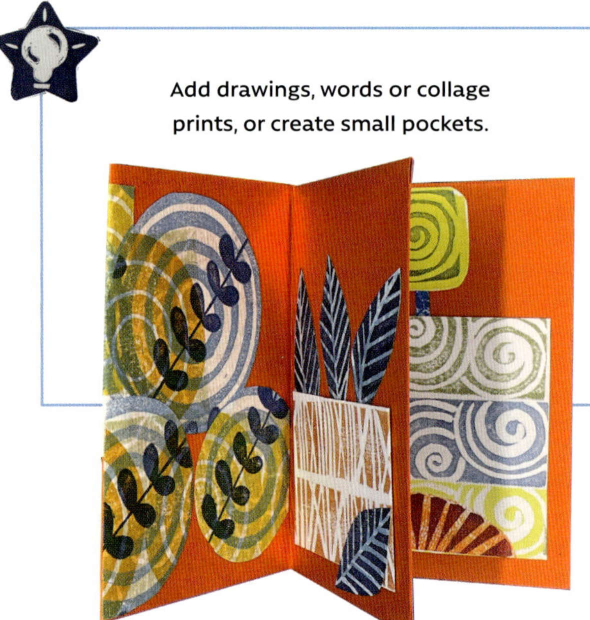

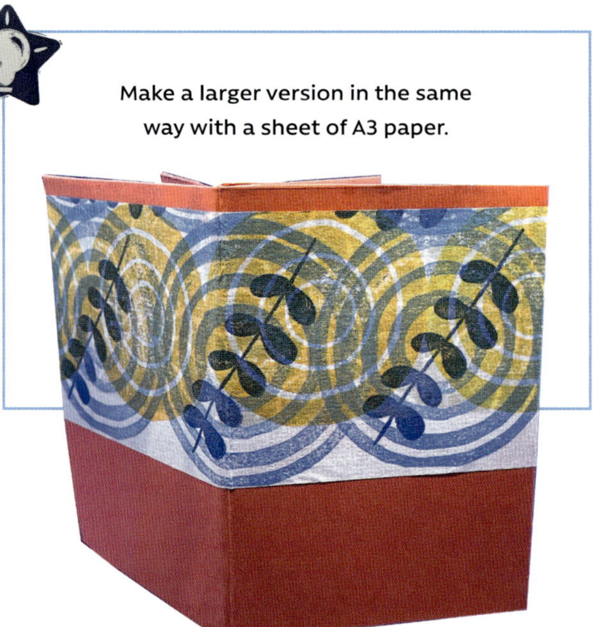

LEPORELLO OR ACCORDION BOOK

These little books are fun to make and are a great way to display your work. The pages are a folded accordion so you can use both sides. Your printed papers make attractive covers. I like to have something of a colour or pattern match for front and back but you could also use contrasting papers. Collage other prints on to the book pages or leave the pages blank to use for linoprints or stamped images, or for sketching.

YOU WILL NEED

- two square pieces of card (mountboard or card from the back of an old sketchbook) (each 12 × 12 cm)
- two square pieces of your printed paper (each 14 × 14 cm) to cover the book boards
- strip of cartridge or mixed-media paper (10 × 60 cm) (or join two strips to make this length)
- scissors
- pencil
- piece of ribbon (30 cm)
- ruler
- bone folder (optional)
- glue (glue stick, PVA glue or bookbinding glue)
- glue brush or applicator (optional)

A leporello book can be displayed on a shelf with a selection of your small prints on its folded pages.

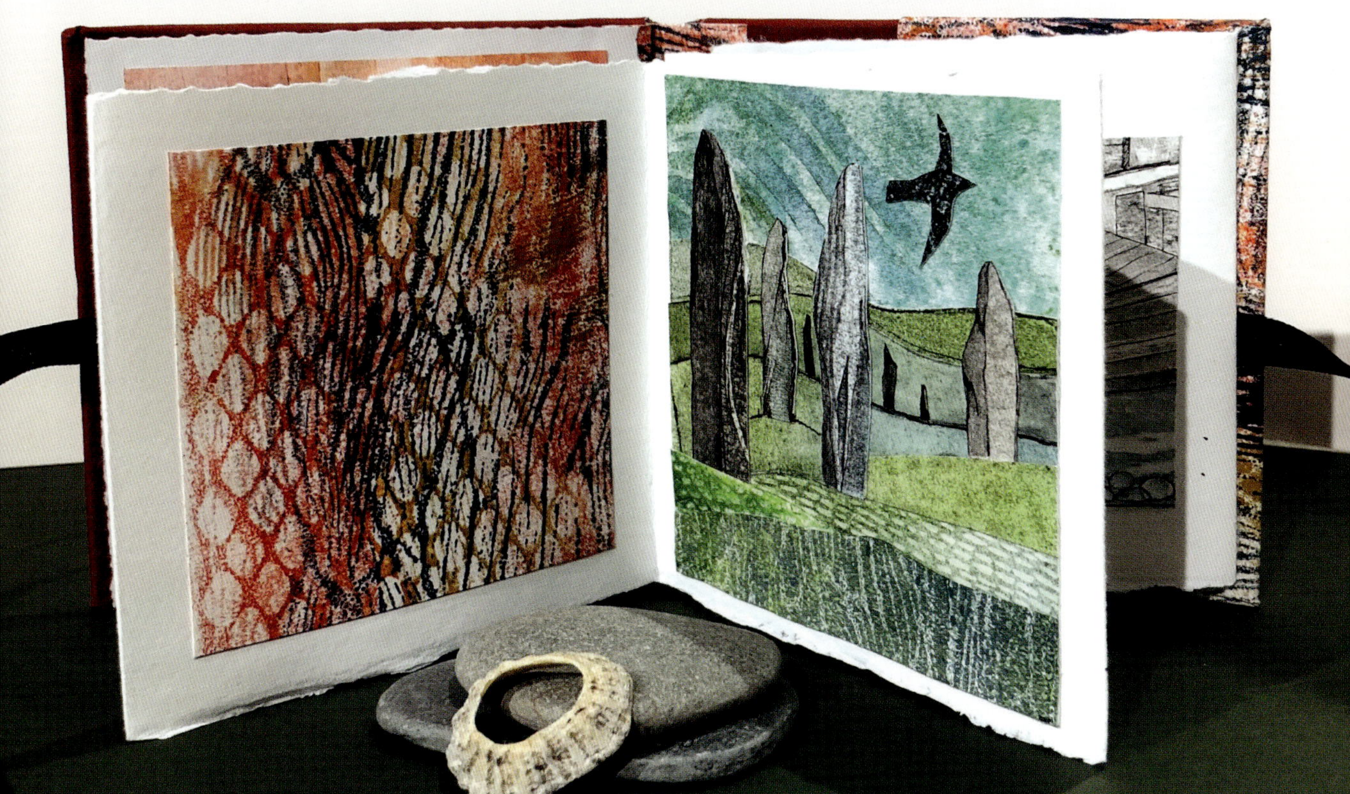

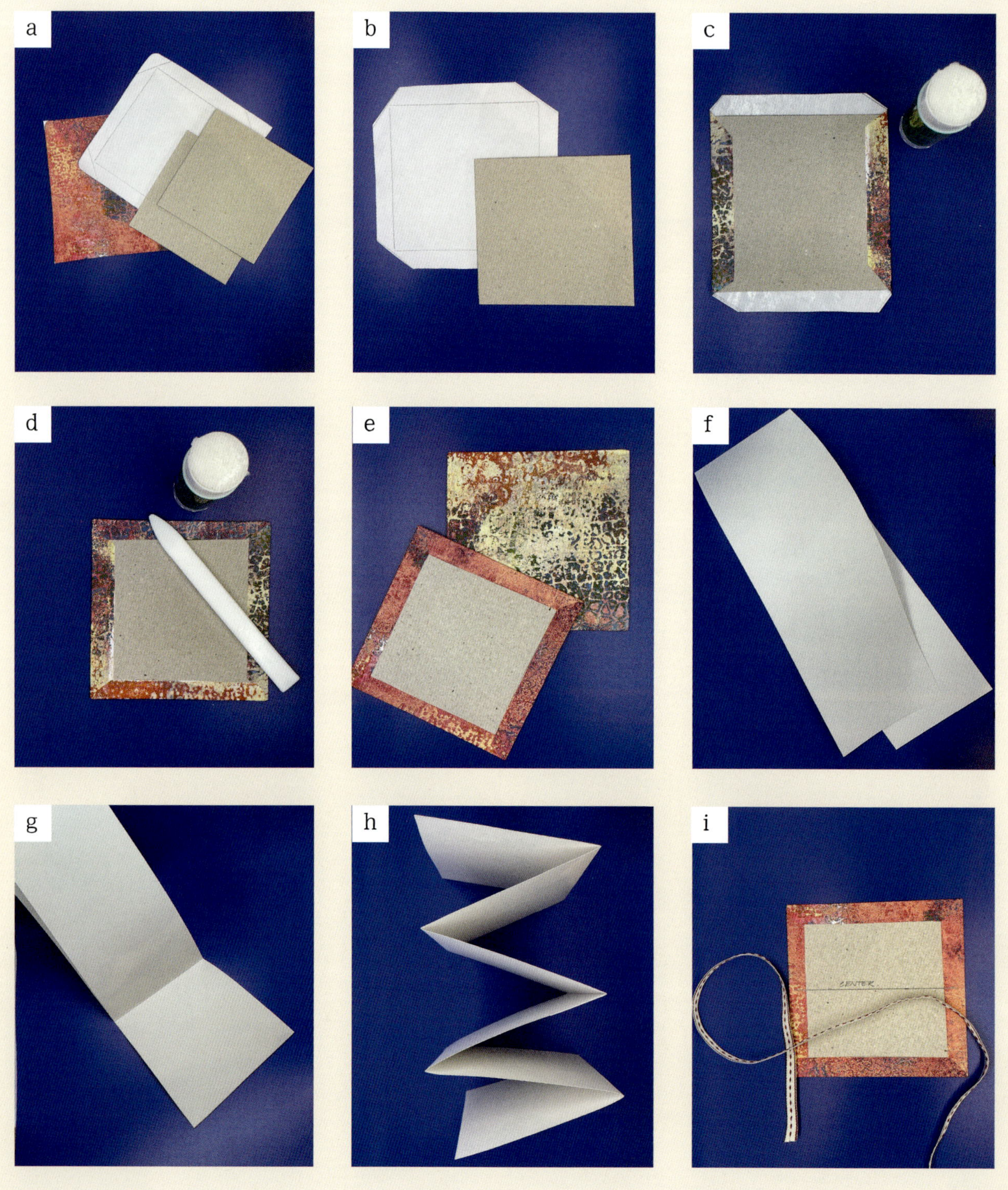

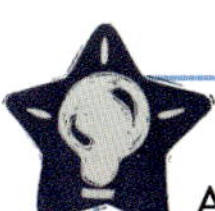

1. Take the paper for the front cover, turn it print side down and place one of the pieces of card centrally on the paper. Draw around the card leaving a margin all around. Draw diagonal lines across the corners, just slightly above each drawn corner, and trim these with scissors. (a) (b)

2. Spread glue all over the reverse side of the paper, taking it up to the edges. Place the card in the centre square. Fold over two opposite edges, wrapping tightly over and smoothing the edges with a finger or bone folder. (c)

3. Fold the other two edges over, pinching in the corners to make a neat fold. (d)

4. Do the same process with the other card and paper. You now have a book cover for each end of the book. Set these aside. (e)

5. Take the long strip of paper and fold it in half, bringing the short ends together. (f)

6. To start your zigzag folds, measure 10 cm from the centre and fold the paper back, creasing it firmly. This will be the size of each of the 'pages' of your book — 10 x 10 cm square.

7. Now fold the paper back on itself. Continue folding and pressing each fold firmly. Repeat the process with both halves of the paper strip so that it forms a zigzag with each folded section matching in size. This will be the accordion part of the book with blank pages on each side. (h)

8. Take the book covers. With a pencil and ruler, draw a line across the centre of one of the covered cards where the covering paper is folded round. Glue a long piece of ribbon across the centre from side to side, leaving lengths on each side that are long enough for you to wrap the ribbon round and tie the book together. The cover with the ribbon attached will become the back cover and the ribbon will tie at the front. (i) (j)

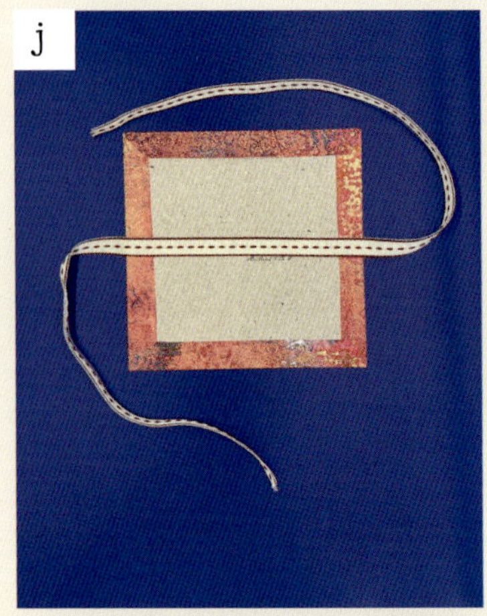

j

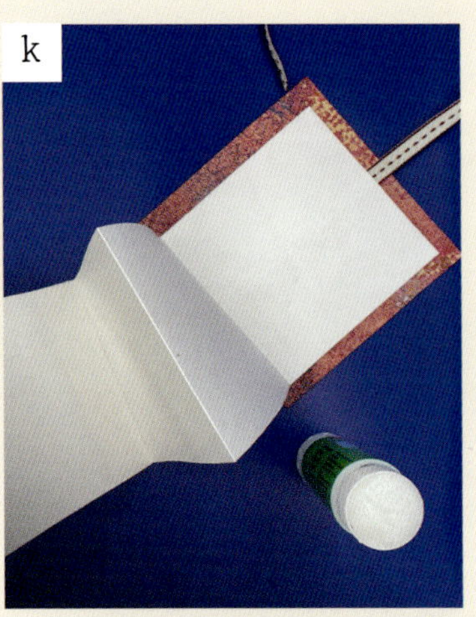

k

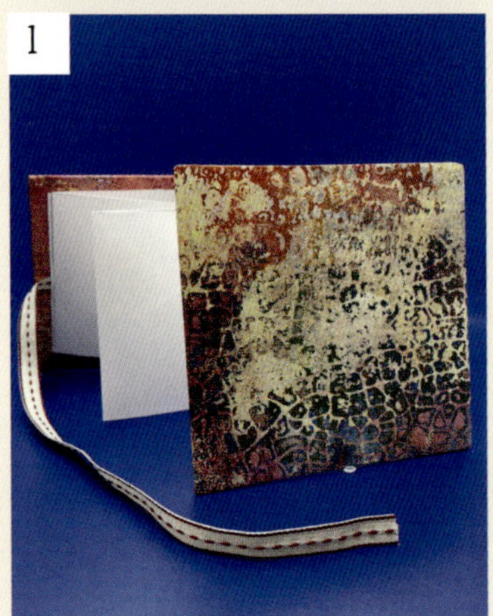

l

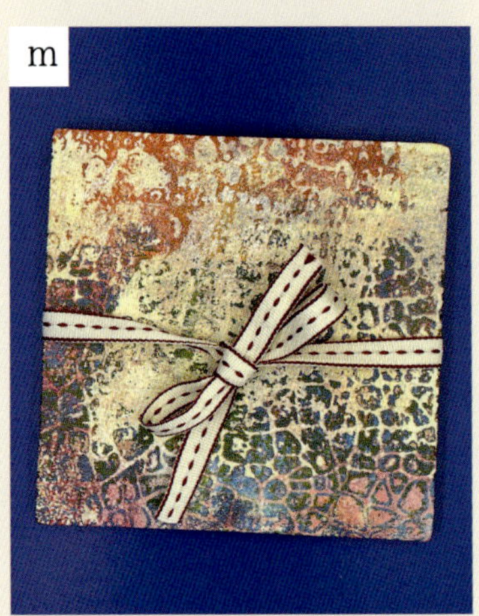

m

Inside the book, write words, add photos, create collage pictures or use your stamping blocks or linoprints to add a design. It lends itself to a sequence of images or a thematic approach — for example, a single colour used for each page or lines from a poem with matching illustrations.

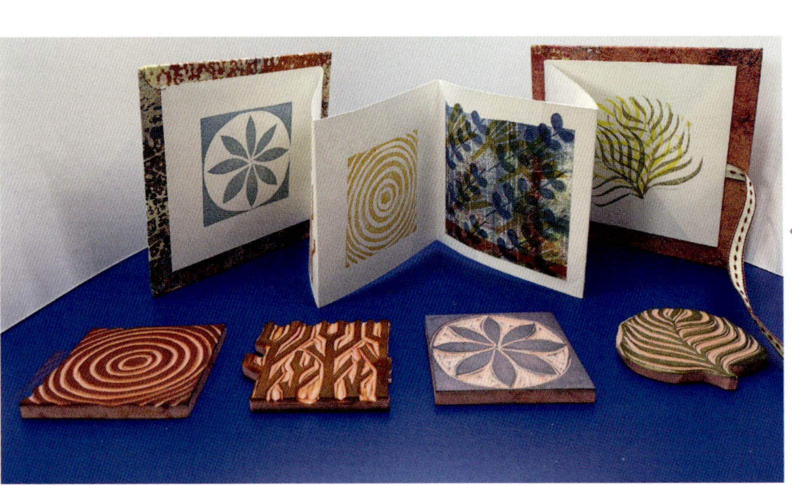

Use a different method for tying the book together, attaching a button on one side or having a loop of elastic to slip over it.

9. Spread glue on the end of the zigzag paper strip and carefully place it on the inside of the back cover. (k)

10. Glue the other end of the zigzag paper strip and carefully attach the front cover to complete your accordion. Wrap the ribbon around and tie in a bow. (l) (m)

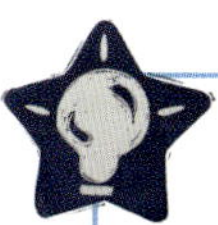

Make a larger version — just increase the size of the paper strip and match the cover to the folded page size.

3D projects

FOLDED BIRD

These little birds are easy and quick to make from a strip of hand-printed paper. Printed copy paper works well if the bird is going to be used on a card or collage picture. If it will be a hanging decoration, printed cartridge paper is more substantial, although a bit harder to fold neatly.

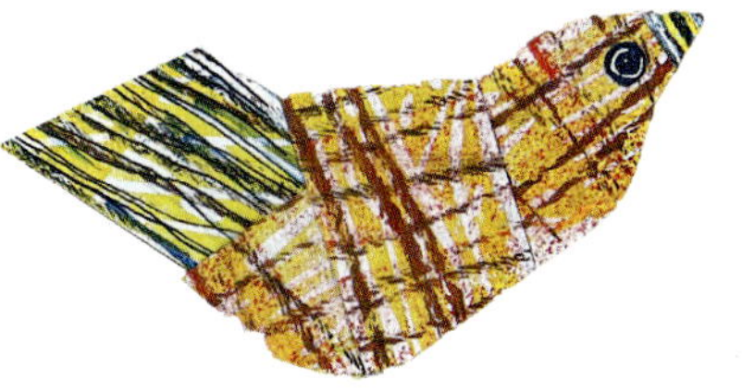

YOU WILL NEED

- strip of paper (25 × 210 mm), printed on both sides
- small pieces of contrasting printed paper (optional)
- scissors
- fineliner pens (optional)
- bone folder or ruler for creasing the folds
- glue (optional)

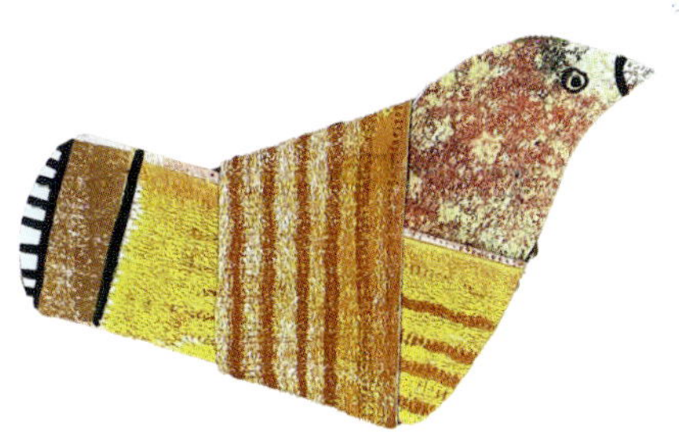

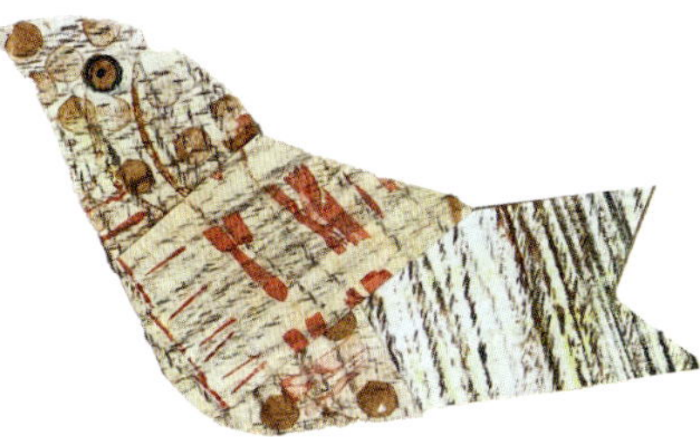

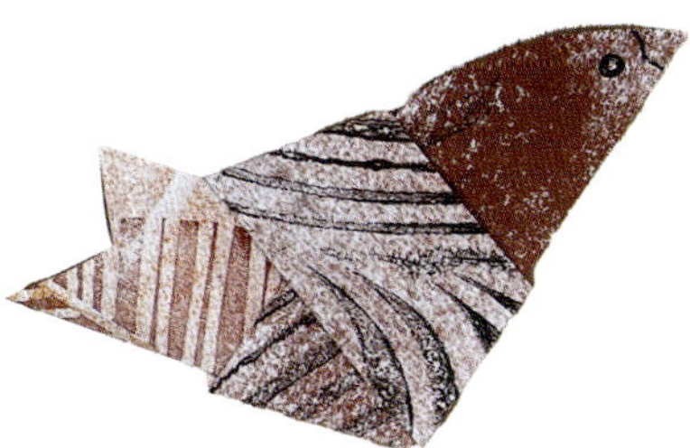

1. Take your strip of paper and bring the two ends together, overlapping them. (a) (b)

2. Tuck one end over the other and through the loop in a loose knot. Be careful not to tear or crumple the paper. Flatten the knot gently. You should now have two ends of the paper strip poking out of the folded knot. One end will become the bird's head and the other the tail. (c)

3. Take the scissors and shape one end to form the head and beak. Shape the other end to create a tail — simply cut at a slant or into a 'V' shape. (d)

4. Draw an eye and beak or collage pieces of contrasting paper to the bird's head on one or both sides. (e)

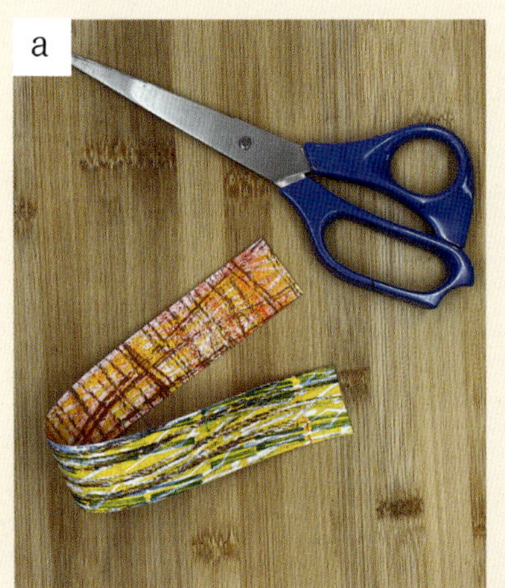

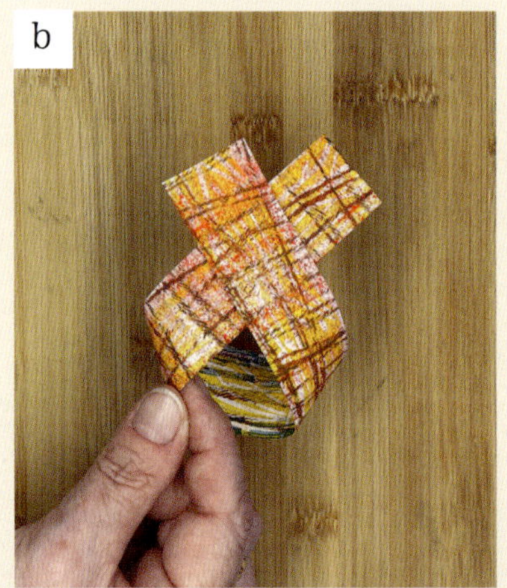

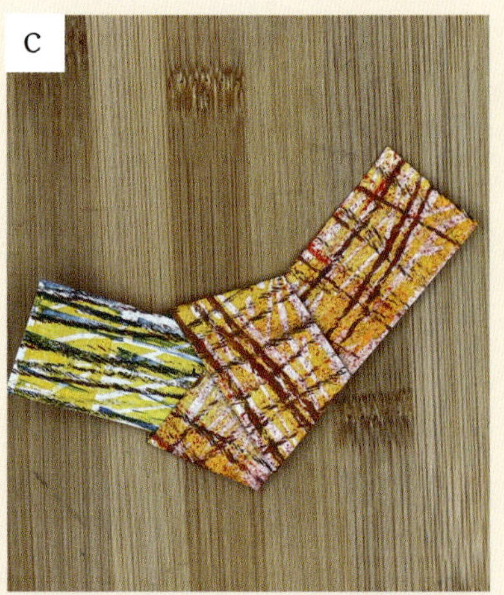

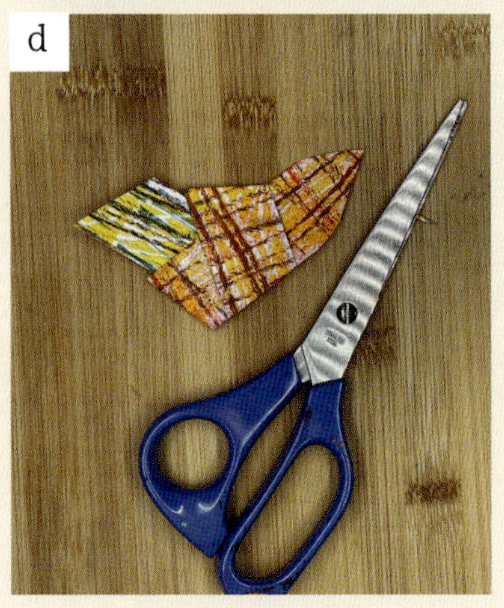

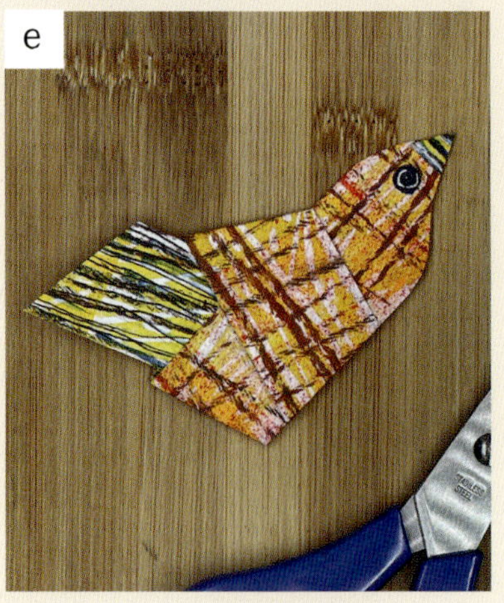

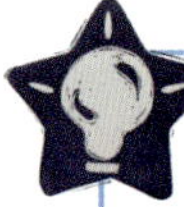

Add a wing on one or both sides, depending on how you plan to use the bird. You could also draw legs or add a twig in its beak.

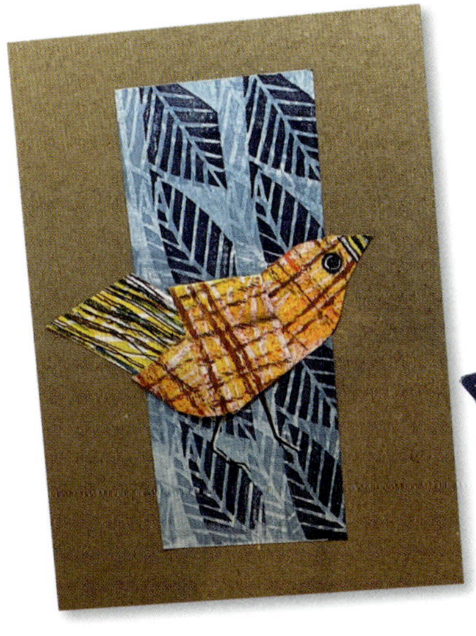

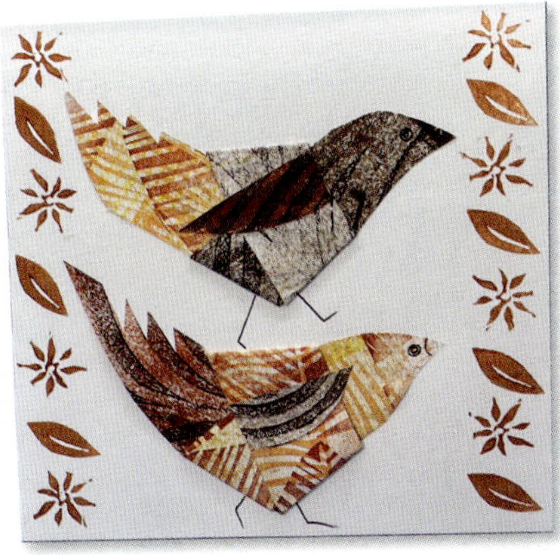

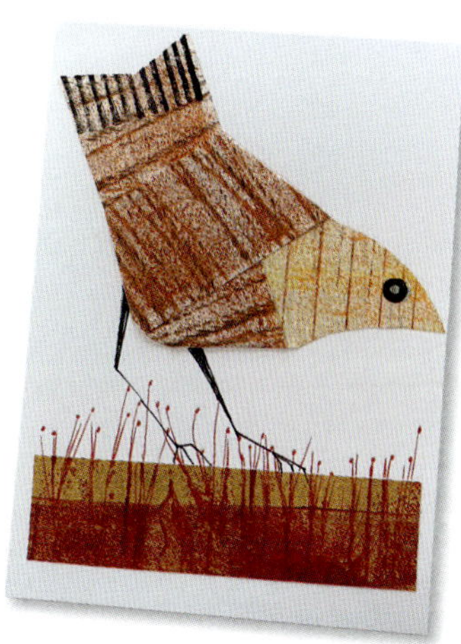

You can make lovely cards with these folded birds, but because they are double-sided they also look great as hanging decorations or on a mobile.

ORIGAMI HEART

A heart-shaped image is always rather special, particularly when it is made from your hand-printed papers. It can be used to hold a message or a gift of money or jewellery, or it can be used on a card.

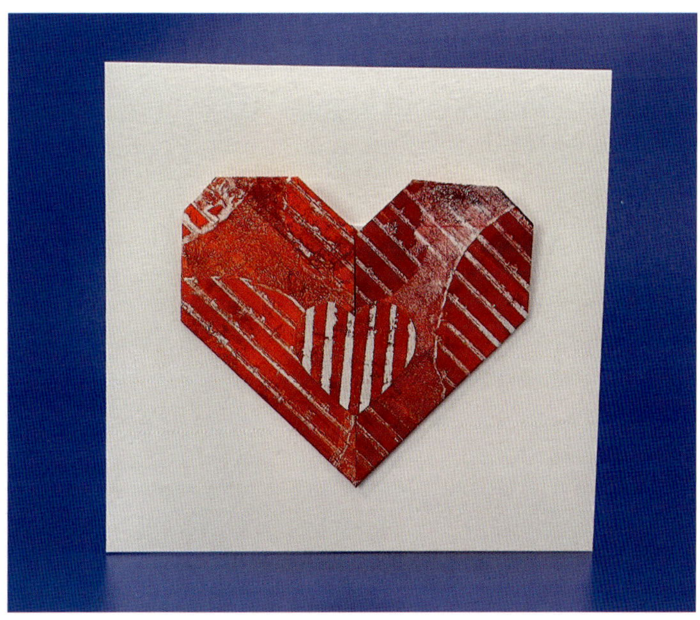

YOU WILL NEED

- square piece of printed paper (15 × 15 cm)
- small heart-shaped piece of paper (optional)
- scissors
- bone folder or ruler
- glue stick

1. Place the paper printed side down on the work surface and fold it in half diagonally, corner to corner. Press the fold with the bone folder. (a)

2. Open the paper and repeat, folding the other opposite corners together. (b)

3. Open the paper out and position it in front of you in a diamond. Fold the top corner down to the centre and press the fold flat. (c)

4. Fold the bottom corner up to the top fold and press flat. (d)

5. Take the right lower corner and fold it up from the centre. (e)

6. Repeat with the left corner, matching the folds exactly along the centre as they meet. (f)

7. Turn the paper over. (g)

8. Fold the two upper points down to the horizontal fold and crease firmly. A dab of glue can be used to secure them in place. (h)

9. Fold the two points at each side in and secure with a dab of glue. (i)

10. Turn the paper over. You can stick a small heart-shaped piece of paper on to your heart to hold the sides of the central fold together.

Stick down the sides of the heart to the front of a card and pop a message or small gift into the pocket.

Use a sticker with a word on it, or a flower cut from a magazine to hold the central fold together.

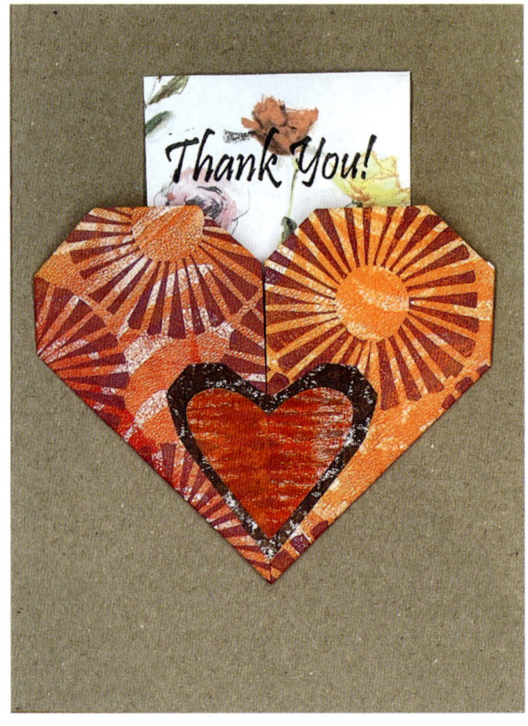

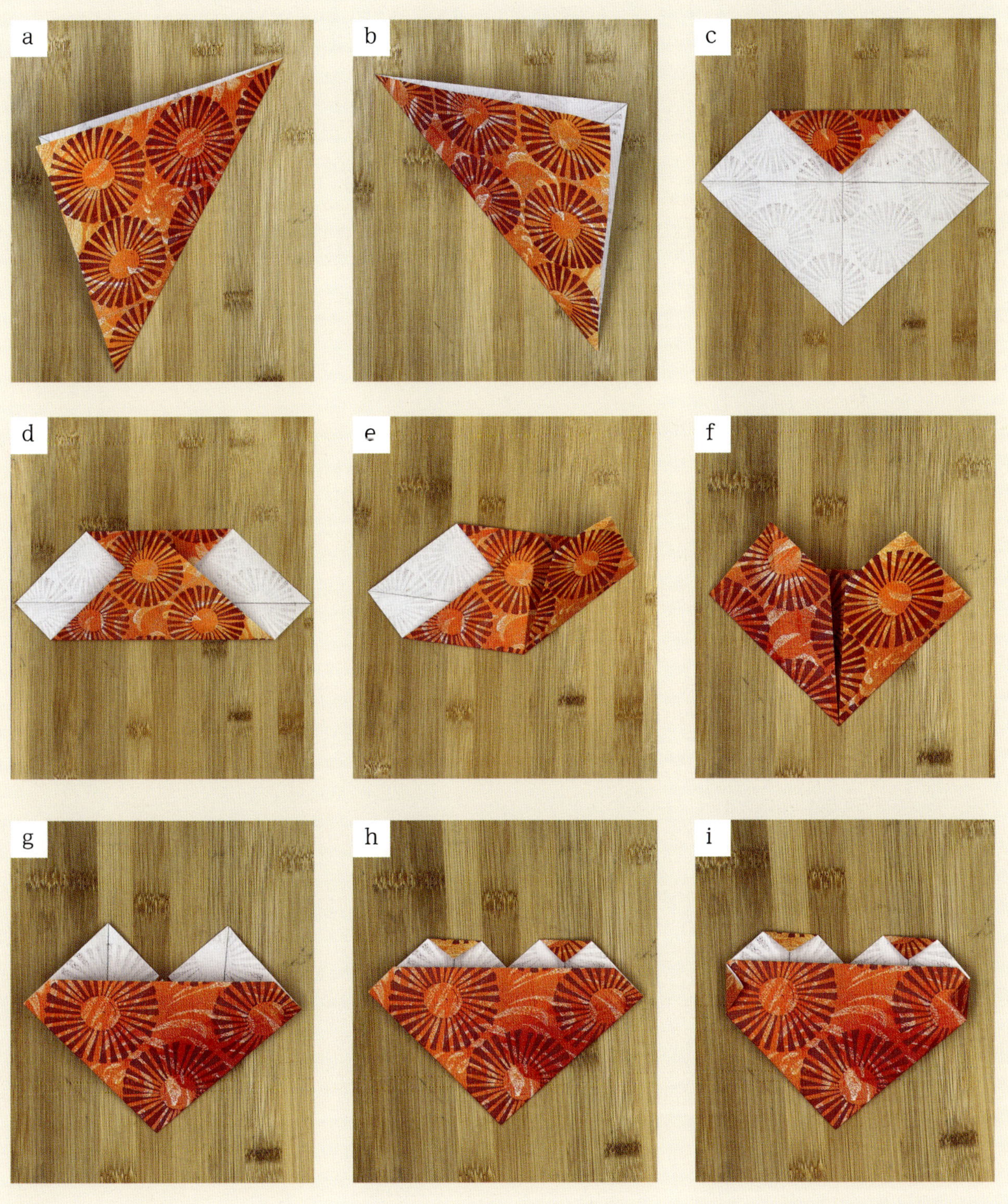

13

THINGS TO THINK ABOUT

Editioning and signing your prints

If you are creating your prints just for yourself, family and friends or for making cards, you will not need to edition them. However, if you plan to sell your work in shops, galleries, craft fairs or online, making an edition and numbering your prints helps to distinguish your original prints from reproduction prints which are digitally produced.

A 'limited' edition of prints means that once you have printed a specific number of identical prints, no more copies will be made. Editioning does not apply to monoprinting, as each monoprint is unique, but linoprints can be printed many times and limiting the number produced makes them special. It is worth knowing how to edition, number and sign your prints. You are establishing that an edition of prints is consistent in quality, each print is identical and that only a specified number of these prints has been produced. There will be some prints that don't quite make the grade for inclusion in an edition. These can be used for cards or collage, so don't discard them.

Once you have established how many prints you will produce in a limited edition and these have been printed, you can give each print a number, sign it and give it a title. If you have made reduction prints, you will have decided on the number of prints to produce right from the start, but with other methods you can be more flexible.

When you are ready to sign and number your work, make sure that the ink has dried, your hands and your work area are clean, and that you use an HB pencil for signing. Pencil is traditionally used rather than pen as it is harder to forge and is less likely to fade.

NUMBERING

The prints are numbered at the foot of the print on the left-hand side. The x/y format is used, with y as the number of prints in the edition and x as the individual number of the print being signed. An edition of ten prints would be labelled 1/10, 2/10, 3/10, etc.

If you are not printing the whole edition in one go, keep a note of the ones that have been numbered so that you can continue adding the numbers later when you finish printing the edition.

If there are variations in the way you have printed your design – for example, a change of colour or printing over a background – these prints will not be part of the main edition and can be labelled V/E for 'Variable Edition'.

I have a printed label which explains my printing process and editioning. I stick this on the reverse of the backing board when packing up my prints for sale.

SIGNING

Your signature should be written below the print on the right-hand side using a pencil. Many printmakers carve themselves a small printing block with a design using their initials and print this in the right corner of their print instead of signing the print. Decide on how you are going to sign and be consistent to avoid any confusion. Some artists include the date of the print below their signature, but this is optional.

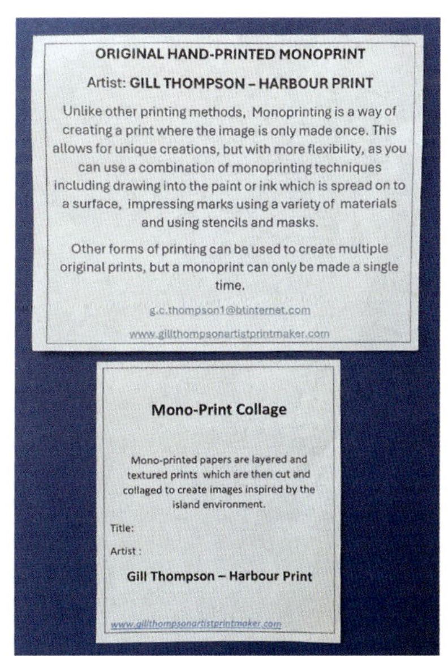

ORIGINAL HAND-PRINTED MONOPRINT

Artist: GILL THOMPSON – HARBOUR PRINT

Unlike other printing methods, Monoprinting is a way of creating a print where the image is only made once. This allows for unique creations, but with more flexibility, as you can use a combination of monoprinting techniques including drawing into the paint or ink which is spread on to a surface, impressing marks using a variety of materials and using stencils and masks.

Other forms of printing can be used to create multiple original prints, but a monoprint can only be made a single time.

g.c.thompson1@btinternet.com

www.gillthompsonartistprintmaker.com

Mono-Print Collage

Mono-printed papers are layered and textured prints which are then cut and collaged to create images inspired by the island environment.

Title:

Artist :

Gill Thompson – Harbour Print

www.gillthompsonartistprintmaker.com

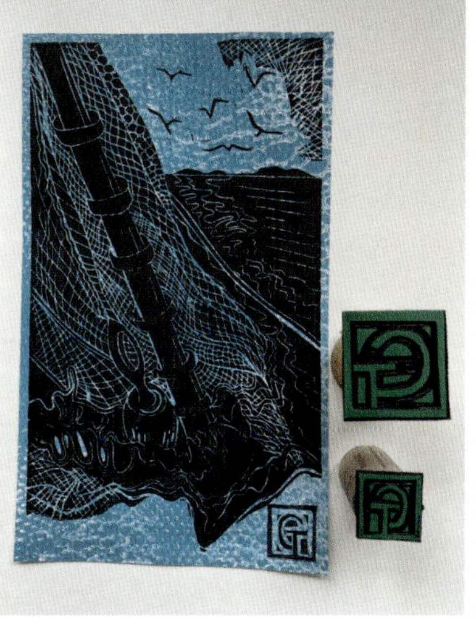

TITLE

The title of the print is written in inverted commas in the centre, between the edition number and the signature. Each print in an edition will have the same title.

Presenting your work

If you decide to sell your work, you will want it to be displayed and presented in a professional way that shows your prints to their best advantage. It is also worth packaging them in a way that protects them, using acid-free materials.

There are several ways to present your printwork — it can be framed, mounted and enclosed in bags or, in the case of cards, bagged or enclosed in a paper wrapper. The best way is to give potential clients the option to buy a piece of work ready to hang on the wall or mounted and bagged for them to frame themselves. Hand-printed cards can also be framed as they are small, original pieces of art and can be grouped in a frame to great effect.

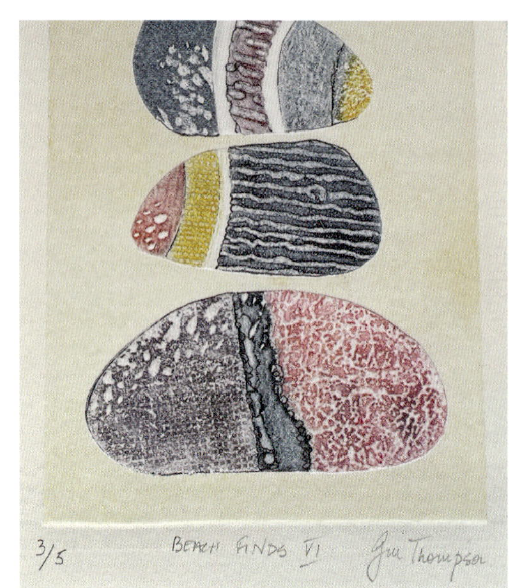

MOUNTS

Mounting your work gives it protection and enhances a print for display. Ready-cut art mounts can be bought from art shops or online, and come in standard sizes so they can be fitted into frames.

Check that mounts are made from acid-free conservation board, as cheaper mounts will yellow and fade in time and can stain the paper around your print. Some mounts come with a backing board — if not, use a piece of acid-free card the same size as the dimensions of the window mount.

Ordinary self-adhesive tapes should not be used for mounting artwork. Masking tape and sticky tape tend to dry out and lose adhesion over time, and can leave stains and sticky residue if removed. Acid-free conservation tape will not leave any residue and is available online and from art suppliers.

The window mount should be hinged to the backing board along the longest edge using acid-free tape. The paper with the print needs to be larger than the

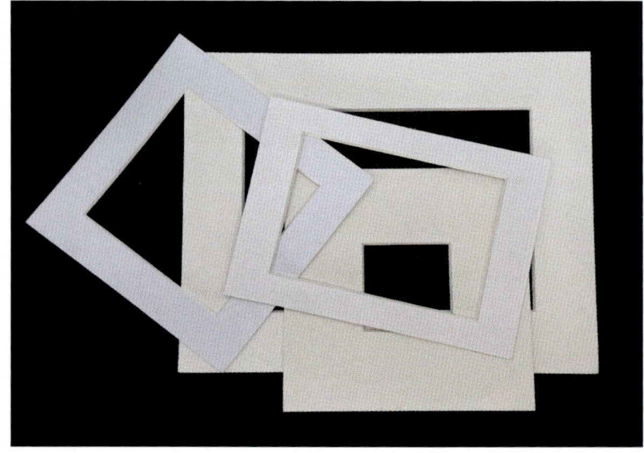

aperture in the mount so that there is enough of the print paper to attach it to the back of the mount. The print can fit exactly in the aperture or can have a margin around it. Position the print on the backing board so that it sits under the window mount correctly. Attach the print to the backing board with pieces of acid-free tape, with only 5 mm of tape adhering to the artwork. Enclose the mount package in a cellophane bag for protection.

FRAMES

Framing is a very personal issue. A good frame shows your work off well. A poor frame can do the opposite. Sometimes it is best to let the purchaser select the frame they want, but it is always worth having a few pieces of work that are well framed on display.

Frames come in standard sizes and a range of prices. Ready-made frames are acceptable, providing they are well made, and the mitred corners fit snugly. Cheaper frames can look 'cheap' which does not give a professional look to your work, particularly if the corners are not done well and they use thin acrylic rather than glass.

Simple black, white or natural wood frames work well on most prints and a group of prints in identical frames looks great.

Bespoke frames from a framer are worth investing in if you are submitting work for an exhibition, but make sure that you include the cost of the frame when calculating the selling price as it is an integral part of the artwork.

When submitting work for an exhibition, check with the gallery to find what they prefer in the way of hanging fittings. As a rule, D-rings and cord are acceptable but some galleries like mirror plates, which fix the picture flat to the wall. Avoid using screw eyes or screws on the back of the frame as these can damage the wall and risk scratching or denting other pictures during transportation or in storage. D-rings are flat so damage is less likely. When stacking or moving your work, it is always advisable to place pictures back to back or front to front.

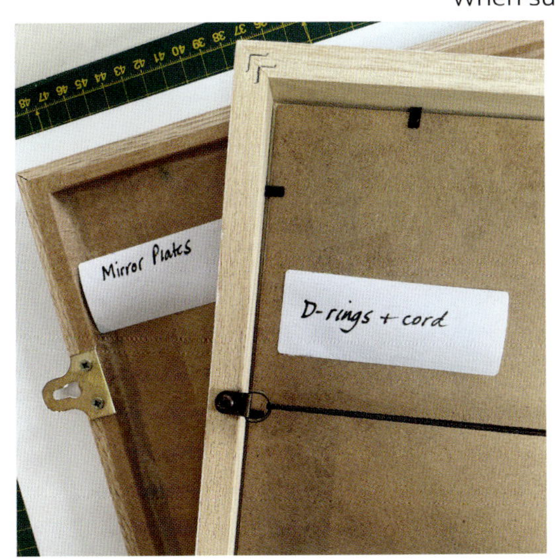

BAGS

Bags for cards and mounted work are available in compostable cellophane or glassine (a recyclable and biodegradable paper). Rolls of biodegradable cellophane are also available. For presenting your cards, cello bags protect the cards from damage when handled. You can also use a band of paper to hold card and envelope together, printing your name and/or logo on the band. Raffia or ribbon can also be used. This works well if you are selling packs of cards.

Business cards

It is worth having some business cards to provide customers with your contact details. These can be commercially printed or you can make your own using your hand-carved stamps or linoprints.

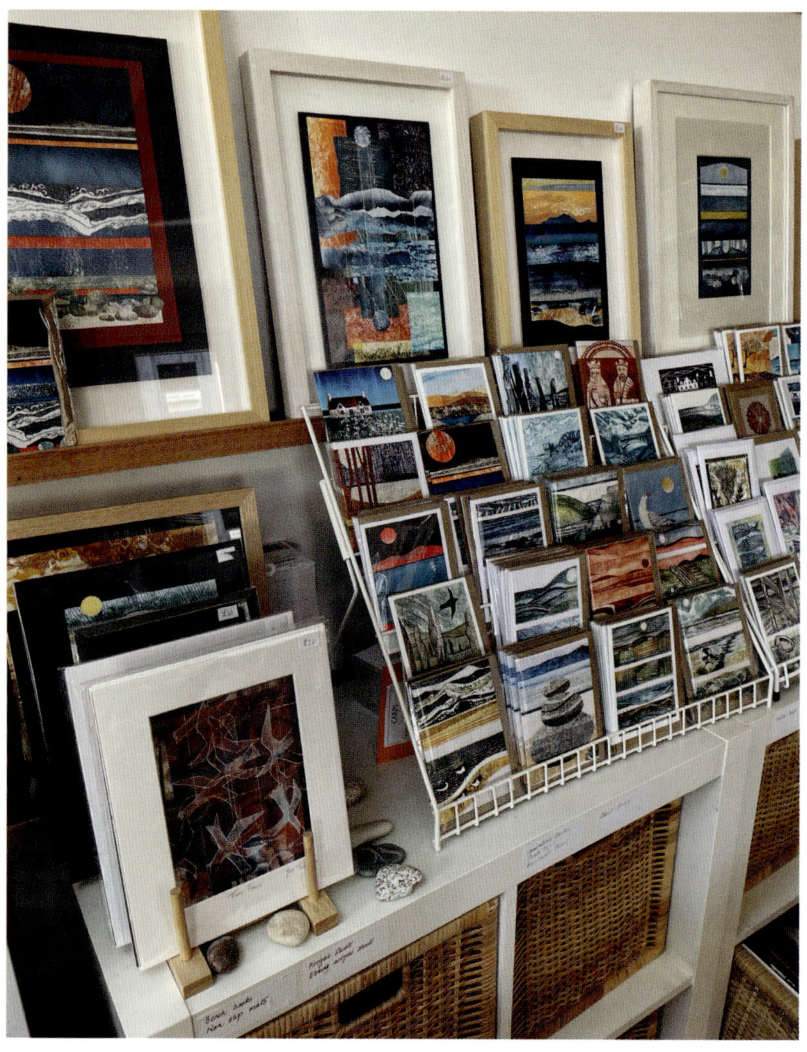

14
WHAT NEXT?

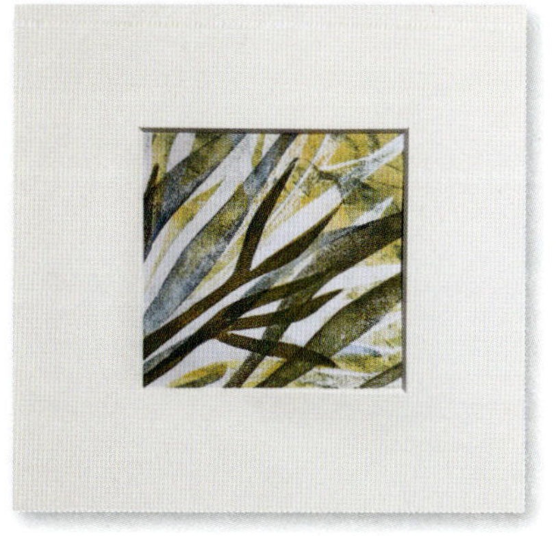

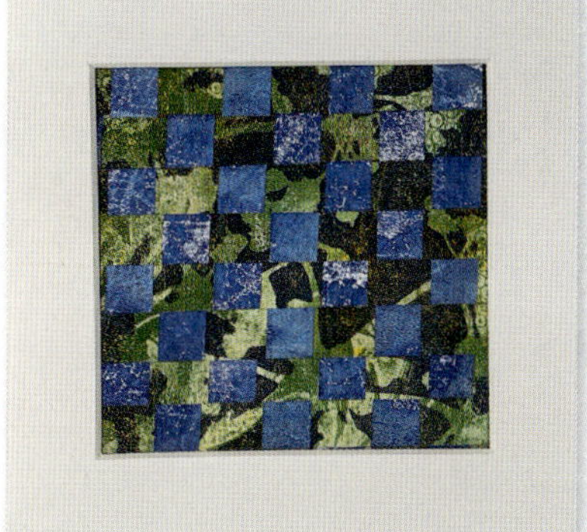

You may have worked through all the printmaking activities in the book or just dipped into some of them. I hope that you have found inspiration and will go on to develop one or more of the techniques.

You may think of printmaking as a hobby and print some cards for friends and family or dabble with some of the projects for fun and relaxation. You might, however, decide to take it up in a more serious way.

Many printmaking methods require a press, which is a considerable financial outlay, and a dedicated space for you to work in. It is worth finding a printmaking studio in your area where you can take some classes, meet other printmakers and use a printing press, which will allow you to expand your printmaking practice. There are many more types of printmaking to explore, such as drypoint, woodcut and screen printing.

Take time to develop your skills and build your confidence – look back at your work and your sketchbook and see how you have progressed over time and how much you have learned.

Art can give meaning to our lives and is an essential part of our culture. It helps us to look more closely at the world around us and, in my opinion, is essential for our physical, emotional and mental wellbeing. Whether you dabble or take printmaking up in depth, I wish you enjoyment and success on your printmaking journey, and I hope you will find time to develop your creativity and maybe share your work with others.

Gel plate recipe

You can purchase ready-made gel plates (see p.172), which come in a variety of sizes and, if looked after, will last you for years. I buy these in different sizes for my own artwork and for classes as they are robust and durable. Alternatively, you can make your own. Homemade gel plates are more fragile than commercially made plates, but you can break them up, melt them in the microwave and reform them.

A gel plate can be made by using a shallow Tupperware®-style container or glass dish for a mould; it needs to have a smooth flat bottom. (I have used a rectangular plastic container with a flat area measuring 15 × 24 cm, which produces a gel plate that is 2 cm in depth.) Lining the bottom of your mould with cling film will make the plate easier to remove but may leave some wrinkles in the underside of the plate. This is not a problem as you will use the top, flat surface for printing.

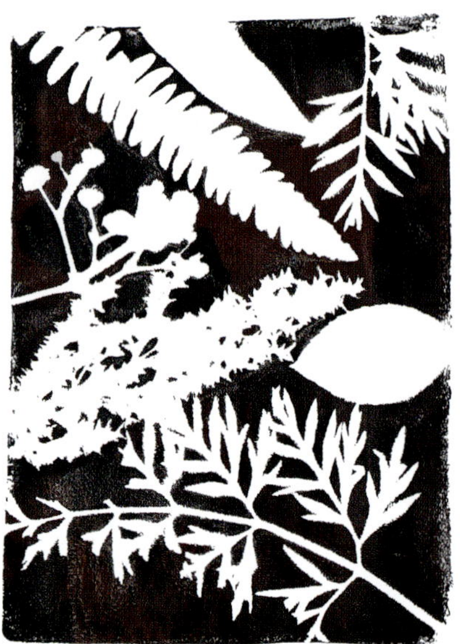

YOU WILL NEED

- strip of paper
- 115 g powdered gelatine (unflavoured) (from the baking section of the supermarket)
- 375 ml glycerine (from a pharmacy)
- 120 ml cold water
- 375 ml boiling water
- glass or acrylic sheet or a large ceramic floor tile
- spatula
- knife
- plastic or glass container with a flat bottom (approximately 15 × 24 cm)
- bowl
- cling film
- kitchen paper
- washing-up bowl
- warm soapy water
- sanitiser gel

1. Place the cold water in a bowl.

2. Pour approximately half of the glycerine liquid (about 185 ml) into the cold water.

3. Use a spatula to stir and mix thoroughly but slowly — try not to create bubbles in the mixture.

4. Once thoroughly mixed, sprinkle all the gelatine powder into the water/glycerine mix. Mix, keeping a slow and steady stirring motion to reduce the addition of bubbles, until all lumps of gelatine have disappeared.

5. Carefully add the boiling water and continue to stir slowly, until all the gelatine crystals have dissolved. (If you stir too vigorously, you will create bubbles which rise to the surface and pop, leaving a pitted surface on your plate.)

6. Once all the crystals have dissolved, add the remaining glycerine.

7. Carefully pour the mixture into the mould, taking care not to let bubbles into it. If some bubbles rise to the surface, skim them off with a strip of paper.

8. Allow the mixture to solidify by leaving it undisturbed until It sets, and then place in the refrigerator until it is completely set.

9. You will need to remove the solidified gelatine plate from the mould before trying to print. First, prepare a flat, firm surface for your new gelatine plate – this could be a glass or acrylic sheet or a large, smooth floor tile on your worktop. Dip a knife in warm water and run it carefully along the inside of the mould, then invert and shake the mould lightly. If you lined the mould with cling film, peel this off carefully. Invert the gel plate on to your prepared firm surface. It is now ready to be used for printing.

CLEANING UP

- Clean your container and mixing utensils with warm soapy water.

- The gel plate is best cleaned by spraying lightly with water and using a piece of kitchen paper to wipe the surface. Smear a small amount of sanitiser gel on both sides and around the edges to prevent the growth of bacteria. Cover with cling film, making sure no bubbles of air remain between the cling film and the surface of the gel plate, and store in the fridge.

RE-FORMING YOUR GEL PLATE

Once the surface of a homemade gel plate begins to deteriorate, break the whole plate up into small pieces and place in a microwaveable bowl. Microwave in small bursts until all the pieces have melted, and then pour slowly into a shallow flat container that is lined with cling film. Leave it to solidify and reuse as before.

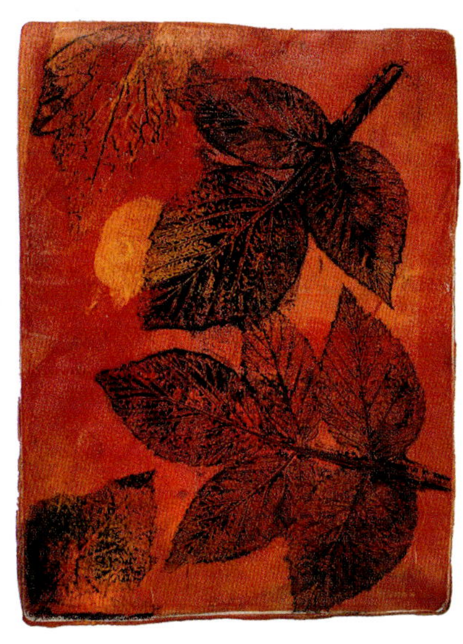

SOURCING TOOLS AND MATERIALS

Here are some of my preferred brands of tools and materials, followed by a list of specialist art and print suppliers. Materials for printmaking are also widely available from local art and craft shops, general stores or online marketplaces.

cutting tools
sets of Japanese carving tools with wooden handles, Abig sets, individual Pfeil tools

cyanotype paper
Sunography paper, LUTER cyanotype paper, coated cyanotype paper

cyanotype sensitizer set
Jacquard

gel plate
Gel Press®, Gelli Arts®

ink pads
Crystal Craft, VersaFine Clair, VersaColor, Tim Holz Distress, Hobbycraft®

mixed-media paper
Somerset® Satin, Fabriano®

sketchbook and cartridge paper
Seawhite®, Daler Rowney®, Hobbycraft®, Artway®

printing inks
Caligo Safe Wash inks

soft lino
Speedy Carve™ (by Speedball®)

white gel pens
Gelly Roll® (by Sakura®)

white Tracedown® transfer paper
Frisk

Suppliers

UK

Cass Art
www.cassart.co.uk

Cowling and Wilcox
www.cowlingandwilcox.com

Cyanotype UK
cyanotype.co.uk

DT Craft and Design
www.dtcrafts.co.uk

Eco-craft
www.eco-craft.co.uk

Handprinted
handprinted.co.uk

Ironbridge Fine Arts
www.ironbridgeframing.co.uk

Hawthorn Printmaker Supplies
www.hawthornprintmaker.com

Hobbycraft
www.hobbycraft.co.uk

Intaglio Printmaker
www.intaglioprintmaker.com

Jackson's Art Supplies
www.jacksonsart.com

Lawrence Art Supplies
www.lawrence.co.uk

London Graphic Centre
www.londongraphics.co.uk

Transpack
www.transpack.co.uk

USA and Canada

Blick Art Materials
www.dickblick.com

McClain's Printmaking Supplies
www.imcclains.com

Opus
www.opusartsupplies.com

Printer's Corner
www.printerscorner.ca

Jerry's Artarama
www.jerrysartarama.com

Art Supply Warehouse
www.artsupplywarehouse.com

Utrecht Art Supplies
www.utrechtart.com

Australia

Art to Art
www.arttoart.net

Eckersley's Art & Craft
www.eckersleys.com.au

Melbourne Etching Supplies (M.E.S)
www.mes.net.au

Senior Art Supplies
www.seniorart.com.au

Union St Printmakers
www.unionstprintmakers.com

Articci
articci.com

The Artist Warehouse
theartistwarehouse.com.au

France

Joop Stoop
www.joopstoop.com/fr

Lefranc Bourgeois
www.lefrancbourgeois.com

Magasin Sennellier
www.magasinsennelier.art

Le Géant des Beaux-Arts
www.geant-beaux-arts.fr

Rougier et Plé
www.rougier-ple.fr

Germany

Gerstaecker
www.gerstaecker.de

Modulor
www.modulor.de

Peters Art Künstlerbedarf
peters-art.nl

Hobby Shop – Wilhelm Rüther
www.hobbyshop.de

Idee
www.idee-shop.com

Edelhoff Kreativkaufhaus
kreativkaufhaus.de

List of contributors

Susan Yeates

www.susanyeates.co.uk

Susan is based in Surrey and has worked as a successful professional artist for over 15 years. She has written six art books and has created over 35 online courses. She has taught sketching and drawing techniques to thousands of aspiring artists from all over the world. She is passionate about inspiring others to get creative.

Karen Komurcu

www.linocutlassie.com

Karen aka Linocut Lassie is an artist and printmaker based in Scotland. She creates her prints at her kitchen table with the simplest of equipment and her main area of work is linocut.

Suzie MacKenzie

www.mackenziefineart.co.uk

Suzie is an award-winning artist printmaker based in the Scottish Highlands; she is an expert in collagraph printing. Her work has been exhibited both nationally and internationally, and her book *Making Collagraph Prints* (Crowood Press, 2019) is an excellent guide to the medium of collagraphy.

Clare Youngs

www.clareyoungs.co.uk

Clare is a designer-maker and papercraft collage artist, illustrator and author, based in Kent. She takes inspiration from a range of traditional and contemporary handicraft techniques to make stunning collage pieces using hand-printed papers. Her book *Creative Collage* (CICO Books, 2017) is a mine of ideas.

GLOSSARY OF TERMS

acrylic wax – A type of acrylic sealant used to seal collage work, eco prints or sun prints (different from acrylic wax for floors).

anthotype – A printed image created using paper coated with photosensitive plant dyes.

baren – A tool used for burnishing relief prints by hand.

blended roll – When ink is applied using a mix of colours on the same roller (graduated colour tones from dark to light or a blend of colours); see also rainbow roll.

block-printing – A form of relief printing where an image is carved into the surface of a block of wood, lino or rubber material and used to print on to paper or fabric.

bone folder – A shaped tool to fold and crease materials in card-making or bookbinding.

botanical printing – A printing technique using natural objects, such as leaves and ferns, to create prints on paper or fabric.

brayer – see roller

burnish – To rub the surface of paper when making a relief print.

button polish – see shellac

collage – Applying various materials to a surface using glue to create an artistic composition.

collagraph – A print technique which uses collaged materials to create a printing plate, which is inked up either for relief or intaglio printing.

cyanotype – A printed image created using paper coated with a photosensitive chemical solution.

drypoint etching – A printing plate made by incising into a surface using a sharp-pointed tool, which is then inked using the intaglio method.

eco printing – A technique which uses leaves and flowers to transfer an image on to paper or fabric without the use of ink or paint.

edition – A set number of prints made from one plate. If the prints are not identical in colour or tone, they are called a variable edition (V/E).

etching – A printmaking technique where ink is applied to the surface of a plate that has been created by incising the image using a chemical process or by scratching the surface with a sharp-pointed tool. The surface is then wiped and printed using an etching press.

ghost print – A second print that is taken from a printing plate without re-inking. This is usually a fainter print.

glassine – A biodegradable and recyclable alternative to plastic packaging, made from wood pulp.

graduated roll – see rainbow roll

hybrid print – An image that is produced using different print techniques, for example, a relief print layered on a monoprinted background.

intaglio – Ink is applied to the printing plate, worked into the lower recesses and then wiped from the surface. It is printed on dampened paper using an etching press.

Japanese Vinyl – An alternative material to traditional lino for printmaking; it is easier to carve and gives good results. It can be recycled.

jigsaw print – A print made with a carved lino plate cut into two or more pieces, which have been inked up separately and then reassembled before printing.

lino – A composite material, originally for flooring, that is made from cork and linseed oil with a hessian or burlap backing. It is widely used by printmakers and is biodegradable.

Mod Podge® – A decoupage-medium glue, sealer and finishing layer.

monoprint or monotype print – A print technique where the image can only be produced once. There are many ways of making these one-off prints which are unique and can stand alone or be used as part of mixed-media work.

mordant – A substance that is used in the process of dyeing or staining fabric or paper to fix the colour.

mountboard – Sturdy cardboard used for mounting artwork and as a base for a collagraph plate.

multi-plate printing – A printing process that uses various different plates in combination; a printing method using several separate printing blocks as an alternative to reduction printing.

plate – A printing plate created using various methods, such as carving into the surface of a block of lino or collaging materials on to the base of card or other material, and/or incising into the surface with a blade.

rainbow roll – A way of combining more than one colour of ink on the roller and applying it to the surface of a relief-printing plate.

reduction print – A multicoloured relief print which is printed in progressive layers, removing more of the surface of the plate with each layer. The number of prints is limited as, by the last layer, there is almost nothing left of the block.

registration – Using tape or a registration device to correctly align paper and printing block so that prints are placed accurately when using multiple layers.

relief printing – A print technique where ink is applied to the surface of a printing block and does not reach the areas that have been cut or carved away.

roller – A tool with a handle and rotating cylinder which can be used to spread a thin layer of printing ink or, when dry and clean, to burnish a print; also known as a 'brayer'.

scrim – A starched cotton fabric with an open weave used for wiping a printing plate during collagraph printing or etching.

shellac – A varnish used in carpentry as a wood finish and in printmaking for sealing collagraph plates; also known as 'button polish'.

Tetra Pak® – A brand of food packaging, usually found in the form of milk, juice or soup cartons. Its waxy inner surface can be etched into and used for printmaking.

Tyvek® – A brand of synthetic material with multiple uses; this paper is ideal for creating stencils.

Acknowledgements

I would like to thank artist Adrienne Craddock whose inspirational approach to printmaking fired my enthusiasm and rekindled my own interest in the magic of making original prints. To An Lanntair Arts Centre in Stornoway for giving me the opportunity to devise and teach printmaking workshops on the Isle of Lewis. To Alex Boyd who encouraged me to get started when I first moved to the island. To all the students, young and not so young, who have attended my printmaking classes, got their fingers inky and been inspired to become printmakers themselves. To the artists who have generously contributed to this book and to Bloomsbury Publishing and Herbert Press for guiding me through the process of putting the book together.

And finally, to my husband Colin – without his support and encouragement for my printmaking projects and his patience with the ever-growing piles of printed papers, cards, bookmarks and handmade books that have resulted from my 'here's one I made earlier' experiments, this book would not have been written.

Photo credits

All images © Gill Thompson unless stated below.

Susan Yeates
22, 23

Karen Komurcu
92, 93

Suzie MacKenzie
100, 101

Clare Youngs
139, 140, 141

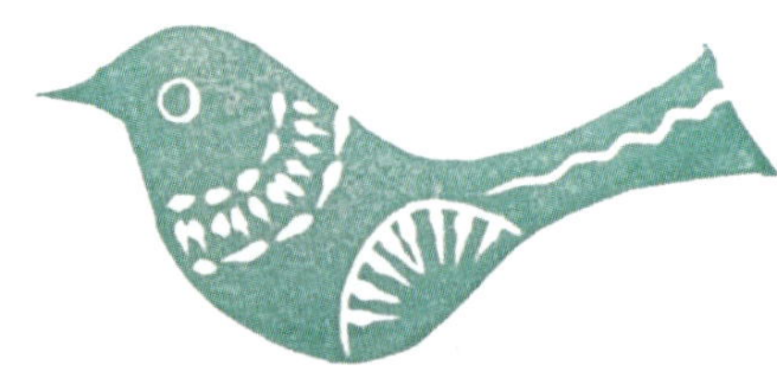